BECOMING A SPORT PSYCHOLOGIST

Sport psychology is a competitive profession with rigorous and demanding entry routes in terms of education, training and accreditation. Once qualified, the sport psychology practitioner will face complex, day-to-day professional challenges of the kind not always covered in conventional sport psychology textbooks. *Becoming a Sport Psychologist* is the first book to reveal the reality of working in sport psychology through the personal perspectives and narratives of some of the world's leading sport psychologists, top professionals with many years experience of working at every level of sport, from amateur to elite, in consulting and support roles, and in sport psychology research.

With each chapter focusing on a key issue or issues in professional practice, each contributing psychologist discusses their own education, training and professional experience, their personal motivation and their approach to consulting and delivery, helping the reader to develop a rounded understanding of how to succeed in sport psychology. The book also explores key professional issues such as intervention style, work–life balance and the commercial aspects of sport psychology practice not covered in other books, plus it offers a summary of typical education and training routes and additional information on professional organisations and accreditation schemes. *Becoming a Sport Psychologist* is invaluable reading for anybody considering a career in sport psychology, or any practising sport psychologist looking to extend and develop their professional skills.

Paul McCarthy is a Lecturer in Psychology at Glasgow Caledonian University, UK. His research examines issues in applied sport psychology and emotional and attentional processes in sport performers. He has previously published a book on single-case research methods in sport and exercise psychology.

Marc Jones is a Reader in Sport and Exercise Psychology at Staffordshire University, UK. He has published over 40 academic papers, mostly in the area of stress and emotion. He is a registered Sport Psychologist (HCPC) and is currently working as a consultant in professional football.

BECOMING A SPORT PSYCHOLOGIST

Edited by
Paul McCarthy and Marc Jones

LONDON AND NEW YORK

First Published in 2014
by Routledge
2 Park Square, Milton Park, Abingdon, Oxon OX14 4RN

Simultaneously published in the USA and Canada
by Routledge
711 Third Avenue, New York, NY 10017

Routledge is an imprint of the Taylor & Francis Group, an informa business

British Library Cataloguing in Publication Data
A catalogue record for this book is available from the British Library

Library of Congress Cataloging in Publication Data
Becoming a sport psychologist / edited by Paul McCarthy and Marc Jones.
pages cm
1. Sports psychologists--Vocational guidance. 2. Sports--Psychological aspects.
I. McCarthy, Paul, 1977-
GV706.4.B42 2014
796.01'9--dc23
2013005048

ISBN: 978-0-415-52521-3 (hbk)
ISBN: 978-0-415-52522-0 (pbk)
ISBN: 978-0-203-11993-8 (ebk)

Typeset in Bembo
by Saxon Graphics Ltd, Derby

Printed and bound by CPI Group (UK) Ltd, Croydon, CR0 4YY

For Lesley, Liam and Euan – Is buaine focal ná toice an tsaoil [A word is more enduring than worldly wealth]. (Paul)

For Helen, Molly, Jacob and all my family (Marc)

CONTENTS

PART V
Clinical Psychology

PART VI
Sport Science

CONTRIBUTORS

Mark B. Andersen, PhD, Victoria University, Australia

Jamie Barker, PhD, Staffordshire University, UK

Sarah Cecil, MSc, English Institute of Sport, UK

Richard L. Cox, PhD, private consultant, Scotland, UK

Burt Giges, MD, private consultant, New York, USA

Sandy Gordon, PhD, University of Western Australia, Australia

Chris Harwood, PhD, Loughborough University, UK

Brian Hemmings, PhD, private consultant, UK, www.golfmind.co.uk

Ken Hodge, PhD, University of Otago, New Zealand

Marc Jones, PhD, Staffordshire University, UK

Zoe Knowles, PhD, Liverpool JMU, UK

Roger Mace, PhD (deceased), Sport in Mind, UK

Paul McCarthy, PhD, Glasgow Caledonian University, UK

Aidan Moran, PhD, University College Dublin, Ireland

Shane Murphy, PhD, Western Connecticut State University, USA

Al Petitpas, EdD, Springfield College, MA, USA

Ronald E. Smith, PhD, University of Washington, USA

Rebecca Symes, MSc, private consultant, UK, www.sporting-success.com

David Tod, PhD, Aberystwyth University, Wales, UK

Robert Weinberg, PhD, Miami University, Miami, Ohio, USA

ACKNOWLEDGEMENTS

We are most grateful to Routledge for the opportunity to publish this book. Their staff were immeasurably supportive, especially Joshua Wells and Simon Whitmore. They clarified our idea for this book at the outset, offered sensible and insightful suggestions for the content and guided us throughout the publishing process. Regretfully, one of the contributors to this book, Dr Roger Mace, died during the time that this book was being prepared. His chapter is based on material he wrote and was originally printed in *From Balls to Psychology* by Sport in Mind, Worcestershire, UK. We are grateful to Sport in Mind for permission to reprint this material. Finally, we are especially thankful to the authors in this book for their open, engaging and educational stories about becoming a sport psychologist.

1

INTRODUCTION

Paul McCarthy and Marc Jones

This book is about the journey to become a sport psychologist; not only is it a journey with notable landmarks such as academic qualifications, professional accreditation, and contracts with athletes and teams, but it is also a journey navigated through expanses of uncharted waters. We are, therefore, becoming sport psychologists: constantly learning, developing and refining our knowledge and skills for the betterment of our profession. Whether you are beginning your journey as a sport psychologist or have travelled far, this book brings you face to face with fellow sport psychologists and their unique accounts of the field.

The discipline of sport psychology

The academic study of sport psychology is over a century old with university courses recorded as early as 1891 (Kornspan, 2012). Triplett's classic work on the performance of cyclists (Triplett, 1898) is often cited as the first study in sport (and more broadly social) psychology. The practice of sport psychology, in the sense of someone employed as a 'sport psychology consultant', is more recent. The first recorded example is Coleman Griffith's work with the Chicago Cubs baseball team between 1938 and 1940 (Green, 2003). As a discipline, sport psychology did not really grow until the foundation of professional bodies in the 1960s (e.g., the International Society of Sport Psychology, the North American Society for the Psychology of Sport and Physical Activity, the European Federation of Sport Psychology) with sport psychology journals (e.g., the *International Journal of Sport Psychology*; the *Journal of Sport Behavior*) following in the 1970s (Lavallee *et al.*, 2012). Today, the practice of sport psychology is widespread, with consultants employed with many elite teams and athletes. However, this book is not about the discipline; it is about the people who make the discipline.

Why was this book written?

We are, by our own taxonomy at least, sport psychologists. And we think that how we practise our vocation overlaps meaningfully with the practices of other trained professionals. Though there are many edifying textbooks (e.g., Andersen, 2000, 2005; Hanrahan and Andersen, 2010; Kremer and Moran, 2013; Tenenbaum, 2001) and quarterlies demonstrating the practice of sport psychology, only a few authors have strayed across the boundary to meet the person behind the practice. With so much autobiographical substance missing in our field, we thought we could set a keystone in the gap and so began our journey to bring the storyteller to the people. The aim of this book, therefore, was to gather the tales of the field from a cross-section of sport psychologists in the early, mid and late stages of their careers. This list is not exhaustive; rather, it offers a variety of careers to the reader. We felt that abridged life stories, from different career stages, could reveal the predictable and unpredictable passage through one's career, offer hope and direction to those who seek to join the profession as well as those who are in the profession but would like to know how others laid their path. We hoped this book would be a font of inspiration and guidance for aspiring and experienced practitioners. At the very least, it would illustrate how sport psychologists have learned, developed and grown as people and practitioners; how their personal experiences have shaped their professional lives and how they have overcome the challenges they faced.

About the title

We shamelessly borrowed the title of this book from Carl Rogers' classic text: *On Becoming a Person* (Rogers, 1961) (although you will notice that we lost the battle to keep the preposition). At my (Paul McCarthy) first counselling seminar, my tutor recommended we read Carl Rogers' book. As I began to read his book, I realised features of his life chimed with mine. For instance, he grew up on a farm (just like me), he was the fourth of six children (just like me), he had a strong ethical and religious background (just like me), his parents cared deeply about their children's welfare (just like me), and he considered studying agriculture at university (just like me). But one sentence in particular was jarringly similar with my early childhood. Rogers said: 'I remember my slight feeling of wickedness when I had my first bottle of "pop".' Oddly enough, I had a Proustian moment when I read that sentence because there was a grocery shop just a few hundred metres from our farm and whenever I passed by, the old shopkeeper would bring me treats. On this particular day, she gave me a bottle of Coca-Cola; I can still remember drinking some of the Coca-Cola and then hiding the bottle in a breeze block near one of the sheds on our farm. Such parallels were enough to connect me with Carl Rogers, his philosophy and teachings. The more I learned about client-centred therapy, the more I felt it 'suited' me – my personality, my goals in sport psychology practice and that ultimately, I could be an effective client-centred therapist.

Why is this book important?

You might argue that this book is unadulterated self-indulgence. But from one perspective at least, exploring the lives and careers of sport psychologists is necessary and discerning. We are, on balance, responsible for our profession. Most sport psychologists believe optimistically in the merits of their profession and whom it represents. They continue to establish solid educational foundations, respond to contemporary ethical challenges and instruct prospective sport psychologists to meet the needs of the clients they serve. Yet, despite these gallant efforts, the connotation of the compound noun 'sport psychology' among the social milieu ranges from 'dark science' to 'blatant pilfering'. When asked if he has ever considered using a sport psychologist, the professional golfer, Ian Poulter, explained: 'Why pay somebody 10 percent of what I earn to tell me how good I am?' (Dixon, 2012, p. 56). Although this is the fate of many professions, those who choose to involve themselves in sport wear a 'high visibility jacket'. When the media discovered that Tottenham Hotspur football club were employing a sport psychologist in the early 1980s, they splashed the headline: 'White coats at White Hart Lane'. Wearing the club colours at least gave the sport psychologist some integrity! Such scepticism has yet to disappear entirely but attitudes have changed regarding the value of sport psychology. Why has this happened? There are several reasons to explain this shift in perception but one reassuring testament has come from those who have been helped by sport psychologists, especially those in professional sport who receive abundant media coverage. Before 2012, tennis professional, Andy Murray, openly expressed his reluctance to work with a sport psychologist; however, after winning the 2012 US Open, it emerged that he had begun to work with a sport psychologist earlier in the year:

> [It's been about] learning how to deal with people a little bit better. Obviously, I've known a lot of the guys I've worked with for a very long time. We are also friends, so it can sometimes be hard to open up if there's something you're not necessarily happy with, something you want to change. That's probably what's helped most.
>
> *(Newman, 2012, p. 62)*

To move away from the 'dark science', sport psychologists can do more to increase their transparency. After all, sport psychologists are people with a set of skills; skills that can be learned by other people. The simplicity of the services we offer should further demystify 'sport psychology' but not diminish the time and experience necessary to counsel athletes effectively.

Why do we need to know about the sport psychologist?

There is a paradox that although psychology practitioners are technically diverse in their practices, there is no differential effectiveness (Stiles *et al.*, 1986). In other words, psychotherapy is effective but it does not matter which technique you use, the results are similar. In 1936, Saul Rosenzweig suggested that so pervasive were the common factors across psychotherapies, there would only be small differences between the outcomes of different forms of psychotherapy. When Luborsky, Singer and Luborsky (1975) examined around 100 comparative treatment studies, they found that Rosenzweig's hypothesis was right. The title of Rosenzweig's (1936) paper had a quote from *Alice in Wonderland*. It was the Dodo bird's verdict after judging the race in which a number of characters who had got wet were to run around a racecourse until they were dry. No one bothered to measure how far they had run or for how long, so when they asked who had won, the Dodo could not answer without a great deal of thought, then he said: 'Everybody has won and all must have prizes.' Similarly, in psychotherapies, the Dodo Bird Verdict suggests that all therapies are winners, they all produce comparable outcomes. If we accept this line of argument, perhaps it is one's personal variables such as the ability to shape and sustain a therapeutic alliance with clients that could explain differential therapeutic outcomes (Stiles *et al.*, 1986). Continuing this 'personal' theme, we sought to illustrate the process of becoming a sport psychologist by inviting sport psychologists to write about this theme from their experience. In outlining their journey, we also get to learn the skills and techniques that make them successful. The contributing sport psychologists include men and women from different therapeutic backgrounds, at different stages in their careers, working on both sides of the Atlantic as well as the Antipodes.

The unique journey

What will be apparent in the contributions to this book is that the journey to become a sport psychologist is idiosyncratic. To illustrate in the UK, the 'simple' career pathway is to attain a primary degree in psychology with an accredited postgraduate degree followed by two years of supervised practice. This answer, however, only represents a recent development in the professionalization of our practice in applied sport psychology in the UK and brushes over the nuances of requirements from specific bodies in other countries such as Australia, Canada, and the United States. It also brushes over the different ways in which people in the UK can, and have, become sport psychologists. For example, some sport psychologists completed a psychology conversion course after an undergraduate degree in sport science. Because sport psychology has its roots in psychology, physical education and sport science, it is not surprising there is no singular pathway to become a certified sport psychologist. Many people call themselves sport psychologists and support athletes and teams across the globe; some are certified to do so, some are not. This debate is mentioned in many chapters in this book (e.g., Chapter 10 by Andersen, Chapter 9 by Petitpas) and is likely to run indefinitely. That is why we have arranged the book in the way that we have to illustrate the many different starting points from which our contributors became sport psychologists. We hope you enjoy their contributions.

References

Andersen, M. B. (2000) *Doing Sport Psychology*. Champaign, IL: Human Kinetics.

——(2005) *The Practice of Sport Psychology*. Champaign, IL: Human Kinetics.

Dixon, P. (2012) Poulter remains focused with designs on his maiden jacket; Englishman takes a single-minded approach to Augusta, with advice from form champions regarded as a major distraction. *The Times*, 3 April, p. 56.

Green, C. D. (2003) Psychology strikes out: Coleman R. Griffith and the Chicago Cubs. *History of Psychology*, 6: 267–283.

Hanrahan, S. J. and Andersen, M. B. (2010) *The Routledge Handbook of Applied Sport Psychology: A Comprehensive Guide for Students and Practitioners*. London: Routledge.

Kornspan, A. S. (2012) History of sport and performance psychology, in S. Murphy (ed.) *The Oxford Handbook of Sport and Performance Psychology*. Oxford: Oxford University Press, pp. 3–23.

Kremer, J. and Moran, A. (2013) *Pure Sport: Practical Sport Psychology*, 2nd edn. London: Routledge.

Lavallee, D., Kremer, J., Moran, A. and Williams, M. (2012) *Sport Psychology: Contemporary Themes*, 2nd edn. London: Palgrave Macmillan.

Luborsky, L., Singer, B. and Luborsky, L. (1975) Comparative studies of psychotherapies: is it true that 'Everyone has won and all must have prizes'? *Archives of General Psychiatry*, 32: 995–1008.

Newman, P. (2012) Andy Murray needed a psychologist to end his Grand Slam misery and win the US Open. *The Independent*, 12 October, p. 62.

Rogers, C. P. (1961) *On Becoming a Person*. Boston: Houghton Mifflin.

Rosenzweig, S. (1936) Some implicit common factors in diverse methods of psychotherapy. *American Journal of Ortho-psychiatry*, 6: 412–415.

Stiles, W. B., Shapiro, D. A. and Elliott, R. (1986) Are all psychotherapies equivalent? *American Psychologist*, 41: 165–180.

Tenenbaum, G. (2001) *The Practice of Sport Psychology*. Morgantown, WV: Fitness Information Technology.

Triplett, N. (1898) The dynamogenic factors in pacemaking and competition. *American Journal of Psychology*, 9: 507–533.

PART I
Psychiatry

2

ON BECOMING A SPORTPSYCH PRACTITIONER

Burt Giges

Beginning in sport

I like beginnings. So this time, I'm going back 75 years to the beginning of my involvement in sport. In my early years, "street games" were my chance to play, compete, and sometimes win. The games were literally played in the street, and included roller skate hockey, stick ball and box ball (the last two patterned on baseball). Because we played in the "gutter," we frequently had to stop to let the cars go by. Then I added neighborhood football, played not in the street, but on the nearby park grass. I was grateful for that grass when I injured my knee trying to tackle a ball carrier who kept running. I was a chubby kid, and I played fullback, with a fierce determination to get that extra yard. What I did not know then, but observed repeatedly over the ensuing years, was that in both sport and my professional life, I was intensely competitive. I not only had an inner drive for excellence, to be the best that I could be, but also a hidden desire to be "first"— better than anyone else.

During high school, I was manager of the high school track team, and assisted the coach with timing the runners' laps. I also helped by carrying the medical box, and when athletes were injured, I was right there to help the trainer or the coach tend to the athlete. Back then, I had no idea I would eventually become a physician. In college, I continued my participation in sport as a member of the fencing team, a foil fencer. I once made the mistake of substituting for a teammate who was not able to compete in a sabre match. In foil, the head is off-target; not so in sabre. My opponent's first point was all he needed. It came from a slap (read "slam!") on the side of my head, hard enough for me to see stars. I gracefully withdrew from the rest of the match (lesson learned).

My involvement in sport changed many years later, when I was a resident in psychiatry. A friend of mine, who was the coach of a high school football team, appointed me their team doctor. That's where I first learned about coach stress (he told me first-hand), parental involvement (I heard the father screaming at his son), and the connection between an athlete's emotions and injury (they got hurt when they were starting to lose). Again, I had no idea I would later get involved in sport psychology.

I expanded my own participation in "sport" by adding exercise as a parent of two young girls. In those days, "working out" was not generally considered part of sport. I was drawn into serious exercising because I had virtually no stamina in trying to teach my older daughter to ride a bicycle. At first, the exercises were from the Royal Canadian Air Force group, and then I settled down to indoor bicycling and strength training. Today, at 88, I'm still at it, adding the treadmill two days a week.

Beginning in psychology

My involvement with psychology came first as a patient in psychoanalysis and then as a resident in psychiatry. I was in analytic treatment twice, once before entering psychiatric residency and once after completing my training. I went into analysis the first time because of feelings of anxiety, loneliness, and isolation as a researcher at the Rockefeller Institute for Medical Research, NY. The second time resulted from an unsatisfying ending to the first, and the fact that I had decided to become a psychiatrist knowing that more personal work was needed. There was a significant difference in the style of my two analysts and in my own readiness to change. I think both factors contributed to the very satisfying outcome of treatment. One unexpected result was that after the completion of my analysis, I was able to water ski for the first time in my life—free of anxiety and feeling exhilarated. I loved it!

During residency, we studied psychodynamics, psychopathology, group and family dynamics, child development, and social factors. I found myself much more interested in the psychological issues than in the medical model of diagnosis and treatment of psychopathology. Years later, as a practicing psychiatrist, I came to realize that I had actually become much more of a psychologist than a medical doctor. I had drifted away from prescribing medication and had started referring those who needed drugs or hospitalization to other psychiatrists. Long after sport psychology became my main interest, a colleague, Dan Begel, who was the first president of the International Society of Sport Psychiatry, came to a conference of the Association for Applied Sport Psychology (AASP). We spent some time together, and he invited me to speak at his society's conference. In describing the program for that conference in their Newsletter (Begel, 1996), he wrote, "Burt Giges, my favorite anti-psychiatry sport psychiatrist, will be presenting some provocative ideas regarding our methods and role, based not upon his prejudices but upon quite a few years' work in sport psychology." That was a reassuring confirmation for me that my views and practice were in fact different from those of sport psychiatrists. Here's what I wrote about my own perspective on my website (Giges, 2010).

Although originally trained as a clinician, with a background in medical research, I've come to see myself more as an educator. This change involved a shift from the medical model of illness and disease to a growth and development model, in which problems are seen as the result of learned thinking patterns. The focus of my work with athletes and others is to help them change those patterns that contribute to distressed feelings or troublesome behavior, and to remove the barriers to their optimal functioning. This focus is primarily on present experience, based on the hypothesis that past negative experiences might recede into the background, were it not for the fact that present patterns of thinking and feeling keep them in the foreground. The language used by the person is followed very closely, because it not only expresses present thoughts and feelings, but also contributes to their development. I believe that what we learned in the past can be changed by what we learn in the present.

Merger of sport and psychology

As I reflected back over my professional life, I noticed that it changed direction about every 10 to 12 years. I realized later these career changes were attempts at external solutions to internal problems. Whatever the change, it was a great comfort to me that my wife and two daughters were always supportive. The first cycle included the time I spent in medical research and practice. The research was in liver disease at the Army Medical Research and Graduate School at Walter Reed Army Hospital in Washington, DC, and at the Rockefeller Institute, NY. This was followed by several years of practice in medicine. As an outgrowth of my first psychoanalytic treatment, I changed direction and switched my specialty from internal medicine to psychiatry. At the time, I never imagined that the three years I had spent in medical research would serve me well later on. My years in psychiatric practice were in an office doing psychodynamic psychotherapy. Recognizing a growing restlessness, staleness, and diminished aliveness, I changed again and became involved in the Human Potential Movement, participating in encounter groups, group therapy, gestalt therapy, and transactional analysis. During this time, I became more active in the therapeutic process, and eventually led many group experiences.

The final change came 23 years ago, at the age of 65, when my connection to sport psychology officially began. The suggestion that I explore sport psychology came from my older daughter who was a psychologist and knew of my interest in track and field. The idea seemed to fit my desire for something new; and combining my interest in sport and psychology sounded just right. It must have been right because I'm still involved well after the 10–12-year cycle. Many years before this last change, I had seen several patients who were avid sport participants (in golf, tennis, swimming, and running). I had used techniques that would now be considered sport psychology, but had not yet studied or practiced the psychology of sport. An example was my work with a serious runner who was approaching his first marathon, anxious about whether he would be able to finish. During his sessions, we worked on his maintaining his focus, visualizing his completing the run, and thinking positively about his commitment. He did finish and was very happy, and I was pleased that I was able to help him achieve his goal.

Once I decided to pursue this new career direction in the field of sport psychology, I went at it fiercely. I went to every conference and workshop I could find, including a Continuing Education workshop at an APA Division 47 Conference. I subscribed to sport psychology journals and joined organizations devoted to sport psychology. I began reading avidly and over the years eventually read more than 60 books.

In this new endeavor, I was uncertain about what to call myself. I am not a psychologist, so that term was out. I did not want to be called a sport psychiatrist, with its emphasis on diagnosis, psychopathology, and treatment of illness. Yet I did want to make known my interest in merging sport and psychology. The term that appealed to me was a combination of sport and part of psychology. And so I became a *"sportpsych practitioner."* That allowed me to teach graduate students, mentor colleagues, consult with athletes, coaches, teams, and parents, and write about my experiences.

Early experiences as a sportpsych practitioner

My first official step in the direction of applying my new knowledge as a sportpsych practitioner was to call a local track coach, who was the coach of an international elite track team. I told him I was a psychiatrist with a lifelong interest in track and field, and that I would like to talk with him about the possibility of consulting with the team. I also said I would not charge a fee for my services. I had decided that because I wanted this to be my hobby rather than my business, and that was a freeing experience. In addition, I had a strong urge to give back to others and to feel good about doing that. The coach was agreeable to my coming to practice sessions. I became helpful immediately—when he suggested I join him in timing the runners' laps (still timing laps 50 years later). Some of the runners thought I was an assistant coach, because I was not formally introduced as a psychiatrist (I was glad for that, but not for the fact that I was not introduced as anything else). For one year, that was my contribution.

After that year, the coach asked if I would see one of the runners who had trouble finishing her races. This first referral was a most significant experience for me because it served as a turning point in my thinking about how to consult with athletes. I saw that after only two sessions, the shame that she felt when being passed in a race was no longer present during a four-year follow-up (Giges, 2000). As I mentioned in my keynote address on "How People Change" (Giges, 1995):

> For a psychiatrist, particularly one trained in psychoanalytic psychotherapy, this was an astounding experience. How can important things happen so quickly? Doesn't it take years to get profound change? It was difficult to let go of a long-standing belief I had, that depth of work correlated with length of time.

Another early and important experience was the opportunity to serve on the Psyching Team of the New York City Marathon, which I did for several years. In looking for something special to do, I approached the director of what was called the Family Tent—a large tent that served as a recovery tent for those who did not need serious medical attention. It contained about 50 cots and was staffed by physical therapists, nurses, podiatrists, athletic trainers, massage therapists, and medical students. I offered to talk with the staff about what they might expect to see and what they might do for the runners who might have psychological symptoms, whether or not they finished the race. I would be available to provide back-up support if they needed it, either as a consultant to them or for direct contact with the runners. This consisted of a solution-focused mind set, limited to here and now functioning. It was an exciting and fascinating time.

An unexpected consulting experience I had at the beginning of my new career was that the sport I knew best turned out to be my least effective consultation. Having been on the fencing team at college, I was looking forward to a session with an elite college fencer. As I began to ask questions, I became more occupied with his fencing technique and less with his fencing experience. I was drifting somewhere between a coach and an admiring fan about his technique. I lost the connection that's necessary to be effective as a consultant. There was no real rapport, no beginning relationship. After that first session, he did not return or call. When I called him, he merely said he was not interested in continuing. Another lesson learned.

At the first conference I attended, I was excited and eager to learn, and also anxious about starting something new and wanting to show my competence. I did feel confident, however, that I would eventually find a place for myself and be able to make a contribution. That happened sooner than I expected. When I asked one of the speakers whether his satisfaction depended entirely on the athlete's improved performance, his answer was "Of course it does." That reply told me there was already something worthwhile I could contribute. Drawing from the concept of counter-transference in psychoanalytic theory, I developed the idea of a workshop on "Self-Awareness for Sport Psychology Practitioners." Its purpose was to assure that the athlete's needs, rather than the consultant's, were primarily served. I knew from my earlier experience with the marathon runner that the practitioner would also derive benefit, but that was not the primary consideration. I have since given that workshop at more than a dozen universities around the country, as a Continuing Education workshop at an AASP Conference (2010), and annually at Springfield College for graduate students in Athletic Counseling. In addition, Virtual Brands made a video (Giges, 2011) in which I interviewed two athletes and two coaches, and discussed some of the principles and techniques involving self-awareness in sport psychology consulting.

I met Ken Ravizza at that first conference. He became my friend and mentor in the years that followed. It was Ken who told me not to expect too much in my first year of consultation, making it much easier to tolerate. Among my other important early contacts were the Athletic Counseling faculty at Springfield College, Al Petitpas, Judy Van Raalte, and Britt Brewer, who also became good friends and mentors. This connection led to my being asked to give workshops to the graduate students at Springfield. After a few years of these workshops, the following important conversation took place with Al at one of the AASP Conferences:

Al: You're like one of the Springfield family, Burt.
Burt: Would you be willing to make that official?
Al: What do you want?
Burt: How about an appointment as Clinical Professor?
Al: I'll see what I can do.

A few weeks later I received a letter appointing me to the staff of the Athletic Counseling Program in the Department of Psychology. And so began a long and fruitful affiliation with Springfield College. A bonus to working with Judy and Britt came when they formed their video company and invited me to participate in two of the videos they made (Giges *et al.*, 2002, 2000). I also met Mark Andersen through them, and that led to my writing a chapter in Mark's book *Doing Sport Psychology* (Giges, 2000). The Springfield connection was also a springboard to other valuable experiences; the most important to me was my invitation to be a keynote speaker at an annual AASP Conference (Giges, 1995).

The intervening years

Each conference I attended gave me new ideas about presentations I could give. Among others, I developed workshops about winning, transitions, trust, and working with athletes' emotions. As the years passed, the number of workshops and lectures increased, and I recently did some counting. Somewhat to my surprise, I've given about 75 presentations over the past 23 years. They probably had something to do with being invited to run for election as AASP President. The first workshop I gave at AASP (Giges *et al.*, 1992) was on "Examining the Process of Sport Psychology Consulting." Three of us interviewed different athletes to demonstrate the differences and similarities in the consultant's approach, and Dan Gould led the discussion. It seemed that the differences were more in our behavior, and the similarities were more in the philosophical principles underlying that behavior.

Among the many other presentations, I've selected three for special mention.

1. *The most challenging*: In 2002, I was invited by Professor Jose Maria Buceta to give a workshop at his university (U.N.E.D.) in Madrid, Spain. The idea was for me to give a lecture, and then conduct a live interview with an athlete. The lecture I gave was on "Psychological Barriers to Performance Excellence in Sport: A Counseling Approach to Performance Enhancement." For the lecture, the audience and I were wired for simultaneous translation. (I spoke in English; they listened in Spanish.) No problem. It got more challenging when the Spanish athlete I interviewed spoke "English." So without a translator, I had to translate her "English" into my English. I felt anxious about

how effective I would be with this language difficulty. Fortunately, the interview went very well. In the 30 minutes allotted, she was able to see that she was holding herself back, and this awareness helped her to decide to change that behavior.

2. *The most satisfying*: As President-Elect of AASP in February 2007, it was my privilege to represent AASP at the Annual Meeting of the Joint Commission on Sports Medicine and Sport. I was scheduled to talk on what I had titled "Common Ground: Where Sport Psychology and Sports Medicine Meet" with two other speakers, both from the field of Sports Medicine. Because of last-minute emergencies, neither was able to attend the meeting. As alternatives were discussed, I suggested that if someone from among those attending would volunteer, I would be willing (in fact, eager) to demonstrate a consultation in sport psychology. Someone did volunteer, and after the interview one of the participants in the audience said, "Now I understand what my wife meant about how to listen."

The most fun: For a profession that values and depends a lot on talking, perhaps it is not too surprising that my most enjoyable workshop was one I gave at the AASP Conference in 2006, "When Words are Not Enough: Non-Verbal Approaches to Team Self-Awareness." All of the exercises were completed with no talking allowed, and they varied from interesting to fascinating, and from serious to hilarious. The participants left wanting more.

Another significant activity during these years was my involvement with Springfield College. Being a teacher and mentor to the graduate students and consultant to the Women's Track and Field team was quite enjoyable and very satisfying. I became the track team consultant after the coach had an unsatisfactory experience with one of the graduate students, and we hoped that my serving temporarily in that capacity might bring him back into the fold. What followed, however, was much more than a transition. My work with the coach and the team lasted eight years, unexpected but indeed worthwhile. A few years after I began, the graduate students joined me in working with the team, and took over after I left.

Guiding principles as a sportpsych practitioner

The work I do as a sportpsych practitioner is based on a foundation of guiding principles. In addition, I use the research tools I learned years ago to ask how and why something happened, as well as what possible conclusions follow from the information obtained.

• *Follow, lead, follow*. In every interview, my focus is on here and now functioning. I listen very carefully as the athlete (coach, parent, etc.) describes thoughts, feelings, wants, or problems, until I hear something that may be an opening to further exploration. At this point, an "entry point," I shift from following what's being said to leading (i.e. offering some comment or question that encourages the person to consider an alternative perspective, or a deeper exploration of the issue). I then shift back to following by listening to the reaction to what I introduced. This cycle of following, leading, following, continues throughout the whole session.

• *The importance of beginnings.* When people think of change, they often compare where they are now with where they want to be, and that may involve many steps and much time. If they can see themselves taking a small step, a beginning, they will see that they know how to change, and may feel an early confidence that they can continue. I think that's one of the essential elements of change… the realization that you can begin a change process. A small shift in behavior, if continued, can make a significant difference after time has passed. If one is too focused on a change in behavior or feelings, however, another important beginning change (in awareness or perspective) may go unnoticed.

• *Consultation in sport and therapy.* It is important to make a distinction between a consultation about sport performance and therapy about some underlying issue. In an AASP newsletter in 1996, I wrote the following commentary:

> An important distinction must be made between therapy in a clinical context and intervention in sport performance. In the world of sport, sometimes the symptom *is* the problem. Whatever underlying issues there may be, they are not necessarily the focus of the work. Even the presence of some diagnostic entity does not determine the appropriate intervention. It may not be why the athlete came for help; and sometimes, relieving the symptom removes the problem. I have seen this happen with runners whose performance was impaired by anxiety, anger, self-doubt, or loss of confidence, motivation, or concentration. In such instances, when the symptoms were dealt with directly, no further exploration (of deeper issues) was required. Sometimes a careful follow-up of an intervention may reveal unexpected lasting benefit from what seemed initially to be "first aid." In other situations, where no such benefit is obtained, or when recurrences continue to interfere with performance, underlying difficulties might then be addressed.

• *Experiences outside of sport.* For each problem athletes might have in their sport participation, they may be able to draw on inner resources that were helpful in their lives outside of sport. For example, a runner was having difficulty with his performance and was not feeling successful. He was, however, doing well with a book that he was writing. He felt strong, clear, and competent in his writing ability. In his work in the sessions, he was able to transfer that strength and competent feeling to his running, using his legs to do the "writing" on the track. And a golfer I worked with was able to use his love of learning to change his attitude toward himself from a "lousy golfer" to a great "student of golf."

The present

Currently, I am mostly involved in activities other than consultation with athletes. I continue to do some part-time teaching of graduate students at Springfield College. I have recently created a website that describes my work in sport psychology over the past 22 years. Virtual Brands has produced a new video showing interviews I conducted with two athletes and two coaches, with a discussion of self-awareness. I have also started mentoring at a distance for sport psychology practitioners and graduate students. With the benefit of current technology, I am able to view the work of the person I am mentoring directly using videotape, DVD, or Skype. In addition, I served (with Judy Van Raalte) as co-editor of a special guest issue of *The Sport Psychologist*, for case studies in sport psychology (Dec. 2012).

Thoughts for students

At the beginning of a new career, there is often a mixture of excitement and anxiety: the excitement of venturing into something unknown and the fear that comes with not knowing enough. Most students are concerned about whether they will learn fast enough to be seen as competent. Here is what I wrote in the *AASP Newsletter* in 2006:

> To borrow from Zen teaching, when being a student, just be a student. Be as fully a student as you can be. Soak up new information, whether it matches your prior ideas or not. Be open to differences as an expansion of your knowledge, rather than a threat to your beliefs. Learn from teachers, coaches, books, journals, fellow students, athletes, and especially from your own experience. Being an excellent student is different from being an excellent consultant, teacher, or researcher. As a student, your excellence is in your dedication and commitment to learning, and in your acceptance of what you have not yet learned or cannot yet do. Be mindful of your long-term development as a professional, and consider that every step of the way is preparation for the next step.

In essence, my advice is "Be present. Be open. Be curious."

References

Begel, D. (1996) The president's view. *International Society for Sport Psychiatry Newsletter*, April.

Giges, B. (1995) How people change. Keynote address delivered at the annual meeting of the Association for the Advancement of Applied Sport Psychology, New Orleans, LA. Available at: www.burtgiges.com/Lectures_Workshops.html.

——(1996) Commentary. *Association for the Advancement of Applied Sport Psychology Newsletter*, 11(3): 24.

——(2000) Removing psychological barriers: clearing the way, in M. B. Andersen (ed.) *Doing Sport Psychology*. Champaign, IL: Human Kinetics, pp. 17–32.

——(2006) Ten burning questions with Burt Giges M.D. *Association for the Advancement of Applied Sport Psychology Newsletter*, 21(1): 5–6.

——(2010) My work in sport psychology: Home page. Available at: www.burtgiges.com.

——(2011) *Self-Awareness in Sport Psychology Consulting*. Wilbraham, MA: Virtual Brands. Video.

Giges, B. and Van Raalte, J. (2012) Special issue of *The Sport Psychologist*: Case studies in sport psychology: Introduction. *The Sport Psychologist*, 26, 483–485.

Giges, B., Ravizza, K., Gordin, R. and Gould, D. (1992) Examining the process of sport psychology consulting. Workshop given at the annual conference of the Association for the Advancement of Applied Sport Psychology, Colorado Springs, CO.

Giges, B., Ravizza, K. and Murphy, S. (2000) *Three Approaches to Sport Psychology Consulting*. Wilbraham, MA: Virtual Brands.

Giges, B., Ravizza, K., Van Raalte, J. and Zaichkowsky, L. (2002) *Brief Contact Interventions in Sport Psychology*. Wilbraham, MA: Virtual Brands.

PART II
Physical Education

3

FROM BALLS TO PSYCHOLOGY

Roger Mace

During a discussion on the concept of 'Leisure' and 'Work', a good friend of mine, Professor Bob Davis, looked at me and said, 'Roger, you've never done a day's work in your life.' Given his interpretation of 'Work and Leisure', which takes the stance that if you are doing something that you enjoy, you are not working, he was probably close to the truth. For the first ten years of my working life, I was a physical education teacher (hence the title of the chapter), for the next ten years, I was a lecturer in outdoor pursuits, and for the last 20 years I was a sport psychologist. This chapter is a selection of my experiences working as a sport psychologist which are taken from Mace (2007). Rather than broadly discussing issues around being a sport psychologist, I outline examples of my experiences working as a sport psychologist that illustrate my approach, the type of issues I faced, and how I dealt with them. Through outlining these experiences, I hope there will be something of interest, and use, to aspiring and current sport psychologists.

My path to becoming a sport psychologist began when, after teaching Physical Education, I became a lecturer in outdoor education at Newman College of Higher Education. I was responsible for teaching the outdoor education programme to physical education students. After taking a foundation course students could opt to specialise in outdoor pursuits, games or dance and gymnastics. On Mondays, I spent the day rock climbing, on Tuesdays, I spent the day canoeing, on Wednesday mornings, I taught orienteering skills, Wednesday afternoon and Thursday, I was free and, on Friday, I went in to prepare for a weekend expedition. What a job! I would sit on a mountain and say to the students, 'This is where you learn the important things in life. This is the biggest classroom in the world.' Then, referring to my job, I added, 'All this and money too!'

After six years of working bliss, the Principal asked to see me. 'Teaching is becoming an all-degree profession,' he said, 'I want all my staff to have a Master's degree. I would like you to put yourself on a course and you can have next year off with full pay.' I promptly applied for, and successfully obtained, a place on the MA course at the University of Birmingham. I now had a keen interest in outdoor pursuits and found research methods fascinating. There were so many questions I wanted answers to and shortly after I was awarded my MA, I registered for a PhD in psychology. I returned to college and set up a research programme. Four years later I was awarded a PhD for my research into stress management in sport. For my PhD I had specialised in the use of clinical psychological techniques for the control of emotions in sport. The techniques were based on the work of Donald Meichenbaum (Meichenbaum, 1977, 1985) on stress inoculation training and I utilised a cognitive-behavioural approach in my intervention work (see Mace, 1990, for a review). Shortly after I received my PhD, I received a phone call inviting me to be sport psychologist to the England Netball Team.

Working with my first team

Two weeks after the phone call I joined the England Squad for a day's training session. My main role, initially, was to observe the players and provide feedback to the coach. However, this didn't last long and I was soon throwing in ideas for training and generally interfering during squad training sessions. I believed that training in mental skills should be done on the court/pitch as much as possible and I developed a wide range of on-court practices for improving psychological aspects. This approach was acceptable to players and I tried to ensure that the practices were enjoyable as well as meaningful. I referred to myself as a mental skills coach as the phrase 'sport psychologist' seemed to cause some players to get a false impression of the nature of my work.

For much of the time I was 'flying by the seat of my pants' in a new and exciting aspect of sport. It's not surprising, therefore, that given the extravert personality of athletes we had a number of amusing incidents. In one training session, I had the squad working on developing concentration skills. They were in groups of three; two sitting on the floor alongside each other with their legs stretched out. The third player was standing 6 or 7 metres behind them holding a netball. She would wait for a short while and throw the ball up in the air so that it landed within 2 or 3 metres and bounce up in the air. The two players sitting were not allowed to look but as soon as they heard the ball bounce they competed against each other to see who could get to the ball first. It was nearly lunchtime and two players at the far end were sitting straining to hear the ball. The others nodded to each other and in a pre-planned move they all tiptoed out of the sports hall and went to lunch. The two players sat there for nearly five minutes before they guessed what was wrong.

One of the first things the players took on board was what came to be called the 'England huddle'. After the 15-minute warm-up on court, the team would go into a circle, arms on each other's shoulders and they would visualise themselves playing brilliantly. They told themselves that with everybody playing at their best they were the best team in the world. One player, however, didn't want to do this. She said that she preferred to look at the crowd and soak up the cheering and the atmosphere, and she liked 'the buzz'. I made sure that she was able to continue to do this but still join the huddle. Individual differences between players is common and something I always sought to accommodate in my work with teams.

After a few months of working with the squad, the coach asked me if I would take a session aimed at improving assertiveness. The Australians and teams from the Caribbean would throw a pass and then go in a direct line into a space regardless of anyone in the way. England players would dodge around anyone in the way and apologise if they accidentally brushed against them. They were just too ladylike and other teams were beginning to take advantage of this.

For three hours the players got involved in rugby-type drills and practices involving a lot of contact. Self-statements were introduced as a way of developing assertiveness. Every time they jumped for a 50/50 ball, they shouted 'My ball!'. Towards the end of the session I wanted to demonstrate another practice and reached out to 'borrow' a ball from the player next to me. I started to take the ball and she suddenly flared up, snatched the ball back and shouted, 'Get off…this is my ball, use your own!' I was surprised at the aggressive response but pleased that the training had produced the desired effect. I hoped that the effect was specific to playing netball and didn't cause 20 cases of road rage as they drove home.

Kicking the habit

After ten years of working in a variety of sports I was asked to make an input to the England U21 rugby squad. I started with an introductory session before the evening meal and said that if anyone wanted to see me individually I would be available after the session. When I finished, 22 of the 26 players stayed behind and there was a queue outside my room in the hotel all evening. I felt sport psychology had 'arrived'.

During my work it was not uncommon to be put in situations that required me to 'intervene' quickly. When working with England Colts, it was two hours before the start of the match against Wales. I was strolling along the pitch with Gary (pseudonym), the captain of the England team. The rest of the players in the team accompanied us. Leaning against the end of the players' bench was a bag of practice balls. A few metres away there was a table. A single brand new ball was prominently displayed on the top. It was the match ball. 'Oh no!' he groaned. 'It's a Mitre ball…I can't kick a Mitre ball…I expected a Gilbert ball, that's what we asked for…I'm OK with a Gilbert ball…I can kick it fairly accurately…but not a Mitre ball.'

I looked at him closely; he was clearly very upset about the choice of match ball. In rugby, a good kicker is worth his weight in gold. He can win matches by scoring extra points every time a penalty is awarded and a try is scored. If Gary continued to think this way, there was a distinct possibility that he might perform badly and miss a few kicks. Despite the lack of time for implementing an intervention strategy, I decided to treat the situation as critical and try to modify his beliefs by using a crisis intervention strategy. I mentally formed a plan of action he could work on during the next two hours.

We walked over to the match ball; I picked it up and asked why he couldn't kick it as well as the Gilbert ball. He said something about minor differences in the shape, but he agreed with me when I argued that if it were kicked accurately with a good technique, the kick would be successful. He also agreed that his negative thoughts about a Mitre ball were a form of distraction, which interfered with focusing on kicking successfully. I said, 'OK, we have established that the problem is largely psychological so I can teach you how to overcome this and today is going to be the day you begin to kick a Mitre ball successfully.' I asked him to say, 'Today is the day I am going to start kicking a Mitre ball properly.' I asked him to use this self-statement frequently during the next two hours. We then found a quiet place in the stadium and I gave him some basic training in imagery. He visualised himself kicking a Mitre ball successfully from a number of different positions on the pitch and I suggested that if he felt comfortable with it, he could quickly use it as a mental rehearsal technique just before kicking. I would have liked him to have some physical practices but formalities prevented us from doing this.

I joined the coaching team on the bench a few minutes before the teams came out. They were aware of what I had been doing. Sport psychology was fairly new to them and they had been able to see me working with Gary. In many ways, it had now become a test of the value of mental training and I felt some anxiety creeping in. The match started and it soon became clear that the teams were evenly matched. There was a distinct possibility that the result would hinge on the kickers. Fifteen minutes into the first half with the scores still level, a Welsh player was penalised for making a dangerous tackle. Gary decided to kick for goal. My heart was in my mouth as he placed the ball, stepped back and clearly carried out his imagery of a successful kick. One of the coaches looked at me and said, 'Nervous, Rog?'

'Not me,' I lied.

It was a difficult kick, just ten yards inside the Welsh half and to the right-hand side. Gary finished visualising, his head came up and he ran in and thumped the ball towards the posts. It cleared the crossbar by about 4 metres and went right between the posts. It was a superb kick. Gary turned towards the bench, caught my eye, gave a huge smile and stuck up two thumbs. The feeling that I had was almost as good as when the final whistle went and we had beaten Wales.

After image

While I was working for England Rugby, the management team from the Great Britain and England Men's hockey team asked to see me, regarding me taking on the role of becoming a sport psychologist. I met the senior coach and a couple of the management team and I explained how I would introduce sport psychology. After an hour's discussion he asked me what my commitments were in six weeks time. 'I've nothing special on,' I said. 'In that case, I'll book you on the flight. I would like you to join us on the tour to Italy,' he said.

We arrived at the hotel, went straight in for an evening meal and I was promptly put to the test. I was just finishing my meal when the senior coach said, 'I would like you to give a two-hour session on mental skills training.' With an unconvincing apologetic expression he said that there was no projector or other lecturing aids. I returned the smile indicating that I was aware of his strategy. 'I'll start in two minutes,' I said. I dashed back to my room and collected 20 copies of a specially prepared players' booklet, which I had brought with me just in case I found myself in a situation such as this.

It was also not uncommon to be tested by the players, in addition to the coaches. At an England Rugby U21 Squad training session I was asked about psychological techniques for pain control. I described a couple of techniques. During the evening a small group of players approached on the pretext of discussing a problem. One player was using a battery-operated heat massager for a muscle injury. He handed it to me and asked me what I thought of it. As he did so he turned it up to maximum power behind his back. It was extremely painful but I managed to keep a deadpan face and asked him if it could be turned up any more. They said, 'Hey, his pain control ideas really work.' 'Of course, they do!' I calmly said gritting my teeth. I calmly walked to the toilet and let out a loud 'Aaaaagh' of pain.

Six months after the hockey tour to Italy I was flying to another country again with the GB Hockey team. This time we were going to take part in a pre-Olympic tournament. It was here that I had my first big breakthrough that silenced the 'mickey-taking' players and brought the 'hard men' knocking on my door, asking how to use mental skills to improve their performance.

The breakthrough occurred shortly after we arrived. I was sharing a room with a specialist coach. His role was to constantly monitor the performance of players in his specialist position. One of the players was considered to be the best in the world. It was surprising, therefore, when he came into the room and told the coach that he had lost his confidence and had become very nervous before matches. I knew nothing about this, as he was one of the 'hard men' who had made it clear that he didn't need a shrink. That was for 'softies'. I listened in to the conversation but while the coach came up with some really good ideas for physical practices, I felt that they didn't address the specific problem. The player explained how in a recent international match he had made a fundamental error resulting in the other team scoring and England losing the match. He kept thinking about it and it was destroying his confidence as he anticipated making the same mistake again.

It's never been in my personality to keep quiet when I've got something to say, so I got off my bed and said, 'Oh, if that's all your problem is, I can sort that out in no time. Let's get started.' Inside me, a voice said, 'Here we go again...in with both feet...now you will have to put your money where your mouth is.' I started off by giving an explanation of how the reoccurring image of making a mistake was having a detrimental effect on his performance. It was causing excessive tension and cortical 'noise'. When he thought about the error, he was essentially attending to irrelevant information when his brain should be focusing on what was relevant information regarding the task at the time.

I pointed out that before a match, 'positive best performance' imagery is very useful as it prevents the brain from thinking negative thoughts and visualising negative images. I then explained that I was going to use a crisis intervention strategy based on 'thought stopping', a cognitive-behavioural approach that is aimed at changing a person's thoughts and images. Ultimately the athlete's perception of the problem should be modified. In this player's case, he should recall all the times he had played brilliantly, resulting in England winning.

I asked him to explain in detail the error, which was troubling him. We then discussed what he did and then I asked him to describe what he should have done. I then asked him to stand up and to physically go through the action that he should have made. He struggled for a few minutes saying that he felt stupid standing up in a bedroom pretending he was playing hockey. In order to ease his embarrassment I demonstrated how to do it physically and got the coach to join in. I then asked him to recall the situation in the game just before he made the error. He should visualise what was happening. I then asked him to use positive imagery and replace the mental image of the error with an image of seeing himself making the correct action. For an hour he practised seeing himself in the situation, starting to make the error, then correcting it and seeing himself succeeding.

The next match was against India, a team that would be stiff opposition. During the warm-up the player looked composed and said that he felt confident. He gave a brilliant performance. I had not said anything about the training in order to respect his confidentiality. However, he had spent three hours practising after the hour with me and had openly spent two hours every day practising mental rehearsal until the image of making an error was buried.

Chrissie and the burglar

Chrissie was 9 years old. During the last 12 months she had made incredible progress and, as a result, she had been invited to join the West Midlands Gymnastic Squad. Chrissie had enormous potential. She was recognised as one of the best gymnasts in the country and was likely to be invited to join the National Squad. Then the burglar came and stole her skills. One by one her skills disappeared. Her coaches were very worried and asked me if I could help, as it appeared that Chrissie's problem was psychological.

When I first went to see her, she was at a three-hour training session with the West Midlands Squad. She spent most of the time sitting chatting to the other girls or just watching the others. When she was asked to practise, she did so reluctantly and in some situations, notably on the asymmetrical bars, she would 'freeze' and be unable to perform the skill task. A similar set of responses was occurring on the vaulting horse. She was gradually losing the ability to perform vaults that, until recently, she had been able to perform at a high level.

Her motivation to train was becoming a problem, the lack of progress was evident and, as a result, she was seriously considering giving up gymnastics and quitting. I was particularly interested in her reaction to training on the asymmetrical bars. She seemed to become very anxious and was unable to perform because she had become very tense.

At the request of Chrissie's coach I agreed to work with her. I started a number of sessions with Chrissie but made little progress at first. Gradually I began to get a full picture of how she felt and why. It became apparent that the problem stemmed from the time that she had had an accident on the asymmetrical bars. She was attempting to perform a special dismount which required her to balance horizontally on the top bar then dip the legs, throw them back and up split the legs into straddle push off the hands and dismount forwards to land on the mat. During an early attempt to learn this move, she had caught her toes on the bar and nearly fell, which could have resulted in serious injury. I had frequently asked her about fear of performing difficult and potentially dangerous skills and she had never given a clear answer. It suddenly occurred to me that it was possible that it wasn't fear of performing; it was fear of experiencing the feeling that she had when she nearly fell. She was frightened of fear.

Further investigation confirmed this. We worked on coping skills for dealing with emotions and visualised dealing with the burglar who came to steal her skills. She enjoyed seeing herself lying in bed staying calm, taking a torch from under her pillow and shining it straight at the burglar. At the same time she pressed the buttons on her singing toys and they all started singing their own songs in their distinctive metallic voices. Jack-in-the-box jumped out and the burglar ran away with an empty bag.

Chrissie also said that when she was about to start a difficult move she heard a voice inside her head saying, 'I can't...I can't.' Together we worked out a mental strategy for dealing with this. Chrissie visualised an old turntable with an arm that had a needle in the end. When the arm was lowered and the needle came into contact with the record on the turntable, a voice said, 'I can't...I can't.' She then saw herself reaching out, lifting the arm and moving it to a different place on the record. The voice then said, 'I can...I can.' Chrissie practised this regularly and she started to regain the skills that she had lost.

One Sunday morning a couple of months after I had finished working with Chrissie, the phone rang. I picked it up and a squeaky 9-year-old girl's voice said, 'Guess who's Regional Gymnastics Champion?' It was probably the best sport psychology experience I have ever had.

Acknowledgement

This text was originally printed in *From Balls to Psychology* by Sport in Mind. Sections published by permission of Sport in Mind.

References

Mace, R. D. (1990) Cognitive behavioural interventions in sport, in G. Jones and L. Hardy (eds) *Stress and Performance in Sport*. Chichester: John Wiley & Sons, Ltd, pp. 203–230.
——(2007) *From Balls to Psychology*. Worcestershire: Sport in Mind.
Meichenbaum, D. (1977) *Cognitive Behaviour Modification: An Integrative Approach*. New York: Plenum.
——(1985) *Stress Inoculation Training*. New York: Pergamon.

4

ON BECOMING A SPORT PSYCHOLOGY CONSULTANT

What a long strange trip it's been

Robert Weinberg

"What a long strange trip it's been." This classic line from the Grateful Dead song "Truckin" probably best sums up my career in sport and exercise psychology. It was a career that most definitely was not targeted to sport psychology. Rather, it was supposed to be a career that focused on teaching and coaching; and before that on accounting. But I am getting ahead of myself. So let me start from the beginning.

Early beginnings

Entering Brooklyn College, I was going to be an accounting major since I was pretty good in math in high school. Although I was doing well in my accounting courses, I was not really enjoying my studies. But I knew that what one does on the job is often not that similar to what they have learned in school. Fortunately, a couple of my friends' dads were CPAs (Certified Public Accountants) and that was exactly what I thought I wanted to do. I interviewed them and when they told me what they did on a daily basis, I decided that was not for me. I was in the end of my sophomore year so if I was going to change majors, I needed to do it pretty quickly. So what was I going to study? The only thing that came to mind was something related to sports because I had been an athlete all my life and sports were central to my personality. Thus, I decided to become a physical education major and hopefully become a physical education teacher in the New York City public school system and coach a team.

So I majored in physical education, fully intending to teach and coach. As a junior, I became student co-intramural chair working with a faculty member to organize intramurals. The faculty director (Dr. Bernard Pollack) took an interest in me and convinced me that I should apply to Graduate School because I had good grades, and was capable of graduate work. After researching and visiting several schools, I decided on UCLA where I pursued a Master's in Kinesiology (minor in psychology) and started to get an interest in psychology related to sport.

Remember there were still few, if any, classes in sport psychology at this time, but my interest was spurred by three sources. First was a book (now out of print) called *The Madness in Sport* written by Arnold Beisser, who was a junior Davis Cup tennis player who had an accident and was paralyzed from the waist down. He went on to become a psychiatrist and wrote about some of his clients who had psychological (sometimes clinical) issues related to sport such as fear or success, suicidal thoughts, excess anxiety, and lack of confidence. This really intrigued me, and it related to my sport experience from the standpoint of the importance of the mental side of competition. Specifically, I was able to be fairly successful as a varsity athlete because I felt that I played "smart" (had a good mental game), knew my limitations, made good decisions, and analyzed my opponents' strengths and weaknesses. Third, I received a research assistantship and my major duties were to supervise and run the electromyography (motor behavior) laboratory at UCLA. This spurred my interest into investigating how anxiety affected performance via its impact on muscle tension (and formed the basis for my Master's thesis and doctoral dissertation).

After completing my Master's, I went back to New York and was still intending to teach and coach. But my major professor at UCLA, Dr. Valerie Hunt, encouraged me to think about getting a PhD because she felt I had the aptitude and interest to continue my studies. Although I had not really thought abut a PhD before, this idea intrigued me and I wound up going back to UCLA in the Psychology Department (the Kinesiology Department did not have a PhD) and received a second Master's degree along with a PhD. There was no formal specialization in sport psychology in the psychology department so I formally specialized in social psychology and industrial psychology. This psychology background combined with the sport science background I received doing my undergraduate physical education and the Kinesiology Master's provided me with a solid foundation to study sport and exercise psychology. In addition, I was able to take a couple of sport psychology courses through the Kinesiology Department while studying for my PhD and these were the only formal sport psychology courses I ever took.

I still was not totally interested in research as I started the doctoral program in psychology, but I became interested through my tennis doubles partner (of all things) who was into research and studying motor behavior/control. Once I got my Master's thesis accepted for publication, it really gave me a real boost in confidence. In addition, I started to enjoy discovering new knowledge via research and the research process itself, so for those of you graduate students who are not that interested in research, this might change as you get experience doing research.

Starting my sport psychology career

At the time of the completion of my PhD (1978), there was still little in the way of applied sport psychology opportunities working with athletes but a few programs in sport psychology started to emerge at different universities. After several close seconds, I finally accepted a position in sport psychology at the University of North Texas. My primary job was to build the sport psychology program through research and teaching, although after a few years my name started to get out to the community due to doing workshops, and presenting at coaching conferences. As a result, I started getting calls to do some mental training and sport psychology consulting with athletes. It was now in the early to mid-1980s and applied sport psychology was just starting to take off and get some national publicity.

Of course, there were no courses in applied sport psychology that focused on how to consult effectively. The whole notion of mental or psychological skills training was just being developed, so consulting, frankly, was a little by "the seat of your pants." I did do some reading in the counseling literature, which was helpful in terms of process and communication, but there were still few guidelines on assessment and what to include as part of the consulting process with athletes. My background as a former varsity coach and athlete helped me during the initial consultations. In addition, I started out using some standard psychological inventories that seemed related to sport (e.g., the Test of Attentional and Interpersonal Style, Nideffer, 1976) along with fairly newly developed sport specific inventories including the Sport Competition Anxiety Test (Martens, 1977) and the Psychological Skills for Sport (Mahoney et al., 1987). I employed psychological inventories as my primary method of assessment, although over the years I used more and more interview information as my primary means of assessment. I was knowledgeable about many different sports and this was helpful in connecting with athletes and understanding their unique terminology. As I consulted with more and more athletes, my name became better known, and I continued to receive more and more referrals. Thus, I have always led two sport psychology lives. The first one is my position as a professor with a focus on teaching and research in sport psychology along with professional service. My second life is as a consultant, where I work with individual athletes or teams on the development of mental skills for performance enhancement and personal growth. At this point, it seems appropriate to discuss the evolution of my sport psychology consulting approach.

My consulting orientation

I started my sport psychology consultations with little help in terms of empirical research regarding how to be an effective consultant. I believe the first sport psychology article dealing with the initial contact of meeting and securing a client (although not the consulting process per se) was by Ken Ravizza (1988). But I always take an educational (mental skills) as opposed to a clinical approach to consulting, due to my training in kinesiology and psychology focusing on social psychology and not clinical psychology. I communicate this to clients right at the beginning of my first session along with the notion of confidentiality which helps establish a feeling of trust. In addition, I am usually more "directive" than "detective" as I focus on what has been happening now as opposed of trying to be a detective and find out about things that might have happened in the past.

In terms of a psychological approach to interventions in sport psychology, I have chosen to be fairly eclectic but with a focus on a cognitive-behavioral and social psychological orientation. With this in mind, I have focused on an interactional approach highlighting reciprocal determinism (Bandura, 1997) of people and environments. I try to define the boundaries where the athlete is having a problem. For example, the issue may start for a basketball player when he feels he is pushed and shoved by an opposing player and the official does not call a foul. It may end by the player retaliating in an aggressive manner and getting called for a foul. Thus I may focus on this period of time to teach some mental skills to more effectively deal with the problem. Finally, there are generally two types of clients that come in for sport psychology consultations. One does not have a problem but simply wants to improve his "mental game" and this requires a preventative approach teaching appropriate mental skills. The other has a specific psychological issue and requires a problem-focused approach, teaching mental skills to effectively cope with the problem. Of course, oftentimes, the delineation between these two approaches gets clouded, as many athletes need a combination of these approaches.

A heuristic for my sport psychology consulting

Poczwardowski *et al.* (1998) and Poczwardowski and Sherman (2011) have presented a heuristic that focuses on critical factors in designing, implementing and evaluating sport psychology services that provides a nice structure to situate my consulting. The different aspects of this heuristic will be highlighted and then my consulting practices will be integrated into this structure.

Professional boundaries

One's professional boundaries should be defined by their academic training, and this should help clarify services to prospective clients. As noted above, I take an educational approach, focusing on the development of mental skills. To support my approach, I am bound to the ethical guidelines advanced by the American Psychological Association and further refined by the Association for Applied Sport Psychology.

Professional philosophy

This focuses on the consultant's belief about the nature of behavior change and helps define their intervention goals (e.g., performance enhancement, personal development) and how to accomplish them. Although there are many potential approaches (e.g., behaviorism, rational emotive, psychophysiology), I noted above that I endorse a cognitive-behavioral, social psychological approach. The approach is less important than how it provides guidance to the consultant for conceptualizing and implementing their intervention.

Making contact

As noted earlier, the first article addressing this issue was Ravizza (1988) where he detailed the importance of the coach's or organization's willingness to accept the consultant into their environment. When I make contact with a potential client, it is important that I quickly establish respect, credibility, and trust. By demonstrating my expertise in sport psychology (and maybe in the sport itself), I specify the limits of confidentiality, clarify my role and explain the services I provide. This aspect of making contact can change dramatically if I am speaking with an individual parent (as I often am, because I work a lot with junior development athletes) or if I am speaking with a coach, general manager, or personnel director of a team. In the former, I try to inform the parent of my approach, my ability to deliver mental skills training, and confidentiality. For teams, I usually have a much more detailed plan (written) regarding how I would deliver mental skills training to the entire team, emphasizing my background/expertise, and clarifying my role.

Presently, if you want to be a sport psychology consultant, you have to be assertive in getting the word out about you and your services. Having an excellent website is a must in today's technological world as potential clients often go there first to see what sport psychologists are in their area. If you can do this yourself fine; if not, hire someone with expertise to set up a user-friendly website. I am not technologically savvy but have a website which has generated a lot of business. Things you also can do to enhance business is write applied sport psychology articles and a book, give presentations, join sport and/or business organizations, and volunteer. Sometimes doing something for nothing will get you business, but that's an individual call as to how much sport psychology do you give away.

Assessment

Identifying the athlete's, coach's or organization's needs, wants, strengths and weaknesses with respect to psychological aspects that are critical to individual or collective growth within the sport organization is a key first step in the consulting process. I started with general trait tests of psychological skills (e.g., anxiety, confidence, concentration, motivation), and then began to employ sport-specific tests as well as multidimensional sport-specific tests such as the Test of Psychological Skills (Thomas et al., 1999) and the Athletic Coping Skills Inventory (Smith et al., 1995). Based on the results of the questionnaire and some interviewing, I would write up about a three-page summary detailing the strengths and areas of improvement of the athlete. I end the evaluation with a summary of key points as well as recommendations for the mental skills we would concentrate on based on my evaluation.

However, over the years I have moved more and more to rely almost totally on an in-depth semi-structured interview for my assessment (backed up at times with questionnaires based on the individual athlete). Before I formally begin, I emphasize and explain the concept of confidentiality and my approach to mental training. I use a triangle to explain my approach. Specifically, I note that there are three aspects that are necessary for anyone to reach their potential in sport. First are physical skills and coaches usually helped develop these. Then there is conditioning (strength, flexibility, endurance), which is done by coaches or physical (personal) trainers. Finally, there are mental skills (e.g., concentration, dealing with pressure, goal-setting, confidence). I ask how important each of these is to performance, and athletes typically agree that all are important. I simply add that someone like me focuses on developing mental skills and thus I like to see myself as a mental coach. This usually alleviates athletes' fears about going to a "shrink" who is trying to find something wrong with their mental state.

I typically start off the actual interview asking athletes to describe their experiences in their sport, starting from when they first started, highlighting important positive and negative events. This helps establish trust and allows athletes to start to feel comfortable just talking about their sport experience. Although I would not necessarily get a lot of useful information from this, it serves the purpose of allowing athletes to feel more at ease, as they often do not know what to expect from a sport psychology consultant. Although some athletes get right into their "problem," I usually steer clear of this for a while and then have them focus on what they were thinking and feeling when they had their best and worst performance. This usually results in very disparate feelings and thoughts and athletes start to realize that what they are thinking and feeling is very much related to how well or poorly they perform. I then start to ask them to discuss their strengths and weakness in different mental areas (one at a time). Sometime during these discussions, athletes will start talking about the things that are really causing a problem right now. But often other issues emerge as they get a chance to discuss things on their mind that often they never talked about before. I probe where appropriate but mostly listen to what athletes have to say so I can get the most amount of information for my assessment.

Conceptualizing athletes' concerns and potential intervention

Given this semi-structured interview and any questionnaires I might give, I write up a detailed assessment/evaluation for the different mental skills (e.g., confidence, coping with anxiety, motivation, concentration) and then end with a summary and recommendations for how to proceed with the mental training. It is important to note that this is an individualized evaluation, which I find much more effective (although time-consuming). At the second session, I try to consensually validate the assessment by going over it carefully with athletes, asking them to explain some things and note whether they agree or disagree with the different aspects of the evaluation.

Range, types, and organization of service

After the assessment has been shared with the athlete, a strategy should be developed to determine, how, when, and in what order mental skills should be delivered. To do this, I usually take into consideration such things as the specifics of the organization or the individual athlete (e.g., competitions, training, days off, preseason, informal/formal conditioning, skill level, relationship with coaches, and proximity to myself). I typically start out explaining and working on goal setting, especially the difference between outcome, performance, and process goals as these seem critical to get athletes started in the right direction. The other skills simply are given in a manner individualized to athletes' needs.

Program implementation

The specific mental skills are explained in detail before athletes are asked to practice them and then eventually employ them in competitive situations. Homework assignments, log books, self-monitoring, as well as other assessment and self-awareness techniques are employed so that athletes have something to work on between sessions. They have to bring in their "homework" for the next session and I go over it as it relates to the development of specific mental skills. As athletes learn a mental skill, a new skill is added as appropriate to their individual needs. All athletes are given folders in which they keep my handouts, their assignments, articles, and any other information that I might give them. This becomes a permanent record (I also keep a similar copy of all materials for my files).

Specific mental plans are developed to help athletes manage the different situations before, during, and after competition. These include: (1) pre-competition plans; (2) pre-competition refocus plans; (3) competition focus plans; (4) competition refocus plans; and (5) post-competition plans. Not all these may be relevant for each athlete; again, this is individualized based on the athlete and the situation.

Program/Self-evaluation

In most cases, I do this informally rather than formally. I will typically survey athletes (and coaches and parents, if appropriate) regarding what worked and didn't work. I will also do this for myself as I always try to learn and get better.

Lessons learned

I have learned a great deal over the years to help improve my own consultancy. First, I have learned from coach and athlete feedback as noted above. Their input and suggestions are critical to me and help structure more effective consultations. For example, many years ago, a coach suggested I come to competitions to see the athlete in action and I have made that a staple of my consultancy over the years. I periodically have discussions with outstanding consultants asking their opinions about some of my tougher consultant situations as well as having them share with me how they handled different situations. I have always tried to stay abreast of current literature although that has been harder and harder over the years with the proliferation of so much material and the Internet. Along these lines, I regularly attend sport psychology conferences because that is where the most current information is delivered. I have learned to be an active listener. Consistent with the counseling literature, consultant characteristics play an important role in the success of any treatment. So listen to what the client is saying and reflect back about the meaning of their communications. If you happen to get to consult at a big event (e.g., the Olympic Games, World Championships), don't try to do too much. Much of the time will be spent sitting around; you have to wait for athletes to come to you and have to feel happy sitting on the sidelines most of the time. If you work with a team, try to fit in by being around practice, riding the bus to competitions, and just being around as this facilitates trust. As the old saying goes, "Athletes don't care what you know until they know that you care."

Advice to aspiring sport psychology consultants

Commencing on a career as a sport psychology consultant can be an exciting yet daunting time. First, you have to determine whether you want to pursue an academic career, which would focus on teaching and research, but with an interest to also develop an applied sport psychology practice, or do you want to simply start a practice in applied sport psychology? One of the things I think people wanting to start a sport psychology practice need to do while in school is to take a number of business courses (e.g., marketing, management, entrepreneurship) because you will likely be starting a small business. This requires numerous business skills in addition to your sport psychology skills, as you have to manage an office, billing, phones, advertising, scheduling, and so on. I would also suggest that if you want to start an applied sport psychology business, you get licensed in psychology so you can access insurance payments and increase your potential pool of clients. An educational sport psychologist can primarily consult with athletes on the development of mental skills. Starting a practice focusing only on athletes can be difficult and daunting. Some people trained in sport psychology have started working in the business world using sport psychology skills. If you are interested in this approach, I would again suggest business courses, especially in leadership and organizational development.

Challenges for the future of sport psychology consultancy

I think one of the biggest challenges as well as opportunities for sport psychology consultants will be the important role that technology will play in the future. More and more consultants are using Skype, telephone consults, and online Internet-based consulting (Weinberg et al., 2012). New consultants need to make sure they make full use of technology in their consulting and possibly join a sport psychology organization to help get them started. Tapping into less elite populations (e.g., youth sports, junior development athletes, senior athletes) where finances have not been great and access has not been easy might be a great opportunity to help establish a sport psychology consultant business.

As noted earlier, making a living as an educational sport psychology consultant will continue to be difficult due to the lack of access to insurance and the inability to work with populations needing clinical help. I have seen first-hand that many professional organizations want individuals who can handle both the mental skills aspect and clinical aspects of sport psychology consultancy. Thus, new professionals need to get enhanced training/education, both in the sport sciences and psychological sciences (with a license in psychology) to meet the needs of current clients and organizations and increase their potential for securing employment.

Another potential career path might be more in the exercise than sport domain. Specifically, hospitals and physical therapy clinics are starting to see the need for expertise in the area of the psychology of injury rehabilitation. In the military, there is an increased concern for the mental health ramifications of being in a war (e.g., post traumatic stress syndrome). Similarly, in sport and exercise, the mental aspects of rehabilitation are seen as increasingly crucial for a successful recovery from injury. This is especially the case where an athlete is no longer able to compete in their sport due to injury and their identity is closely tied to their athletic prowess. Athletes also report that the mental aspects of injury recovery are even more difficult than the physical aspects. In our graduate program, we see more and more students, who were athletic training or physical therapy majors as undergraduates, train themselves in graduate sport/exercise psychology to work with patients in rehabilitation settings.

Sport psychology has been a great field to be involved with for me as it combines my interests in sport and my interest in psychology. Because becoming rich is not a high likelihood in this business, I feel that you need to be passionate about the field and doing this type of work (either in the university or as part of the business world). It might take a while to get yourself established as a consultant so you need to have patience and dedication to wait out the bad times. But if you truly are committed to the field, I think you will reap great benefits (many not financial) in helping individuals reach their potential. Enjoy the journey.

References

Bandura, A. (1997) *Self-efficacy: The Exercise of Control*. New York: Freeman.

Mahoney, M., Gabriel, T. and Perkins, T. (1987) Psychological skills and experienced athlete performance. *The Sport Psychologist*, 1: 181–199.

Martens, R. (1977) *Sport Competition Anxiety Test*. Champaign, IL: Human Kinetics

Nideffer, R. (1976) Test of attentional and interpersonal style. *Journal of Personality and Social Psychology*, 34: 394–404.

Orlick, T. (1986) *Psyching for Sport: Mental Training for Athletes*. Champaign, IL: Human Kinetics.

Poczwardowski, A. and Sherman, C. P. (2011) Revisions to the sport psychology service delivery (SPSD) heuristic: explorations with experienced consultants. *The Sport Psychologist*, 25: 511–531.

Poczwardowski, A., Sherman, C. and Henschen, K. (1998) A sport psychology service delivery system: building on theory and practice. *The Sport Psychologist*, 12: 191–207.

Ravizza, K. (1988) Gaining entry with athletic personnel for season-long consulting. *The Sport Psychologist*, 2: 243–254.

Smith, R., Schultz, R., Smoll, F. and Ptacek, J. (1995) Development and validation of a multidimensional measure of sport-specific psychological skills: the Athletic Coping Skills Inventory-26. *Journal of Sport and Exercise Psychology*, 17: 379–398.

Thomas, P., Murphy, S. and Hardy, L. (1999) Test of performance strategies: development and preliminary validation of a comprehensive measure of athletes' psychological skills. *Journal of Sports Sciences*, 17: 697–711.

Weinberg, R., Neff, R. and Jurica, B. (2012) Online mental training: making it available to the masses. *Journal of Sport Psychology in Action*, 3(3): 182–92.

5

DADDY AND THE MEANING OF SERVICE DELIVERY

Becoming an applied sport psychology practitioner

David Tod

As a teenager, I had wanted to be a physical education teacher, and I had not heard of sport psychology. Also, I understood that psychology was anti-Christian, an impression I had gained from the church circles in which I moved. As far as I knew, psychologists used their research to justify a godless and evil existence. Early in my working career, a devout Christian prayed for my soul upon learning I taught sport psychology. My views have changed since my teenage years and I now realise psychologists are not reprobates (well…mostly), but help people with their issues, problems, challenges, and desires. In this chapter, I will discuss my journey from a 'non-believer' to someone working in the discipline, along with some of the ways I have changed as an individual and a professional.

The road to Damascus

To pursue my goal to be a teacher, I enrolled in a Bachelor of Physical Education at the University of Otago in 1988. My initial Damascus road experience occurred in my first year, when Ken Hodge gave a lecture on character development in sport. I was fascinated, because morality was something that I thought a lot about as a God-fearing person, and I wanted to find out more about moral conduct in athletes. In my second year sport sociology course, I also learned about athletes' deviant behaviours, and for the first time in my life I wanted to study a topic for interest, not because it was a requirement. The other lasting lesson Ken taught me during my undergraduate years was that the mind influenced the body. As someone who played rugby union, the notion that mental strategies could enhance my performance was something I wanted to explore.

In my final undergraduate year I decided to apply to do a Master's degree, but was unsure whether I had the grades to be accepted. In addition to working hard to lift my grades, I told Ken of my desire to do a Master's degree and regularly had extra tutorials to discuss the character and moral reasoning papers I read. It was a conscious strategy to impress Ken, but it was also the result of my interest in the topic. I was delighted when Ken told my second Master's supervisor, in jest, he feared that if he had not accepted my application, he would not have ever gotten rid of me. It was during my Master's degree that I started working with clients in both group and individual sessions.

The missionary goes forth

There were no formal applied sport psychology courses or professional accreditation schemes in New Zealand at the time I undertook my Master's. The qualification was research-based, and the modules were focused on methodology and statistics. I wanted to work with athletes, however, and went looking for clients. I initially started helping a basketball player and facilitated some group workshops through the consultancy arm of the physical education department in which I was housed. With Ken's guidance I gained my initial experiences as a practitioner, and my early attempts were firmly based on his text, *Sport Motivation* (Hodge, 1994). He worked for lots of national sporting bodies and had published a book, so I trusted his knowledge. Also, the book had many worksheets I could photocopy and use with clients, providing me with the confidence that I could be helpful to athletes. With my initial earnings I purchased other books, including Martens' (1987) *Coaches Guide to Sport Psychology* and Williams' (1993) *Applied Sport Psychology*, that helped broaden my knowledge in psychological skills training.

Before completing my Master's I started working at the Waikato Institute of Technology where I taught sport psychology/sport science and worked with both student athletes and external clients. I threw myself into the position, working with a large variety of athletes, teams, and squads from a broad range of sports, ranging from weekend warriors to Olympic, professional, and elite performers. I would often have 30 or more hours a week of teaching and consulting. These were just the formal hours, and I did not keep a track of the informal hours I spent at clients' training sessions and competitions observing and interacting with them on an *ad hoc* basis. One of the joys of the job was experiencing new sports and activities, ostensibly so that I could develop insights into the demands athletes faced.

I was excited to be employed in a consulting capacity, and felt I was helping people, offering something that allowed them to perform better. My understanding of service delivery was narcissistic: I thought I had special knowledge that could effect change. Counter-transference was also occurring, although at the time I was unaware of these motivations. When I was 13 years old, my father died seven days before I started high school, an event that had a lasting impression on me. I had no capacity for understanding death and reacted by getting drunk at his funeral. He had been a strict disciplinarian, and as a teenager I missed, and fantasized about, having a father who could teach me how to be a man (and a rugby player) and with whom I could share a beer. To that point, the proudest moments in my life had been playing representative schoolboy rugby in front of him, showing him I was a man like him and worthy of his infrequently expressed approval. After his death, people kept telling me I was the man of the family, but I did not know what that meant; I was a schoolboy whose voice had not yet broken. Also, from that moment life was a struggle financially for my mother who had to raise three young children, and I came to believe that no one really cared about us (me), despite the kind words and promises uttered in the days following the funeral. Subconsciously, working with athletes in a mentoring capacity allowed me to address a deficiency in my life – I could be the mentor (father) for others that I had not had myself.

In addition to excitement and satisfaction, I also experienced self-doubt and anxiety because I was aware I had not been formally trained in psychology or service delivery. I imitated Ken's style, and used whatever I picked up from books, colleagues, and clients. These anxieties stimulated attempts to develop my competence. I enrolled in a Graduate Diploma to give myself the equivalent of an undergraduate psychology degree. I spent a summer writing a 32-page manual on how to work with athletes, a task that served two purposes. I used it in a module I was teaching, but it also became my Bible for working with clients. It summarised a traditional psychological skills training approach. My rigid allegiance to psychological skills training helped me manage my self-doubts. To me, it was the manual and the interventions contained within that helped clients, and as long as I followed its simple, logical, straightforward path, I would be effective despite my anxieties.

The sympathetic friend and disillusionment

Initially, during this early period I operated in ways similar to Rønnestad and Skovholt's (2003) 'sympathetic friend'. I identified problems quickly, provided strong emotional reinforcement, and then gave advice based on my knowledge and experience. I was also superficially aware of the role that I and relationships played in service delivery, but because I lacked an ability to monitor and regulate my thoughts, emotions, and behaviours, I sometimes blurred boundaries between clients and myself, becoming over-involved with individuals. For example, I have recently written about an instance of erotic counter-transference I experienced, because I was unable to monitor and regulate my emotions (Tod, in press). Other similar issues included termination (I was losing 'my' athletes) and accepting too much responsibility for client performance (if they won, it meant I was good at my job).

Despite these limitations, I was helpful to many clients. Clients experienced changes in behaviour, thoughts, well-being, and performance (although I acknowledge the unscientific and subjective basis of this claim). Clients gave me positive feedback, kept returning, gave me money, and told others about me, indicating they thought I had been helpful to them. I found, however, that a psychological skills training approach was not always helpful. For example, simple interventions did not help resolve complex issues, clients did not always complete homework exercises, and the range of their presenting issues was much wider than what was discussed in the applied literature at that time. I also came to realise the need to be mindful of the context within which I worked and the influence it could have on my role. On one occasion I was asked by a colleague, who was the physiotherapist for a provincial netball team, to give an introductory workshop to the squad, whom I knew had been having an unsuccessful season. After they lost the following week, it was reported in the newspaper that a sport psychologist had failed to help them turn themselves around. That I was annoyed, because I had delivered what I had been asked to produce, an introductory workshop, and had not been asked to turn the team into winners, indicated my ignorance of the context in which sport occurs. Another example involved the issue of client confidentiality. I was asked to attend a training camp for a national cycling squad to give a workshop, and undertake some performance profiling and goal setting with the athletes. At the end of the camp, the coach wanted some feedback and kept asking for details I was uncomfortable disclosing because I thought it violated confidentiality. Although the coach said he understood the importance of client confidentiality, I was not asked to work with that coach again.

Change and growth

The disillusionment I had with a psychological skills training approach, and the number of times I came across situations where I felt out of my depth stimulated a desire for learning, and was a prime motivator for the selection of my PhD topic in 2002. I also undertook postgraduate studies in counselling and psychology. Throughout my career, there have been a number of people and events that have helped me develop my understanding of the applied role and a broader appreciation of my approach. A big catalyst for learning was client interaction. Through active experimentation and reflection I developed new skills, along with a greater understanding of service delivery relationships and myself as the practitioner. Early in my career, for example, when reading a New Zealand rugby union player's account of having experienced depression (Kirwan and Thomas, 1992), the player wrote that he didn't find many people's advice helpful, because they often said what they would do in his situation and didn't consider him as an individual. One of my next clients was a squash player, and I took more time than with previous athletes learning about her situation and reflecting back my understanding before we focused on possible solutions. It turned out that her presenting problem was not a lack of motivation, as she had initially described, but the anxieties she experienced due to a poor athlete–coach relationship. She reported that the opportunity to talk had helped her clarify exactly what was troubling her, and we were able to develop ways she could communicate better with her coach and manage her emotions. Another rewarding consultation was when a rugby player told me that he found working with me helpful, because unlike most other people he knew, I didn't tell him what to do, but helped him decide for himself.

Reading a lot more widely than just the applied sport psychology literature also enhanced my development. Albert Ellis (Ellis and Dryden, 1997), Judith Beck

(Aaron Beck's daughter, 1995), Victor Frankl (1959), and Irving Yalom (1989) were, and are, some of the particularly helpful authors. For example, Frankl's autobiography and explanation of logotherapy helped me appreciate the value of assisting clients to find meaning and purpose in their lives and sport. I also learned from pop management and psychology authors, such as Zig Ziglar (1975) and Steven Covey (1989) because their writings often contained creative solutions to problems and ways of expressing ideas clients found helpful.

The poet John Donne's quote 'no man is an island' applies to my development as a practitioner, and there have been a number of colleagues, supervisors, mentors, and friends who have contributed to my growth (far too many than I could discuss in this chapter). Throughout my career I have offered to take individuals out for coffee or lunch so I could talk to them. In most cases, the knowledge gained has outweighed the financial cost. Ken Hodge and Daryl Marchant (a PhD supervisor), for example, were role models in being practical and professional in managing a workload and delivering a service or product. Mark Andersen, my other PhD supervisor, is the closest thing I have had as a father figure as an adult. He challenged me on a number of issues that made me uncomfortable, was happy to be challenged, and has helped me bring together in a somewhat coherent fashion a number of threads in my view of service delivery. I have experienced powerful and mostly helpful transference with Mark. One example has been how to reflect on my own history and issues to help understand my motivations for working with clients (e.g., Tod, 2007).

Another group of people from whom I have learned a great deal has been the cohort of psychologists I have been following since the start of their professional training (Tod et al., 2009, 2011). These individuals have graciously spent several hours with me talking about how they have developed, and have shared their joys, sadness, anxieties, successes, and failures. For instance, the way one individual managed her initial overwhelming anxieties and became an effective practitioner has helped me to reflect on the role that self-doubt can play in identifying and resolving my limitations.

Today versus yesterday: similarities and differences

There are similarities in the way I operate today compared with when I first engaged in service delivery. Broadly, I still aim to learn about clients, the reasons they have approached me, and their circumstances before focusing on helping them effect change, if needed. In this way I still follow the broad service delivery stages I learned about from the psychological skills training literature I read. Related to this process, client feedback, be that verbal, nonverbal, or behavioural, remains central to assessing my effectiveness. The reason clients approach me is because they want assistance and they think I can help them. In addition, although I am more confident in my competence, I still have self-doubts. I have gained comfort from senior practitioners who have told me they also question their competence. If these individuals still had doubts, then I decided it was OK for me as well, and maybe such thoughts might assist me in staying focused on helping clients as best I can and perhaps identify my limitations. Although people present with similar issues, such as feeling hurt, experiencing anxiety, having relationship difficulties, or wanting to achieve more from their lives and sports, each individual has a unique story and ways of reacting to others and the world. Given the tremendous variation in the human condition, my self-doubts help me to constantly establish whether or not I am a suitable person to help each client.

In some ways, however, I operate differently compared to when I first began helping people. I have a deeper understanding of, and confidence in, the helping process, and willingly share it with clients. I am slower to offer solutions and take more time to listen to clients and their stories, as far as time and other constraints allow. Related to this change, I also ask more about their opinions on how they can and have tried to help themselves. Educating clients about the helping process has often enhanced their belief that they can effect change in their lives, be that behaviourally, cognitively, or emotionally. Egan's (2009) helping cycle, as discussed in *The Skilled Helper*, has been a framework many clients have reported finding useful.

I also have a broader and deeper understanding of my worldview that underpins the helping process. For several months during my time working in New Zealand, I kept a diary, in which I would spend 45 minutes two times each week, writing about myself and what I believed about service delivery, the world, etc. Specific questions that I obtained from Jones and Butman (1991) included: What is personality? What is health? What is abnormality? What causes adaptive and maladaptive behaviour? How can behaviour be changed? After moving to Australia in 2002, and during my PhD, I read Yalom's (1980) *Existential Psychotherapy* and I was amazed at the strong similarities between my worldview and the themes in the book. The four major themes covered in the text – death, freedom, isolation, and meaninglessness – resonated with me and I could see applications to sport. The book also helped me understand why my father's death had greatly influenced me and my interactions with many clients.

Although I still use interventions from the sport psychology canon (goal setting, imagery, self-talk, relaxation) where suitable, I use them less and have developed a larger repertoire. For example, clients and I have conducted many behavioural experiments, as discussed in cognitive therapy, and I have recently been learning about mindfulness. Many times interventions are organic and emerge as strategies clients and I identify as potentially useful, rather being prescribed by me. Also, I am more creative and able than I was previously to adapt interventions to suit clients and their situations. For example, I have found that many athletes are not inspired by goal-setting diaries. Instead with one client, we decided she would pin a poster of the national team she wanted to get into on her bedroom wall and replace the face of the current player in her position with her own. The athlete found that poster more inspiring than a diary. Another athlete developed a goal-setting plan for a six-month preparation cycle leading up to an international event on a single side of an A4 sheet of paper. He placed the plan on his office wall and found it helpful for his motivation. Another example of my increased flexibility includes being relaxed if I do not suggest an intervention, because I have found some clients are not looking for solutions and are happy just to express their emotions and worries (which itself is an intervention).

Above I discussed being more collaborative, open about the helping process, and willing to draw on clients' existing strengths and expertise. These attitudes reflect a reduced sense of narcissism in my ability to make differences in people's lives, and a greater belief that if clients change, then it is they who change themselves. I have seen many individuals change, feel happier, and improve their functioning or performance, and these experiences give me belief that people often have the wherewithal to help themselves in some way, to some extent. Reduced narcissism is also related to a greater appreciation of the contribution a support team can make to athletes' competitive preparation and to many areas of malfunctioning. The lesson of a team approach was emphasised in a case with a rugby player experiencing burnout. The player's successful recovery resulted from the combined efforts of a medical doctor, a physiotherapist, a masseur, and me working in a coordinated fashion and meeting on a regular basis.

In addition, I am more self-reflective than I was because I have greater self-insight, I am more comfortable with owning up to my limitations, and I appreciate more deeply how the relationships clients and I share influence service delivery outcomes. Bordin's (1994) working alliance theory helps guide my self-evaluations after client sessions. His theory contains three components to the working alliance: goals, tasks, and bond. I often ask myself, did we focus on a specific goal? Does each of us know our responsibilities? Did we get on with each other?

Conclusion

Rønnestad and Skovholt (2003) suggest that a key theme in counsellors' and psychologists' development is the integration of their professional and personal 'selves'. One way this process has played out in my career has been a movement from trying to be strictly professional (as defined by my understanding of what that meant), to being relaxed myself with clients. Initially, I either denied or lacked awareness of, and was unable to manage, how my needs, desires, issues, personal inclinations, sense of humour, etc., influenced service delivery. With the assistance of others and the opportunities to work with clients, I have come to appreciate and somewhat accept that when I work with clients, I am the instrument of service delivery and not my 32-page Bible. Few complicated instruments, such as watches or measuring devices, are flawless, and yet most still operate within acceptable margins of error despite their imperfections, as long as they are regularly maintained, cared for, and calibrated against some criteria. As my understanding about how I influence service delivery has increased, I have realised that I do not need to deny my own imperfections, personal attributes, or sense of humour, and that despite them, or sometimes even because of them, I can be (and have been) helpful to clients. Accepting that I am a service delivery instrument has made it easier for me to trust my judgements, relax, and be present with clients. With the increased confidence to be myself, however, also comes responsibility, and the realisation that I need to regularly maintain myself, calibrate my thinking, and expand my functionality, through self-reflection, peer supervision, and client feedback, so that I operate within my 'margins of error' and remain focused on helping those individuals who have sought me out in a professional capacity.

References

Beck, J. S. (1995) *Cognitive Therapy: Basics and Beyond*. New York: Guildford Press.

Bordin, E. S. (1994) Theory and research on the therapeutic working alliance: new direction, in A. O. Horvath and L. S. Greenberg (eds) *The Working Alliance: Theory, Research, and Practice*. Chichester: John Wiley & Sons, Ltd, pp. 13–37.

Covey, S. R. (1989) *The Seven Habits of Highly Effective People*. New York: Free Press.

Egan, G. (2009) *The Skilled Helper: A Problem-Management and Opportunity-Development Approach to Helping*, 9th edn. Pacific Grove, CA: Brooks/Cole.

Ellis, A. and Dryden, W. (1997) *The Practice of Rational Emotive Behavior Therapy*, 2nd edn. New York: Springer.

Frankl, V. E. (1959) *Man's Search For Meaning*. Boston: Beacon Press.

Hodge, K. (1994) *Sport Motivation: Training Your Mind for Peak Performance*. Auckland: Reed.

Jones, S. L. and Butman, R. E. (1991) *Modern Psychotherapies*. Downers Grove, IL: Intervarsity Press.

Kirwan, J. and Thomas, P. (1992) *Running on Instinct*. Auckland: Moa Beckett.

Martens, R. (1987) *Coaches Guide to Sport Psychology*. Champaign, IL: Human Kinetics.

Rønnestad, M. H. and Skovholt, T. M. (2003) The journey of the counselor and therapist: research findings and perspectives on professional development. *Journal of Career Development*, 30: 5–44.

Tod, D. (2007) Reflections on collaborating with a professional rugby league player. *Sport & Exercise Psychology Review*, 3(1): 4–10.

——(in press) The erotic adventures of D: interactions with a triathlete, in R. Godfrey, A. M. Lane, M. Loosemore and G. W. Whyte (eds) *Applied Sport Science and Medicine: Case Studies from Practice*. Champaign, IL: Human Kinetics.

Tod, D., Andersen, M. B. and Marchant, D. B. (2009) A longitudinal examination of neophyte applied sport psychologists' development. *Journal of Applied Sport Psychology*, 21(Suppl. 1), S1–S16. doi: 10.1080/10413200802593604.

——(2011) Six years up: applied sport psychologists surviving (and thriving) after graduation. *Journal of Applied Sport Psychology*, 23: 93–109.

Williams, J. M. (1993) *Applied Sport Psychology: Personal Growth to Peak Performance*. Mayfield, CA: Mountain View.

Yalom, I. D. (1980) *Existential Psychotherapy*. New York: Basic Books.

——(1989) *Love's Executioner and Other Tales of Psychotherapy*. London: Penguin.

Ziglar, Z. (1975) *See You at the Top*. Gretna, LA: Pelican.

6

'A FUNNY THING HAPPENED ON THE WAY THROUGH MY PhD!'

Ken Hodge

A 'funny thing really did happen on my way to a PhD in *sociology* of sport'; I changed to psychology of sport and eventually I evolved into an applied sport psychology practitioner (i.e., Mental Skills Trainer). I'm still asking myself: 'How the heck did that happen?' Well, actually I do know in a temporal sense. After completing a Master's degree in sociology of sport at the University of Montana, USA, I moved to the University of Illinois, USA, to pursue a PhD in the same specialization in 1984. But I had something of an epiphany during the first semester of my doctoral studies – I enrolled in a 'Social Psychology of Sport' class at the University of Illinois as an elective course. That class was taught by Professor Glyn Roberts and included a series of guest lectures delivered by Professor Dan Gould. I had always been more interested in micro-sociology topics such as group-level socialization and group dynamics; but I had not been exposed to social psychology of sport during my undergraduate studies at the University of Otago in New Zealand or my Master's degree. Consequently the subject matter in that class at the University of Illinois was more than an eye-opener for me; it was a revelation that left me excited and enthused, but also frustrated that I had not been aware of the depth of social psychological research into sport-related issues beforehand. I had long been interested in the sporting cliché that 'sport builds character' and related issues regarding sportspersonship, fair play, and morality in sport; but now, thanks to my discovery of social psychology theories and methods, I could see a means to examine those issues in a concrete, practical manner. So, halfway through my first semester of doctoral studies I somehow convinced Dan Gould to take me on as an additional doctoral student in sport psychology. Right place, right time and a good slice of luck!

Training and background

I completed a PhD in physical education/kinesiology at the University of Illinois; during my studies I took numerous classes in social, cognitive and behavioural psychology. My doctoral research focused on the development of a conceptual model to guide research into the thorny issue of 'character-building in/through sport' (fact or fiction?). In addition to my formal studies I was fortunate to also receive a rich and diverse 'informal' education in applied sport psychology from my supervisor, Dan Gould, and from a number of fellow graduate students who were focused on applied issues – some of whom were working as interns with university sports teams. Dan was heavily involved with the United States Olympic Committee (USOC) and especially with USA Wrestling. Thanks to Dan, I and his other graduate students received numerous opportunities to 'shadow' him as he worked as a sport psychology (SP) consultant with various athletes and teams; and we were also given guided opportunities to get our hands dirty with some SP consulting work of our own. Dan's generous approach to mentoring myself and his other grad students was absolutely invaluable in my development as a SP consultant. Given my social psychology background, and my mentor's background, it was hardly surprising that I adopted and developed a cognitive-behavioural approach to my SP consulting work. Although I didn't have the terminology at the time I intuitively recognized the connection between mental skills training (e.g., motivation, commitment, mental toughness) and life skills training (i.e., character-building in sport; Hodge *et al.*, in press) – it was my view that mental skills training (MST) should not be conceived as being exclusively focused on sports performance (or on elite performance); instead I believed that the skills we teach via MST were indeed 'life' skills, applicable to any life domain.

Consulting practice

As previously stated, I have primarily employed a cognitive-behavioural or Mental Skills Training (MST) approach to my SP consulting work. In addition, I use aspects of Personal Construct Theory (PCT; Kelly, [1955] 1991) in an effort to engage with my athlete-clients on their level of understanding and as a means to help the athlete identify her/his mental skills needs – their strengths and their weaknesses (e.g., performance profiling; Butler, 1997; Butler and Hardy, 1992; Gucciardi and Gordon, 2009; Hodge, 2004a). In my experience, a strengths-based approach is crucial to help nurture an athlete's self-confidence, resilience and mental toughness (Gordon, 2012; Gordon and Gucciardi, 2011). Finally, I ground my overall SP consulting work in Self-Determination Theory (SDT; Deci and Ryan, 2002; Ryan and Deci, 2008), with a particular focus on the basic psychological needs of autonomy, competence and relatedness. Evidence-based practice is the foundation of my applied work (Hodge *et al.*, 2011; Sharp and Hodge, 2011), which is hardly surprising given that I work full-time as a lecturer/professor in a research-focused university setting.

Consulting philosophy and service delivery model

I employ an athlete-centred, but coach-driven service delivery model. From a PCT perspective, I use performance profiling and intake interviews to identify the mental skills needs for the individual athlete, and then working in collaboration with the athlete we design a MST (Mental Skills Training) programme tailored specifically to her/his needs: 'One size does not fit all!' I often joke that I use a very sophisticated athlete assessment tool called the I.I.I.D.D. (i.e., Interpersonal Idiosyncratic Investigative Deductive Dialogue) – or, in other words, the athlete and I talk to each other! We have a number of conversational chats designed to establish rapport, develop trust, and open the door for uncensored disclosure by the athlete about her/his strengths and also his/her weaknesses. A good old-fashioned yarn/chat is still one of the most effective tools in the SP consultant's toolbox! The same athlete-centred focus also applies in team sports, but necessarily the athlete's needs and his/her MST programme must have a clear connection to the team's needs and the athlete's role within the team. Within the bounds of confidentiality it is crucial that the athlete's coach plays a meaningful role in helping identify the athlete's MST needs and then offers meaningful support to reinforce the MST work the athlete is completing. If ethical issues arise (e.g., confidentiality), I always focus on the athlete's needs first before taking into account the team/squad and the coach – the athlete-client needs to be able to trust me and rely on me to be 'in their corner' first and foremost (i.e., a duty of care; Whelan *et al.*, 2002).

Overall, my MST work with athletes is designed to satisfy their basic psychological needs for autonomy, competence and relatedness. If these basic needs are satisfied, then my experience is that athletes will be engaged, motivated, and committed, as well as being able to develop resilience and mental toughness (Gordon, 2012; Gordon and Gucciardi, 2011). When an MST programme is fully focused on the athlete's individually unique needs, there is greater opportunity for perceptions of both autonomy and competence to develop. In addition, when the SP consultant develops a trusting SP-athlete relationship through concerted efforts to: (1) listen to the athlete's needs; (2) develop an individualized MST programme that explicitly focuses on the athlete's needs; and (3) honour confidentiality, then the basic need for relatedness will also be satisfied. Finally, an important aspect of my SP consulting is my stated intention for planned redundancy – I plan to teach myself out of a job, so that the athlete becomes largely self-sufficient with respect to their MST training. If I achieve my goal of planned redundancy, then the athlete's basic needs for autonomy and competency should be satisfied.

MST skills vs MST methods

I have found the distinction between MST skills and MST methods to be a particularly useful structure to use as a means to plan a MST programme (Hodge, 2004a; Vealey, 1988, 1994). An MST skill is something that needs to be developed (see Table 6.1). Skill in this situation means competency, capability, or ability level (e.g., attention-concentration, confidence). Skills are developed via the use of a number of different methods and techniques (e.g., goal setting, centring). MST skills may be divided into foundation, performance, and facilitative skills (Hodge, 2004a; Vealey, 1988). First, foundation skills, as the name suggests, are skills that must be developed as the 'MST foundation' (e.g., motivation, commitment) before other skill areas can be consistently developed. Unfortunately, athletes and coaches often overlook these skills and focus solely on performance skills. Second, performance skills are those that are necessary during the actual game or event for successful performance (e.g., concentration, controlling activation/arousal). Third, facilitative skills such as team cohesion and communication skills are vital for the performance skills to be effectively utilized. Like foundation skills, facilitative skills are often overlooked by athletes/players and coaches as they focus on performance skills (see Table 6.1).

MST method(s) are the techniques that are used to help a player develop a particular skill, just like a physical 'drill' is used to develop a particular physical skill (Hodge, 2004a; Vealey, 1988). Method in this sense means a procedure, technique, or drill (e.g., imagery, self-talk).

The usefulness of the distinction between MST skills and MST methods is especially evident when one realizes that there is no 'set' MST programme. To be able to effectively develop a MST programme for an athlete, it is vital that the athlete's existing MST skill levels be assessed, then the skill weaknesses can be addressed via a well-planned programme of specific MST methods. Too often players/athletes and coaches focus totally on the teaching and learning of particular methods (e.g., centring/relaxation; goal setting) and lose sight of the specific MST skill that the method is designed to improve (e.g., activation/arousal control; motivation). It is easy to be seduced by the method as the 'end' itself, rather than as a 'means' to an end (i.e., MST skill development). The methods chosen must have a planned purpose or the desired skill development is unlikely to occur.

TABLE 6.1 Mental skills training programme structure

Mental skills	Mental methods
Commitment	Goal setting
Confidence	Self-talk
Concentration	Imagery (visualization)
Controlling activation	Relaxation/centring
Coping with pressure	Pre-game mental preparation
Intuitive decision-making	Coping plans
Team cohesion	
Captaincy	

Source: Hodge (2004a); Vealey (1988).

Example MST issues

Elsewhere I have provided detailed accounts of my perceptions of the common MST issues at pinnacle events such as the Summer and Winter Olympics (see Hodge, 2010; Hodge and Hermansson, 2007, 2009). While my SP consulting work at the Olympic and Commonwealth Games forms a key foundation for this chapter, my applied practice in my home country of New Zealand initially developed out of my history as a player and coach in the sport of rugby (the national sport in New Zealand). While I have subsequently worked as a SP consultant with a range of other team (e.g., netball, hockey, rowing, basketball, curling), and individual sports (e.g., golf, swimming, snowboarding, skiing, skeleton), my initial work with rugby led me to develop a particular focus on team dynamics and team-building (Hodge, 2004b; Hodge et al., 2005). Also, given the interactive, dynamic, continuous action nature of rugby (and netball), I developed an interest in athlete decision-making as a crucial aspect of the MST skill of attention-concentration (Hodge, 2004a, 2009).

Rugby is an interactive, continuous, contact/collision, team sport. The interactive, continuous nature of rugby is characterized by players having to 'switch' between attack and defence many times during a game, as well as having to concentrate on the 'role(s)' required by their playing position (Hodge et al., 2005). As a team sport, rugby has both individual (e.g., goalkicking, tackling) and team play components (i.e., playing offence and defence; tactical decision-making). Rugby is a 'systems' team game, with each of the 15 playing positions having a role within the team 'system' and the team as a whole having a sophisticated game plan with tactics and strategies for both attack and defence – these structural aspects of the game of rugby place considerable demands on each player's mental skills. In addition, rugby has no 'time-outs', a short half-time period (5 minutes at club level; 15 minutes at representative level) and coaching from the sidelines is prohibited – consequently, players are required to make many tactical decisions 'on the move' during the game without support from coaches (ibid.).

Team-building

The key focus of my MST work in this area has been on both task cohesion (teamwork) and social cohesion (team spirit). I have developed a number of simple intervention exercises/activities that promote optimal team coordination and avoid social loafing via increased task and social cohesion (Bloom et al., 2003; Hodge, 2004b; Hodge et al., 2005). Successful teams have players who work toward common goals. The culture of the team will dictate these goals and whether or not they are accepted by all members. Therefore, the team vision and values must be carefully moulded. Many methods can be used, however, any session designed to establish a team's vision and values should include: (1) the opportunity for all members of the group to contribute to the process; and (2) concrete examples and strategies that ensure the vision and values will manifest themselves in the day-to-day operations of the team.

I have developed a number of workshops/exercises that can be used to shape a team's vision and values. For example, the 'Team Legacy Speech' where the team is divided into groups of five or six players. Each group is asked to write a 'team legacy speech', mimicking the one they would deliver at the end of a stunningly successful winning season. Each speech must include acknowledgement of (only) four important people and focus on 'how and why' the team accomplished its ultimate goal of winning the championship. The purpose of this exercise is to encourage the group to define success for themselves (vision) and examine the ways in which they can enhance success (values).

Another effective activity is an exercise called 'Team Destruction', where small groups are given the following instructions: 'Imagine you are part of the management team for our main opponents – your mission is to send a saboteur or spy into our team for the season in order to sabotage and destroy our season. What would your instructions be? What would you get the spy to sabotage?' The sabotage plans of each group are then pooled together and the entire team decides on the most 'destructive schemes' (many are usually quite innovative and humorous!). Each group is then encouraged to devise ways to 'spy-proof' the team against the best efforts of the spy/saboteur; 'What plans can we put into place to prevent the spy/saboteur from being successful or to cope with problems if they arise?'

The final exercise is termed 'Build the Ideal Teammate'. Small groups are instructed to design the 'ideal' teammate for their current team by brainstorming about the behaviours/actions/values that they want this teammate to demonstrate at fitness/individual skill training sessions, at team training sessions, before the game, during the game, after the game (social activities), and when we are 'Off-Duty' as a team (away from our sport).

The 'Team Legacy Speeches', 'Team Destruction' and 'Ideal Teammate' exercises typically result in a variety of ideas concerning the team's vision and values. With the assistance of the coach and senior leaders, these ideas can then be moulded into an overall Vision and Values for the team. The team's Vision is defined as the 'why' of the team and questions such as 'Why are we together?' and 'What sort of team do we want to be?' are used as prompts. The team's Values are defined as 'how we do things around here' and the players are encouraged to think of their team values as a set of philosophies that could be used to help guide their team processes both on and off the field.

Intuitive decision-making

Given the interactive, dynamic, continuous action nature of rugby (and netball), I have developed a number of simple intervention exercises/activities that enhance player decision-making as a key aspect of the MST skill of attention-concentration (Hodge, 2004a, 2009). Based on Klein's (2003) Recognition-Primed Decision

Model (RPD), I have focused on helping athletes develop their 'intuitive decision-making'. Within the RPD framework, intuition is not regarded as a mystical gift that cannot be explained; rather, intuition is viewed as a representation of 'skilled anticipation'. Intuition is how we 'read the game'; intuition is how we translate our experience into action. Our experience lets us recognize what is going on (making judgements) and how to react (making decisions). Because our experience enables us to recognize what to do, we can therefore make decisions rapidly and without conscious awareness or effort. We don't have to deliberately think through issues in order to arrive at good decisions – we learn how to 'read the game'. Intuition isn't mysterious, it is a natural outgrowth of experience; therefore, it is possible to accelerate the process of developing it (i.e., 'training' via MST).

The RPD framework starts with a focus on pattern recognition and pattern recall; a 'pattern' is a set of cues (signs) that usually chunk together so that if you see a few of the cues, you can expect to find the others. When you notice a pattern, you may have a sense of familiarity – yes, I've seen that before! (you 'read' the signs). As we play our sport, we accumulate experiences and build up a reservoir of recognized patterns. The more patterns we learn, the easier it is to match a new situation to one of the patterns in our reservoir. When a new situation occurs, we recognize the situation as familiar by matching it to a pattern we have encountered in the past. We know the 'language', we can 'speed read' the language, or even use a 'txt' form of labelling the language/patterns (signs). Once we know what patterns to expect, we can move our decision-making thinking from 'what am I looking *at*?' to 'what am I looking *for*?' We can then begin to prime the decision-making process by being able to anticipate key challenges and likely options before they actually occur (Hodge, 2009).

Activities and exercises designed to enhance this skill of intuitive decision-making include the MST methods of imagery and self-talk, as well as specific decision-making activities such as: (1) the Video Evaluation Exercise (pause an action video and then predict the next 10 seconds of action using pattern recognition and recall); (2) the Decision Requirements Exercise (What decisions are difficult?, What kinds of errors are often made?, How would an expert make this decision better?); and (3) the Pre-Brief Exercise (the opposite of a Game De-Brief; imagine a complete and utter failure of the game plan, why did it fail? Brainstorm ideas to minimize or prevent the problems occurring) (Hodge, 2009).

Conclusion

Becoming a sport psychologist, or more accurately a 'mental skills trainer' (the terminology used in New Zealand for someone who is not a registered/certified psychologist), was certainly not a linear, goal-directed process for me. In many ways I stumbled across sport psychology by chance, but once I had discovered 'gold', I was motivated to 'mine' it!

As previously stated, I clearly saw the connection between mental skills training (e.g., motivation, commitment, mental toughness) and life skills training (i.e., character-building in sport), and it was my view that mental skills training (MST) should not be conceived as being exclusively focused on sports performance; instead I believed that the skills we teach via MST were indeed 'life' skills, applicable to any life domain (e.g., school, sport, home, job, career, relationships). For example, the two MST issues outlined above (team-building and intuitive decision-making) should be viewed as being applicable to many life situations; sport may offer us an opportunity to test and develop these skills but they should be regarded as being portable and transferable to other life domains (Hodge *et al.*, in press).

With respect to the last point above, I welcome the recent emphasis in general psychology on a strengths-based approach to positive psychology and the recent widening of the scope of practice in our field to 'performance' psychology (Martin, 2012), not just sport/exercise psychology. By expanding our definition of 'performance' to life skills, I believe we have a wonderful opportunity as a field to deliver more meaningful contributions to the psychological well-being of our athlete-clients and to society as a whole.

References

Bloom, G. A., Stevens, D. E. and Wickwire, T. L. (2003) Expert coaches' perceptions of team building. *Journal of Applied Sport Psychology*, 15: 129–143.

Butler, R. (1997) Performance profiling: assessing the way forward, in R. J. Butler (ed.) *Sports Psychology in Performance*. Oxford: Butterworth-Heinemann, pp. 33–48.

Butler, R. and Hardy, L. (1992) The performance profile: theory and application. *The Sport Psychologist*, 6: 253–264.

Deci, E. L. and Ryan, R. M. (eds) (2002) *Handbook of Self-Determination Research*. Rochester, NY: University of Rochester Press.

Gordon, S. (2012) Strengths-based approaches to developing mental toughness: team and individual. *International Coaching Psychology Review*, 7: 210–222.

Gordon, S. and Gucciardi, D. F. (2011) Strengths-based approach to coaching mental toughness. *Journal of Sport Psychology in Action*, 2: 143–155.

Gucciardi, D. F. and Gordon, S. (2009) Revisiting the performance profile technique: theoretical underpinnings and application. *The Sport Psychologist*, 23: 93–117.

Hodge, K. P. (2004a) *Sport Motivation: Training Your Mind for Peak Performance*, 2nd edn. Auckland: Reed Books.

——(2004b) Team dynamics, in T. Morris and J. Summers (eds) *Sport Psychology: Theory, Application, and Current Issues*, 2nd edn. Sydney: Jacandra Wiley, pp. 210–233.

——(2009) Intuitive decision-making for rugby. Unpublished MST coaches manual, Highlanders Professional Rugby Franchise, Dunedin, New Zealand.

——(2010) Working at the Olympics, in S. Hanrahan and M. Andersen (eds) *The Routledge Handbook of Applied Sport Psychology*. London: Routledge, pp. 406–413.

Hodge, K., Danish, S. and Martin, J. (in press) Developing a conceptual framework for life skills interventions. *The Counseling Psychologist*.

Hodge, K. and Hermansson, G. (2007) Psychological preparation of athletes for the Olympic context: the New Zealand Summer and Winter Olympic Teams. *Athletic Insight: The Online Journal of Sport Psychology*, 9(4). Available at: http://www.athleticinsight.com/.

——(2009) Psychological preparation of athletes for the Olympic context: team culture and team-building, in R. Schinke (ed.) *Contemporary Sport Psychology*. New York: Nova Science, pp. 55–70.

Hodge, K., Lonsdale, C. and McKenzie, A. (2005) 'Thinking rugby': using sport psychology to improve rugby performance, in J. Dosil (ed.) *The Sport Psychologist's Handbook: A Guide for Sport-Specific Performance Enhancement*. Chichester: John Wiley & Sons, pp. 183–209.

Hodge, K., Sharp, L. and Heke, J. I. C. (2011) Sport psychology consulting with indigenous athletes: the case of New Zealand Māori. *Journal of Clinical Sport Psychology*, 5: 350–360.

Kelly, G. A. ([1955] 1991) *The Psychology of Personal Constructs: A Theory of Personality*, vol. 1. London: Routledge.

Klein, G. (2003) *Intuition at Work: Why Developing Your Gut Instincts Will Make You Better at What You Do*. New York: Doubleday.

Martin, J. (2012) Editorial: about sport, exercise, and performance psychology. *Sport, Exercise, & Performance Psychology*, 1: 1–2.

Ryan, R. M. and Deci, E. L. (2008) A self-determination theory approach to psychotherapy: the motivational basis for effective change. *Canadian Psychology*, 49: 186–193.

Sharp, L. and Hodge, K. (2011) Sport psychology consulting effectiveness: the sport psychology consultant's perspective. *Journal of Applied Sport Psychology*, 23: 360–376.

Vealey, R. (1988) Future directions in psychological skills training. *The Sport Psychologist*, 2: 318–336.

——(1994) Current status and prominent issues in sport psychology interventions. *Medicine & Science in Sport & Exercise*, 26: 495–502.

Whelan, J. P., Meyers, A. W. and Elkins, T. D. (2002) Ethics in sport and exercise psychology, in J. L. Van Raalte and B. W. Brewer (eds) *Exploring Sport and Exercise Psychology*, 2nd edn. Washington, DC: American Psychological Association, pp. 503–523.

7

SUCCESS IS A JOURNEY, NOT A DESTINATION

Richard L. Cox

Background: my school years

I guess my journey began at the age of 7 when I moved from an infants school to an all-age school. 'All-age' meant that if you didn't pass the 11-plus exam in the fourth year of primary school you were obliged to continue in the same school until reaching the leaving age of 15. The 'all-age' school I went to was an all-boys school and I think being terrified of 15-year-old boys when I was only 7 kept me working hard. Consequently, I passed the 11-plus exam, at 10 years of age and was in the first year of a grammar school aged 10 and a half.

Eight years later and after three years in the sixth form, I had an interview with my headmaster who wanted to know what I wanted to do as a career. I told him that I wanted to be a Customs Officer. He also wanted to know what I would do if I failed to pass the entrance exams for the Customs and Excise and, in order to get out of his office as quickly as possible, I answered his next question – "Have you ever thought about teaching?" – by saying that I wouldn't mind being a PE teacher, which was the first time I had even thought about the possibility! However, being lazy (more like 'disinterested') about school work and passionate about sport, I was offered a place at Borough Road College of Education to study Physical Education and Geography two weeks before the exams for the Customs and Excise were scheduled to take place and so it was an easy decision to opt for the former.

Teacher training

After two years at Borough Road College, I applied to do a third year Diploma course at Carnegie College of Physical Education in Leeds and was accepted. This was a one-year course that I enjoyed very much and, looking back on the experience, I realise that it served me well for the future because of the depth of knowledge about sport and performance we were exposed to on a daily basis.

In 1962, I started my professional life as a teacher of physical education in a small secondary school in Wellingborough, Northamptonshire, which is where I was born and grew up, and, for the next six years, was idyllically happy in this post. However, after six years I became restless and, as much as I loved it, I wasn't sure that I wanted to devote the rest of my life to being a PE teacher. While at Carnegie College, I had become aware of a one-year course in PE that was termed an 'Advanced Diploma' and was run by Dr H.T.A. Whiting (John) at Leeds University. I made inquiries through our county Adviser in PE as to the possibility of going on this course and he supported me wholeheartedly. Thus, in September 1968, I began a second term as a student under 'John' Whiting and that is when my academic career in psychology began.

Academic training

The course that Whiting ran was actually an intensive study of skill acquisition and this opened my eyes to other possibilities, not least of which was an opportunity to go to Newcastle University to work as a research assistant to Dr Gerald H. Fisher in the University Department of Psychology. This opportunity arose through someone who had been on the Advanced Diploma course at Leeds the year before me and who had gone on to work for Dr Fisher at Newcastle during the year I was at Leeds. His name was (and is) Ian Cockerill and, not surprisingly, to me at least, he went on to become a lecturer at Birmingham University and one of the country's leading sport psychologists. There were two reasons why I wanted to follow in Ian's footsteps. The first was the attraction of gaining a Master's degree by research and the other was the opportunity to learn more about psychology in all its guises from someone who was a renowned researcher in the subject.

The first year I was in Newcastle (1969–1970) I had to work in the evenings and weekends in a local sports centre because there was no financial help to be had from the university – I was a volunteer! This meant that I worked in the Psychology Department during the day and in the sports centre in the evenings, which resulted in little spare time for socialising in any shape or form. However, at the start of my second year, Dr Fisher offered me a research contract and so I became a paid member of staff in the department. It also meant that I had time to play rugby, which I did for Newcastle Northern. This club ran six teams at that time and, after three matches, starting in the sixth XV, I found myself in the first XV alongside several international players and travelling as far south as Esher in Surrey and north to Edinburgh. Again, this experience stood me in good stead for my future career insofar as I gained valuable experience of what was, at that time, top class rugby and what it demanded of players both physically and psychologically.

At the start of the academic year 1971–1972, I was promoted to Senior Research Associate in the Psychology Department and was having the time of my life. Unfortunately, everything came crashing down at Christmas 1972 when the Social Science Research Council cut back on the number of grants it had been issuing and the one I was working on was a victim of those cuts. Thus, I had three weeks to find work elsewhere as, by this time, I had a mortgage and a family to provide for. (I was told at the local Social Security [welfare] office that I would be supported in paying my mortgage if I left my wife and family!) Fortunately, I spotted an advert in the local paper for 'A teacher of General Subjects' in a local secondary school for boys. I served two terms in that school, which was tough by anyone's standard, and I was glad that, by the summer holidays, I had been offered a post at what was then Dunfermline College of Physical Education in Edinburgh to lecture in the psychology of teaching physical education. This seemed to be the perfect marriage between PE, teaching and psychology that I had hoped for since 1968.

The early days of sport psychology in GB

It should be noted that, in the late 1960s, the British Society for Sport Psychology (BSSP) had been formed, principally by John Whiting of Leeds University and Billy Steel of Manchester University, and they had organised an annual conference for the subject. Thus, sport psychology was beginning to make its mark, although in its infancy at that time. Nevertheless, I was invited to address the 1973 BSSP Conference in Leeds and spoke about the research I had been doing at Newcastle. Over 300 delegates attended that conference and, among them were a good number of sport coaches looking for help with their coaching. They didn't get it, primarily because of the academic bias in the papers presented, of which mine was one. With hindsight, this wasn't surprising because a brand new organisation had to be established as meaningful and acceptable to the world of sport and its leaders chose to do so through academic credibility rather than applied knowledge. Indeed, there was little application of knowledge to sport performance in the country at that time because hardly anyone in the UK had ventured into that side of psychology; that was to come much later.

The fallow years

From 1973, when I started lecturing in Higher Education, to 1990 not a lot happened in the world of applied sport psychology in Britain and certainly not so in Scotland. Yes, there were developments in the academic side of the subject and several universities around the country began to offer Master's degree courses in Sport Science, of which sport psychology typically made up between one quarter and one third of the course. Initially, these were one-year, full-time courses leading to MSc, though two-year, part-time courses also came into being to facilitate those who wanted to study but couldn't afford to go full-time. Also, due to the gradual demise of the BSSP, which, as suggested above, was most probably due to the lack of applied work being published and publicised, a new association was formed in 1984, which became known as BASS – the British Association of Sport Sciences – and represented the merger of psychology, physiology and biomechanics. It was to become BASES in 1993 due to the emergence of Exercise Psychology as a legitimate field of study in its own right and the enthusiastic lobbying of influential people such as Stuart Biddle and Ken Fox who were, and still are, working in this field. In the early part of this period I completed an MEd by research (1973) and, somewhat laboriously, a PhD (1982) in the field of human perception. The latter had taken a very long time to complete because of trying to hold down a full-time lecturing post in Edinburgh and doing research part-time. With hindsight and for reasons that should be obvious, this is not a course of action I would recommend to anyone and, had it been financially and logistically possible, I would have completed my academic studies as a full-time student.

Kevin Hickey's contribution

As BASS gained strength and importance in Britain, so more presentations at its annual conference were focused on the applied side of sport psychology but not significantly so before 1990. I had done some work with the Scottish netball team in 1987 in preparation for a forthcoming World Cup but, it is fair to say, I was learning as much from them as they from me! However, in 1989, a landmark event happened in British Applied Sport Science when Kevin Hickey was appointed Technical Director for the British Olympic Association (BOA). Kevin had been to five consecutive Olympic Games as the Head Coach to the British Amateur Boxing Association and one of his first goals in his new post was to set up Advisory Groups in the three main sport sciences. He did this because working at five successive Olympic Games had made him realise that there was a need for science to be applied to sport in a helpful manner for both athletes and coaches. Thus, upon his appointment, he set about identifying those who were working in the sport sciences and invited them to serve on the appropriate committee. I was one of those who were invited to serve on the Psychology Advisory Group, which was chaired by Lew Hardy of Bangor University. Our remit was straightforward. We were charged with drawing up a programme of applied work that we believed would help our Olympic athletes to perform better. This was a tall order, given what had been happening, or rather *not* happening, in sport psychology in this country up to that point in time. Furthermore, there were time constraints placed upon us because Kevin was already planning to encourage as many Olympic Governing Bodies of Sport as possible to take up the BOA's offer of sports science help in preparation for the Olympic Games in Barcelona in a little over two years time. What is more, this help would be free to the Governing Bodies (GBs) because the BOA promised to finance the arrangement. Not surprisingly, several GBs, though not all, did take up the offer and, as a member of the Psychology Advisory Group, I was invited to work with the GB Swim Team from the beginning of 1990 to the Olympic Games in Barcelona 1992.

My 'baptism of fire'

There were four reasons why working with the GB Swim Team proved to be a real challenge in every sense of the word. First, I was to go with the squad wherever it went in the world, which meant that, on these occasions, I was a full-time, applied practitioner. I had never had that kind of experience before, particularly as I was on call for up to 16 hours each day (at the Olympics themselves, I often did 18-hour days and thereby accrued a level of fatigue not even experienced during my time in top-class rugby!). Second, it was quite daunting to find myself trying to help previous Olympic medal winners, of which there were two on the team – Adrian Moorhouse and Nick Gillingham – who had won Gold and Silver respectively in the 1988 Games in Seoul. Third, there were 30 swimmers and 11 other members of staff on the Olympic Team and I had a responsibility for all 41 in Barcelona. Fourth, due to the Olympic Trials taking place only a few weeks before the Games themselves, and the selection policy of 'first past the post' (and so was the second placed swimmer if he, or she, made the qualifying standard), I was faced with six swimmers out of the 30 selected who had not been in the squad at all until those final few weeks. (From this point onwards only the male personal pronoun is used. This is not to imply a gender bias but simply to avoid the somewhat tiresome use of 'he, or she', throughout the chapter.) Thus, I had little time to get to know them, let alone help them in any way. Finally, I was a novice applied practitioner in the world of high performance sport and had to learn the language of swimming, its structure, what the country's expectations were for the Olympics, the work ethic required of international swimmers and our (GB) place in the rank order of excellence in the world of swimming, all very quickly! For instance, one shock to the system was the fact that one of our men, who became British Champion in his event in the Trials, didn't even finish in the top 20 in the Olympics themselves and yet his performance there was only fractions below his best ever! All of this adds up to the fact that you have to immerse yourself in the sport you are working with if you have any hope of being successful in the eyes of the athletes and staff concerned.

An oversize bite of the cherry?

I realise now that I had probably compounded the difficulties involved in trying to deliver a first class service for my clients because I had previously agreed to take on another team before being appointed to the GB Swim Team. This was the Scotland Ladies Bowls Team. In the summer of 1989, the manager of that team had approached me privately to ask if I would be willing to work with 'her girls' in preparation for the Commonwealth Games in Auckland, New Zealand, which were due to take place in the first two months of 1990. I accepted the invitation even though there were only five months to go before those Games were due to start. Not surprisingly to me, the ladies did not win a medal of any colour in Auckland but that didn't prevent me from agreeing to work with them in preparation for their World Championships, which were scheduled for the summer of 1992, in the same month as the Olympics were due to begin. Working with two teams during the same period of time is difficult to say the least but I can't think of many sport psychologists I know who would have turned down the opportunity of working with two international teams in those early days of the applied form of the discipline. Nevertheless, it proved to be something of a 'balancing act' and I was actually in Barcelona when the Scotland's Ladies team won the World Bowls Championship in Ayr. Not to be with them on that marvellous occasion was, and remains, a major disappointment for me but I learned a lesson from the experience that has stood me in good stead ever since. That is, I always check the timetable for major competitions for one sport before taking on another in case there are clashes because I would always want to be present at their competitions, regardless of predicted prospects and outcomes. After all, isn't this why sport psychologists work with athletes in the first place? I now believe that to be absent when the athletes you are working with are involved in competition borders on dereliction of duty and, over the intervening 18 years or so, I can honestly state that I have spent at least one hour watching my clients compete for every hour I have been occupied in consultations and workshops with them and only illness and family bereavement (thankfully rare) have kept me away from competitions.

My CV since 1992

Since those heady days of working with international bowlers and Olympic swimmers I have worked with six professional football clubs in Scotland, four of which were (and still are) in the Premier League (the other two were in the First Division). I have also worked with the Scotland Men's National Rugby Team on two separate occasions, the first from 1995 to 1997 and the second from 2009 to October 2011. I can also include the Scotland men's golf team during the past eight years and over 30 professional golfers, one of whom, Paul Lawrie (I can name him because he spoke to the media about the work we had done together over a five-year period), won the British Open Championship at Carnoustie in 1999. In total, during the past 20 years, I have worked with over 200 international athletes from 28 different sports and this is a statistic about which I feel proud because I have never asked any athlete or Governing Body if I can work with them; the approach has always come from them to me. Much of this work was facilitated by my leaving academia in 2001 and becoming a full-time practitioner with the Scottish Institute of Sport; a post I held for nine years until, at Christmas 2010, I decided to become self-employed on a part-time basis.

My theoretical approach

What has been my theoretical approach? I am in a small minority who believe passionately that Radical Behaviourism, as proposed, researched and promoted by B.F. Skinner from the 1930s to the late 1980s, still offers the most clear and effective method of changing behaviour without medical intervention. Admittedly, the new sciences of psychobiology, neurology and neurophysiology are leading to ways of attributing 'cause' to events and behaviour hitherto unforeseen but it will be a long time before they can account for the motivation of human behaviour as it is understood today. This is not to say that I believe other major schools of theoretical thinking, such as psychoanalysis and humanism, cannot help anyone to live their lives better than before, for considerable evidence exists to support their contribution to psychological health. Rather, it is to say that I found Behaviourism more helpful and clearer in terms of how to practise psychology than any other theory of human behaviour, and what's more, I still do.

Five important lessons learned

So, what have I learned during these past 20 years while working as an applied sport psychologist? Well, there are several answers to this question, not least of which is the appreciation that there is a 'shelf life' for working with any athlete or group of athletes. If the squad doesn't change and the staff remain the same, then I reckon two years, or two seasons, is about the ideal time to spend with them. Admittedly, this depends a lot on how often the sport psychologist is able to meet with them (please note that 'the sport psychologist' in this sentence is in the singular. I cannot imagine how two sport psychologists would fare if they were both working with the same group of athletes). More than two seasons and there is a danger of complacency setting in, due mainly to familiarity factors. Athletes learn quickly where the sport psychologist is coming from and what form his communications are likely to take. Thus, it can so easily become a process of 'fine-tuning' after the initial ground-work has been done and this can lead to the perception that 'you can't help me any further'. Of course, where the personnel change (or are changed, as in professional football) regularly, then much more can and should be done. This is particularly true of international teams where, for instance, the make-up of a squad can change by as much as 50 per cent within the space of two seasons; international rugby teams are a good example of this.

A second lesson has been to work under pressure of time and availability, particularly during the days leading up to a major competition. For instance, during the Six Nations Championship for Rugby Union, five international matches take place in the space of seven weeks. This might not seem a lot but, given the nature and frequency of injuries, some of which are severe, and the availability of the players, which is carefully negotiated between the National Governing Body and the clubs to which the players belong through their contract, the time left for the coaches to do their work and the medical staff to do theirs, does not leave a great deal of time for the sport psychologist to do his work, despite just about everyone concerned believing that he can and should make a significant and positive difference to the fortunes of the team!

A clear third lesson is that the sport psychologist is not a messiah! In my early days of working with international athletes and coaches, there is no doubt that I thought I could help everyone in the squad, including the medics, nutritionist, video analysts and, most definitely, the strength and conditioning coaches because of my background in PE and competitive sport. This attitude was borne out of naïve enthusiasm and a fervent belief that what I had to offer was not just worthwhile but essential for everyone. Fortunately, I learned very quickly that it is more effective to be more laid-back in approach and, for a long time now, I have waited to be asked to do whatever the coaches, other staff members and athletes want me to do. If nothing is asked for, then I have a lot of free time!

Fourth, I have learned to appreciate that changing behaviour rarely happens as a result of one session with an athlete. It can happen and has happened as a result of a single consultation but, in my experience, it is a very unusual occurrence. More often than not, the process of change is initiated during the first session but seldom completed. This is due to the fact that so many 'problems' that athletes bring to a sport psychologist are deeply ingrained in the psyche and were caused either by some traumatic event on the field of play or through repeated 'hurt and insult' from one other, or others (sometimes team mates!) over a long period of time. This doesn't prevent me from trying to improve matters for the client in the first session. Indeed, my aim is always to send them away with some things they can do to help themselves deal with the issue, or problem, better than ever before but I usually want to see them again and soon, if only to ascertain how things are progressing, or not as the case may be.

Fifth, and perhaps the most important lesson learned of all, has been to work with and to report to the Head Coach on every opportunity. It is easy to forget sometimes, and particularly when working with an athlete on a one-to-one basis, but it must never be forgotten that it is the Head Coach who probably hired the sport psychologist in the first place and it will be his 'head on the block' first should the team's fortunes not be satisfactory for the Board of Directors who employed him. In other words, the sport psychologist should know his place and, in the pecking order of seniority and importance, he often comes some way down the list in many people's eyes.

Reporting to the Head Coach does raise one issue for the sport psychologist that is of vital importance and that is protecting the confidential nature of the consultation. This is an issue I would always discuss with the Head Coach before starting to work for and with him. I would tell him that the majority of my work is likely to be confidential but that, if I sense something told to me is likely to affect the functioning of the team in any way, I will ask the athlete's permission to relay that particular point to him, without naming the individual concerned. If the athlete refuses to give his permission, then I will invite him to relate the point to the Head Coach himself because I believe he has a moral duty to do so for the sake of every other member of the team.

The final chapter

As I write this short account of my life's work, the first month of January 2012 is drawing to a close. Perhaps I should have retired some time ago but I continue to work as a consultant for two reasons. First, my services are still in demand from a number of agencies and individuals and, indeed, I am having to turn work down because I don't have the time to do a lot of it and, second, because I love every minute of it! Yes, it can be a lonely and frustrating way to earn a living but, for every moment I have felt down, for whatever reason, there have been more than enough 'highs' to compensate. I have travelled the world with various teams and squads and I have worked with some very famous people. However, the biggest thrill of all is to know that you have helped an athlete, or a group of athletes, to perform better than ever before. This is why the only sources of feedback that mean anything to me are the client's satisfaction and the outcome of his competitive performances.

I have deliberately refrained from referencing this personal account, for I never looked upon it as an academic treatise. However, this is not to say that I 'ploughed a lone furrow' for nothing could be further from the truth. Instead what follows below is a selection (in no particular order) of those works that, over the years, I found to be most helpful, interesting, illuminating and persuasive. It is a testimony to the effects the authors of these texts have had in shaping my views, opinions and beliefs about human behaviour that I still return to them, quite often, to this day.

Allport G. (1961) *Pattern and Growth in Personality*. New York: Rinehart and Winston.

Bannister D. and Fransella F. (1971) *Inquiring Man*. London: Penguin.

Brunswik E. (1947) *Perception and the Representative Design of Psychological Experiments*. USA: University of California Press.

Darwin C. (1872) *The Expression of the Emotions in Man and Animals*. London: Murray.

Hall C.S. and Lindzey G. (1970) *Theories of Personality*. New York: Wiley.

Kelly G. (1955) *The Psychology of Personal Constructs*. New York: Norton.

Aronson E. (1972) *The Social Animal*. New York: W.H. Freeman and Co.

Bandura A. (1997) *Self-Efficacy: The Exercise of Control*. USA: W. H. Freeman and Co.

Skinner B.F. (1968) *The Technology of Teaching*. New York: Appleton-Century-Crofts.

Skinner B.F. (1976) *Walden Two*. USA: Hackett.

Skinner B.F. (1974) *About Behaviorism*. London: Jonathan Cape.

Skinner B.F. (1953) *Science and Human Behavior*. New York: The Free Press.

Skinner B.F. (1969) *Contingencies of Reinforcement. A Theoretical Analysis*. New York: Appleton-Century-Crofts.

O'Donohoe W. and Ferguson K.E. (2001) *The Psychology of B. F. Skinner*. London: Sage Publications.

Milgram S. (1974) *Obedience to Authority*. UK: Tavistock.

Rushall B.S. (2007) *Think and Act like a Champion*. California: Sports Science Associates.

Sheehy N. (2004) *Fifty Key Thinkers in Psychology*. London: Routledge.

8

WHEN YOU COME TO A FORK IN THE ROAD, TAKE IT!

Sandy Gordon

Introduction

I begin this story of how I became a sport psychologist by acknowledging early influences of 'place and people' and explaining the significance of 'timing' in the quote from Yogi Berra (2001). I then switch focus to Canada and the many positive experiences and influences there before arriving in Australia, highlighting how my consulting approach changed, and how I use positive psychology with each consulting opportunity that comes my way. Finally, I share some concerns regarding consultants' capacity to add demonstrable value, and offer some lessons and tips for aspiring sport psychology consultants.

Background and early influences

> Hard indeed must a man be made, by the toil and traffic of gain and trade, who loves not the spot upon where as a boy he played.
>
> *(Bobby Watt, 'Homeland')*

Born and raised in Huntly (Aberdeenshire, Scotland), I was sport daft at school – too much sport was never enough. I remember running round the table at meal times before dashing out again to play football or golf all year round. No time for 'mindful' eating or meaningful dining table conversation in those days. I feel the same way today and often wonder how some colleagues (researchers and practitioners) can sustain their vocational interest in sport when they publicly proclaim (even trumpet) their disdain for it?

My hometown had amazing facilities for such a small village (population ~4,000) and my school, The Gordon Schools, had a proud sport tradition courtesy of my colourful Physical Education (PE) teacher, James (Jimmy) Cullen. He came to

Huntly when I was primary school age and had an immense impact on me and my interest in and attitude towards sport. In addition, three of my father's bakers, who had been part-time professional Highland League footballers, influenced me. They taught me, among other things, how to kick a ball with both feet. They conveniently ducked for cover each time I broke a window, which happened often, however, when I also became a part-time professional player in the Highland League, aged 16, I realized how rare a phenomenon I was being competent in using both feet. In golf, one of my sister's boyfriends turned professional as soon as he could. I spent hours at Huntly Golf Club trying to model everything he did and when I was just about to leave school, he asked me to be his assistant at a prominent golf club in Ayrshire (Scotland). This was my 'fork-in-the-road' moment and at the time I was alone. My parents were on a Mediterranean cruise, my sister was at university, I was enjoying playing Highland League football and was waiting on school exam results, which would determine which of the five conditional offers to universities I would consider. To this day, particularly during the 'marking season' at my university, I often wonder what life would be like had I selected the golf option instead of education/academe?

On reflection, these and other early sport experiences influenced both my career direction and research topic choices. For example, I realized Jimmy Cullen's ambition for me and became a PE teacher. My part-time professional football career, which ended prematurely due to injury, also led to positive outcomes. The type of leadership/coaching I 'endured' during five seasons was so poor that the focus of my initial sport psychology research, and title of my PhD thesis, just had to be 'Behavioural correlates of effective coaching'. I also became interested in the area of mental toughness (e.g., Gucciardi and Gordon, 2009; Gordon and Gucciardi, 2011) and because the psychological sequelae of my career-ending injury, and subsequent knee operations (five), were so debilitating and challenging, I devoted considerable time examining the psychological aspects of sport injuries, and continue to do so today (e.g., Mankad and Gordon, 2010). Transitions in sport careers that typically involve critical decisions made at critical moments, also impacted me personally. Subsequently, together with students and colleagues, I remain very interested in developments in career transitions research (e.g., Chambers et al., in press). Interestingly, some of the issues I deal with most today also reflect the same personal experiences: ineffective coaching, coping with injuries, developing mental toughness, and transitions.

'Purpose motive' and mentors

Prior to my current appointment at the University of Western Australia (1987), my undergraduate training was in Physical Education (DipPE) at Jordanhill College in Glasgow, which preceded post-graduate degrees in Education (DipEd, MEd) at the University of Aberdeen, and in Sport Psychology (MA, PhD) at the University of Alberta, in Edmonton, Canada. I had enjoyed two years teaching senior high school Physical Education in Aberdeen and six years on staff at Aberdeen University, where my interest and accreditation in sport coaching (golf, sailing, soccer, squash and volleyball) flourished. However, while studying at the University of Alberta (U of A) several professors influenced the 'professional platform' (consulting approach) and research areas I have chosen. For example, Terry Orlick (University of Ottawa) and Cal Botterill (University of Winnipeg) had recently completed their PhDs at U of A and their text (Orlick and Botterill, 1975) and Orlick's (1980) 'classic' remain on my recommended book list today. Rick Alderman (1974) was one of my lecturers and Garry Smith (PhD coordinating supervisor) and Murray Smith (PhD supervisory committee member) had both been effective coaches in the Canadian university system (basketball and Canadian football respectively). Their passion for psycho-educational approaches to effective leadership in sport coaching immediately attracted my attention.

While the aforementioned mentors initially influenced 'what' I do (teaching and research) and 'how' (research methods, consulting approach), the 'why' only became clear and relevant a few years later. During a flight from Calgary to Manchester in 1983, I had the great fortune to be sitting next to a Scottish nun who at one stage asked me the most profound question I had ever been asked up to that point in my postgraduate education: 'What is the intention of your work?' She didn't ask 'what are you researching?' or 'how are you going about it?' Instead she asked me 'why?' and 'what was my purpose motive?' Eventually I was able to stumble out a six-word reply 'personal growth, enhanced performance, in sport', which remains the reason and explanation for what I do today. In other words, I like to help all my students and clients get better at whatever they want to get better at, but at the same time enjoy more whatever it is they are doing. Unfortunately, I have found that, in professional and elite levels of sport in particular, the former is easier to achieve than the latter.

How my consulting practice developed

It was only when I moved to Australia in 1987 that I considered becoming a 'psychologist' and even though I'm glad I did, I still regard myself more as an 'educator' with a strong psychology background. For almost 20 years, like the majority of practitioners, I employed what resembled a cognitive-behavioural approach to consulting, which seemingly served both my private and sport clients (teams and individuals) well. I also assumed that 'best practice' was identifying weaknesses and helping both teams and individuals improve in these areas. In sport, I began consulting at the Western Australian Cricket Association (WACA: 1987–2009) as 'mental skills coach' for the Western Warriors in 1987, and in 1998 was appointed by the Australian Cricket Board as 'sport psychologist' to the Australian cricket team (1998–2001). Around that time, upon reading Martin Seligman's (1999) call for psychologists to consider 'positive psychology' approaches to both practice and research, I became a devotee of strengths-based coaching psychology. Historically human endeavours have been characterized as 'fixing weaknesses', and I believe that both sport coaching as well as psychological consulting approaches in sport are no exception. It seems to me that current sport psychology practice and traditional psychological skills training still typically focus on identifying a team's or athlete's weaknesses and fixing them. Strengths-based coaching and psychological consulting, on the other hand, are about spotting and exploiting a team's and athletes' strengths. In 2000, I also acquired accreditation in coaching psychology, which I now introduce to my students as an accompaniment to applied sport psychology. By 2004, after a stint with India's national cricket team (2001–2004), I had completely changed my consulting approach in my work with the Sri Lankan national cricket team (2004–2007), which I have reported elsewhere (Gordon, in press; 2012a).

In addition to introducing positive psychology to my private and sport consulting practice, I believe both *coaching psychology* and organizational psychology, specifically *positive organizational scholarship* (POS), have immensely influenced how I operate in the field of applied sport psychology. While there are numerous approaches to coaching psychology (see Cox *et al.*, 2010), including positive psychology (e.g., Biswas-Diener, 2010), sadly I'm not certain graduates of current applied sport psychology programmes are as aware of them as they could or should be. I also don't think POS (see Cameron and Spreitzer, 2012) is introduced to aspiring practitioners either, yet applications of positive organizational psychology are very relevant and useful when working with both teams/groups and individuals in sport. I am particularly drawn to Appreciative Inquiry and its transformative potential within sporting associations, clubs, and individuals (see Gordon, 2011, 2012a).

Challenges ahead: project management and personal de-briefs

Over the years I have discussed with several colleagues the myriad professional service challenges that occasionally create frustration and disappointment in consulting roles in elite sport. One example is continuity or maintaining contractual work with clients. Another is how to embed positive coaching conversations within sporting cultures at a macro-level (see Gordon, 2012b). However, I feel the main issue for consultants concerns how to *add demonstrable value*. Sport psychology consultants need to ask themselves 'what is my unique value proposition to a team or athlete?' 'What specific value will I add and what do I not do or what value will I not add?' 'How will my contribution be measured?' 'How will I differentiate myself from other contributors – coaches, doctors, physiotherapists, trainers?' About 10 years ago I realized I needed to keep defining my value proposition as each team evolved and developed their mental skill capabilities. I needed to scan horizons for new inputs (e.g., business) and engage in constant assessment of team needs and where I could add value. I also needed to constantly challenge myself, measure what I do, which is difficult, and seek out sources of feedback so I could grow.

In Australia, after the 2000 Sydney Olympics, where there were 12 Australian sport psychologists accredited with the Olympic Federation, John Coates (the Australian Olympic Committee Chief) stated that many did not add value. Some coaches made similar comments to me during the final days of those Olympics. So sport psychologists in Australia, and worldwide, have a few challenges ahead. These include the inevitable familiarity with coaches and athletes that leads to diminished criticality, perceptions of an empty toolbox, 'the team outgrows me', and lack of personal assertiveness and capability to challenge. Sport psychologists need to be constantly relevant and in the executive coaching and business consulting world, we refer to this concept as 'being two (PowerPoint) slides ahead of the client'. Sport psychology consultants always need to add something new that enhances capability, to be constantly challenging, moving coaches and athletes out of their comfort zone. As teams and athletes evolve, so too must sport psychologists develop ahead of them. Otherwise we will become irrelevant, not adding value. If nothing changes, nothing changes.

The philosophy I am referring to is akin to being customer-driven rather than product-driven. How often do we do a rigorous diagnostic at the front end to define what the team requires to transform to a higher level of performance? Too often we arrive with a set of products (mental skills) that we promote within the team rather than assess the team against a set of benchmarks/dimensions that will form the basis for a transformation programme. The mental skills menu is just one lever for transformation – there are *many* others. We need to be regularly reassessing the team against relevant benchmarks to identify both strengths and areas in need of development. At the start we often write a contract with the coach/team but after we have been with the team for a period of time, we tend to roll from one tour to another tour, season to season, phase to phase. We need to set clear specific objectives defined by specific value added.

A *project management approach* sets out specific tasks to be performed, deliverables, milestones and interdependencies. In consulting practice, project management disciplines are a basic competency. Many large corporations are attempting to develop internal project management capability to increase the focus on speedy delivery of outcomes. A project management approach would assist sport psychologists to deliver, and be seen to deliver, specific outcomes. There are numerous people who impact our success – coach, captain, senior players, manager, CEO, doctor, physiotherapist. They are our key stakeholders. The perceptions and behaviours of the key stakeholders need to be constantly evaluated and managed.

Some applied sport psychology research, in my opinion, simply does not stack up to reality. Despite excellent reviews of professional practice in sport psychology (e.g., Hanton and Mellalieu, 2012), consultants need to acknowledge that behavioural science will never be an exact science. The business of people development is as much an art as it is a (behavioural) science and 'if the map (research) doesn't agree with the ground (reality), the map is wrong' (adapted from Livingston, 2004, p. 1). Several years ago, based on their extensive and collective experiences, Wayne Halliwell, Terry Orlick, Ken Ravizza and Bob Rotella (1999) penned an excellent compendium for consultants on the art of working with performers in any domain (school, workplace, health, performing, sport). I hope I do not dilute the generalizability of the principles they identified from their research because instead I want to highlight how significant the 'doing of sport psychology' – not the 'doing of applied research' – actually is.

Halliwell *et al.* (1999) reported that coaches and players identified four basic types of *ineffective consultants*. First, 'the Shrink' imagines or actively seeks out pathological problems among players and coaches, attempts inappropriate 'clinical interventions' and generally has a limited understanding of high performance cultures and the mental demands and mental skills training required to be successful in these domains. I am not suggesting that clinical issues do not exist – they often do – but the capability to only deliver clinical interventions is hardly likely to be the sole basis for contracted work. Second, 'the Ivory tower researcher' engages in loads of testing (administering questionnaires) and yet provides limited if any useful feedback. Third, 'the Coach' as consultant attempts to either undermine or actually take over the head coach's role; and, finally, 'the Hot shot' loves photographs, seeks attention, claims undue credit, and is unwilling to be or stay low-profile.

In contrast, *effective consultants* are perceived to just blend in or fit in. They ask meaningful questions and really listen to coaches and players, and to *their* solutions and suggestions. They actively participate at camps and competition sites, offer practical advice and spend quality time 1:1 with everyone, including support staff. They know, understand and accept their on-site job, from preferences discussed with coaches and players, and play effective supportive roles at competitions. Some personal attributes and qualities of effective consultants were also identified by Halliwell *et al.* (ibid.) and include: passion, drive, vision, discipline, confidence, focus, high tolerance for ambiguity and uncertainty, being creative, patience, and responsiveness to failure. Interpersonal qualities include: inspire confidence and trust, compelling, empathic, air of competence and confidence, assertive, comfortable socially, and effective communicator. Some important professional or applied skills that may be caught as well as taught include the ability to write, speak, present to groups, listen and problem-solve.

I have had the privilege of working with several professional teams and individuals and at the completion of their games, tournaments, and seasons I oblige them to review and reflect on their performances. I have only recently begun to apply a *personal de-brief process* for myself, one that I designed to both evaluate my own performance and help me prepare for other tournaments and/or consultancies in the future. I have worked with teams that have won World Cups, national titles and some that haven't. I've also been retained on long-term contracts and experienced disappointment at losing others. So I'm keenly aware that 'Sandy Gordon' has no unique gifts or traits or magic wands to offer, only expertise, experience, and a strong desire both to do my best and to continue to learn. While wins and losses are clearly not the most relevant measures of how well sport psychologists do their job or dictate how they should continue to operate in the future, our clients/employers often use outcomes and results during their considerations of retaining our services. Consequently, to get away from evaluations based solely on a player's or team's performance, I decided to create personal de-brief questions that tapped into the aforementioned key behaviours and personal skills of effective consultants as identified by Halliwell *et al.* (ibid.). The list of evaluative questions I use, illustrated in Table 8.1, is designed to promote *value add* to all the work I am privileged to be offered as well as to facilitate my own professional development and personal growth.

Lessons learned and some advice for aspiring sport psychology consultants

From a long list of lessons, three stand out. First, my most significant learning experiences have been from success NOT failure. Problem is that, unlike losing experiences which are like Velcro and 'stick', winning experiences are like Teflon and 'slip away' and are quickly forgotten. In sport, we default to analysing failure to death (what went wrong) – we are champions at this! – and we spend very little to no time at all analysing success (what went right). Yet, regardless of how bad results and performances appear, all teams and individuals get something right – called the 'exception' rule. I have found that identifying 'what works' sparks both the best learning experiences for individuals and the most helpful attitude to move forward. Yes, you can learn and succeed by fixing problems and weaknesses – you cannot ignore them – but *only* when you are also making most of your successes and strengths.

Second, I have also learned how important the role of effective transformational leadership is when developing and sustaining high performance cultures (see Gordon, 2012b). The worst consulting experience I had, in Australian football, involved an old-school coach butting heads with a modern/new-school club culture and senior player leadership group. When the coach was eventually fired, a year after I was (thankfully) relieved of a two-year contract, the club Chairman wrote to me to express his regret at dismissing the concerns I had raised with him within four weeks of my appointment regarding the effect of poor leadership. I have been very fortunate to have worked closely with excellent coaches, particularly in cricket, whose sustainable style and ability to engage people easily outlasted naïve opinions of talented individual players who claimed they didn't need a coach and thought they 'did it themselves'.

Third, I have learned that I need to keep learning, and that in addition to applied sport psychology literature, I need to access information from other performance environments, e.g., coaching, exercise, health, positive organizational psychology, positive psychology, rehabilitation psychology. In this respect recent attendance and participation in non-sport psychology conferences have been both refreshing and very useful. Giving advice to aspiring sport psychology consultants is a precarious business; however, here are three offerings. First, I am aware that to fulfil registration requirements we must initially log specific numbers of hours of supervised practice. However, rather than flit from practicum to practicum, or job to job, I suggest that early career consultants endeavour, if at all possible, to pick one sport or performance environment that they like and immerse themselves totally in it. Seems some newbie consultants burn out from

TABLE 8.1 Personal de-brief inventory

Code of Ethics

Professional responsibility
1. decisions and actions used were appropriate   yes/no/NA
2. highest (Australian Psychological Society) standards maintained   yes/no/NA

Competence
3. used appropriate skills based on qualifications and training   yes/no/NA
4. refrained from offering services/advice beyond personal competence   yes/no/NA

Client welfare
5. confidentiality of information respected   yes/no/NA
6. obligations and duties towards clients delivered   yes/no/NA
7. ongoing service arrangements made (post-termination)   yes/no/NA

Assessment
8. chosen, administered, and interpreted appropriately   yes/no/NA

Relationship with clients
9. professional nature of relationship clarified   yes/no/NA
10. clinical problem/condition referred to appropriate source of expertise   yes/no/NA

Behaviours/Personal skills	rarely				always
1. determined athlete/coach preferences for my role *(planning, effective communication)*	1	2	3	4	5
2. accessible to everyone *(planning, flexibility)*	1	2	3	4	5
3. approachable to everyone *(flexibility, comfortable socially)*	1	2	3	4	5
4. listened well *(effective communication, empathy)*	1	2	3	4	5
5. asked meaningful questions *(social support, quality 1:1 time)*	1	2	3	4	5
6. offered concrete and practical advice *(practical, helpful)*	1	2	3	4	5
7. pitched in with other non-mental skills tasks *(flexibility, team building)*	1	2	3	4	5
8. creative and intuitive *(vision, passion)*	1	2	3	4	5
9. solution-focused *('always a better way', anxiety management)*	1	2	3	4	5
10. blended in *(low profile/high impact, personal stress management)*	1	2	3	4	5
11. effective member of support staff *(team player, self-confidence)*	1	2	3	4	5
12. had fun/retained sense of humour *(reality testing, positive mental momentum)*	1	2	3	4	5

chasing any job, anywhere at any price and wonder at their disenchantment with their profession. Second, develop a 'why' or 'purpose motive' as soon as possible. While 'what' and 'how' are obviously important, having a 'why' will sustain engagement in sport psychology consulting more effectively. Finally, seek wisdom beyond the usual literatures (e.g., coaching, organizational, positive psychology) and sport environments, and earn a reputation for 'sharing' your stuff.

> We must go beyond textbooks, go out into the bypaths and untrodden depths of the wilderness and travel and explore and tell the world the glories of our journey.
>
> *(John Hope Franklin)*

References

Alderman, R. B. (1974) *Psychological Behaviour in Sport*. Toronto: W. B. Saunders.

Berra, Y. (2001) *When You Come to a Fork in the Road, Take It!* New York: Hyperion.

Biswas-Diener, R. (2010) *Practicing Positive Psychology Coaching*. Hoboken, NJ: Wiley.

Cameron, K. and Spreitzer, G. (eds) (2012) *The Oxford Handbook of Positive Organizational Scholarship*. New York: Oxford University Press.

Chambers, T., Gordon, S. and Morris, T. (in press) Australian athletes in transition: from retirement to education and beyond, in N. B. Stambulova and T. V. Ryba (eds) *Athletes' Careers Across Cultures*. London: Routledge.

Cox, E., Bachkirova, T. and Clutterbuck, D. (eds) (2010) *The Complete Handbook Of Coaching*. London: Sage.

Gordon, S. (2011) Building the optimal cricket operation. *Appreciative Inquiry Practitioner*, 13(2): 60–64.

——(2012a) Strengths-based approaches to developing mental toughness: team and individual. *International Coaching Psychology Review*, 7(2): 210–222.

——(2012b) Creating an effective organisational culture, in F. Pyke (ed.) *Coaching Excellence*. Adelaide: Human Kinetics, pp. 59–69.

——(in press) Roar of the lions: strengths-based consulting with Sri Lanka cricket, in P. Terry, M. Bar-Eli, Z. Li-Wei, Z. Young Ho and T. Morris (eds) *Secrets of Asian Sport Psychology*. Asian-South Pacific Association of Sport Psychology.

Gordon, S. and Gucciardi, D. (eds) (2011) *Mental Toughness in Sport: Developments in Theory and Research*. London: Routledge.

Gucciardi, D. F. and Gordon, S. (2009) Development and preliminary validation of the Cricket Mental Toughness Inventory. *Journal of Sports Sciences*, 27: 1293–1310.

Halliwell, W., Orlick, T., Ravizza, K. and Rotella, B. (1999) *Consultant's Guide to Excellence*. Chelsea, QU: Orlick Excel.

Hanton, S. and Mellalieu, S. D. (eds) (2012) *Professional Practice in Sport Psychology: A Review*. London: Routledge.

Livingston, G. (2004) *Too Soon Old, Too Late Smart*. Sydney: Hodder.

Mankad, A. and Gordon, S. (2010) Psycho-linguistic changes in athletes' response to injury after written emotional disclosure. *Journal of Sport Rehabilitation*, 19: 328–342.

Orlick, T. (1980) *In Pursuit of Excellence*. Windsor, ON: Human Kinetics.

Orlick, T. and Botterill, C. (1975) *Every Kid Can Win*. Chicago: Nelson-Hall.

Seligman, M. E. P. (1999) The president's address. *American Psychologist*, 54: 559–562.

PART III

Counselling Psychology

9

IT'S ALL ABOUT RELATIONSHIPS

A counseling approach to sport psychology consulting

Al Petitpas

I am a Professor in the Psychology Department at Springfield College. In that capacity, I co-direct the Athletic Counseling Master's program, teach several graduate courses, and head Springfield College's Center for Youth Development and Research. Throughout my career, I have tried to promote traditional counseling psychology beliefs and practices in the fields of sport psychology and positive youth development. In this chapter, I will explain how I got involved in the field of sport psychology. I will outline my beliefs about how athletic counseling fits into the practice of exercise and sport psychology and I will describe my approach to working with athletes.

On becoming a sport psychologist

My journey to a career in sport psychology began long before I knew the field existed. As a tall, but overweight 11-year-old boy growing up in Cambridge, Massachusetts, I was fortunate that the Catholic Youth Organization (CYO) started youth basketball and baseball programs at the local playground. I joined and quickly became addicted to sports. I practiced after school every day and sport became my all-consuming passion. Over the next several years, I began to receive recognition and other personal benefits from my athletic successes. When it became time to select a high school, I based my decision on where I was most likely to fit in athletically. My success in sport continued in high school where I earned All-Scholastic recognition and several offers to play basketball in college. I selected a Division 1 program located about an hour from my home. However, for the first time in my life, I was not the best player on my team. In fact, I saw only limited playing time. I began to question my choice of college and started to realize that I had little understanding of who I was as a person or what I wanted to do with my life. For me, college was the next sport league, not a place to prepare for a future career. As I struggled to decide what to do, I had a chance meeting with an Academic Dean at a Division III college. Fortunately, he was a sports fan and had remembered seeing me play in a high school tournament. After I explained my current situation, he told me that I would have no problem getting playing time at his college and he invited me to transfer. I finished out my Freshman year at the Division 1 school and transferred to start my Sophomore year. The decision to transfer proved to be a good one athletically. During the next three years, I was a starting player in both basketball and baseball, served as captain of both teams, and earned Most Valuable Player awards and regional All-American Honorable Mention in basketball.

I graduated from college with a degree in social science, but I had not engaged in any career planning and lacked a sense of direction. In retrospect, I would classify myself as being in a state of situational foreclosure. I had not engaged in exploratory behavior and still held on to the belief that athletics was my identity. In reality, my formal sports career was over and I had not taken the time to consider what I wanted to do for a career.

Fortunately, one of my former basketball coaches became a Dean of Students and offered me a position as Assistant to the Dean on the condition that I pursue a degree in counseling or student personnel administration. Over the next several years, I earned a Master's Degree in College Counseling, began doctoral work in counseling psychology, got coaching experience with a college basketball program, and began teaching as an instructor in school guidance.

I enjoyed my experiences teaching and coaching at the college level, but I eventually came to accept the fact that my athletic career was over and it was time to pursue something different. I decided to leave my position as Assistant Dean and pursue a doctoral degree full-time. I enrolled at Boston University during the time that the Counselor Education program was transitioning to Counseling Psychology. I spent two years in Boston University's Advisory Resource Center providing counseling and career development services to undergraduate and graduate students. Although there were no sport psychology courses available to me, I was able to participate in year-long training seminars in process consultation, assessment, supervision, and sex therapy. These experiences help to shape my worldview and laid the foundation for my current beliefs about sport psychology practice.

During my studies, I had come across the construct of identity foreclosure. The more I learned about the concept, the more convinced I became that I was in a state of situational foreclosure. I had not engaged in exploratory behavior, but had made a commitment to the role of athlete. So when it came time to select a dissertation topic, I decided to examine identity development in male intercollegiate athletes. Without going into detail, I designed a study comparing the ego-identity status of athletes and non-athletes at freshman and senior year in college. I found no differences between the senior athlete sample and the freshman athletes and non-athletes groups on several psychosocial variables related to foreclosure. However, the participants in the senior non-athlete group displayed a more positive psychosocial profile. My interest in the concept of identity foreclosure continued over the years and it was gratifying to see that foreclosure was listed as a core knowledge area in the sport psychology proficiencies of the American Psychological Association (2008).

After finishing my coursework at Boston University and spending a year as a psychology instructor and counselor at a community college, I accepted a position in the Psychology Department at Springfield College as Director of the graduate training program in Student Personnel Administration in Higher Education. Springfield College was very attractive because the Psychology Department was open to and supportive of new faculty initiatives, and the college had a long history of excellence in athletics and the sport sciences. During my first two years at Springfield, I focused on growing the Student Personnel program, but also became acutely aware of the problems that were coming to light in college athletic programs across the United States. It seemed that a new academic scandal surfaced each week. College athletes were graduating with less than third grade reading abilities. College professors were suing athletic departments because of pressure to change grades for student-athletes. Colleges were placed on probation by the National Collegiate Athletic Association (NCAA) for admitting student-athletes with forged high school transcripts. As a result of all of these problems, a group of college athletic administrators met to discuss what could be done to bring academic integrity back to collegiate sports. This group pushed for academic reforms and urged college athletic departments to employ individuals to provide academic and other support services for their student athletes. In response, many colleges assigned assistant coaches and hired tutors to assist their student-athletes. Several years later, this group became an official organization called the National Association of Academic Advisors for Athletics (N4A).

During its early years, the leadership of the N4A sought to position academic advising for athletes as a professional specialty, even though there were no specific competencies identified or training options available. In response to the need for trained professionals and because of my own beliefs about the importance of a quality helping relationship, I developed the Springfield College graduate training program in Athletic Counseling in 1982. This program incorporated a traditional educational/developmental counseling approach into the preparation of counselors who would work with individuals who participate in sport and physical activity. The curriculum included courses in basic counseling and career development competencies, developmental dynamics, sport sciences, performance psychology, and professional practice. This curriculum also became the basis for the Sport Counseling Competencies that I developed for the American Counseling Association in 1983.

My entry into sport psychology probably began in 1982 when I became a licensed psychologist in Massachusetts and opened a small private practice, housed in a large Sports Medicine Clinic in Springfield, Massachusetts. Although my initial clients were individuals seeking help with marital and personal problems, my case load soon filled with athletes who were referred by the sports medicine staff because of difficulties coping with their injuries. My experience as an athlete and coach helped me to understand some of the unique challenges athletes faced in coping with injuries, dealing with stress, and managing forced and unforced transitions, but I was also being asked to assist with performance issues, communication problems, and other sport psychology concerns. To fill some of the voids in my training, I immersed myself in the sport psychology literature and attended numerous related conferences and meetings. I did find some comfort as I began to realize that my doctoral training in process consultation and sex therapy had introduced me to many of the theories and techniques that were being used in the practice of sport psychology. I will describe some of these techniques in the section on my approach to consulting with athletes.

My beliefs about sport psychology were shaped by several important events during the 1980s. First, the N4A expanded its focus beyond academic advising to include personal and career development, life skills, and wellness. In order to meet the need for additional training in these areas, I organized the Conference on Counseling Athletes. This annual conference attracted sport psychologists, athletic counselors, and coaches, and has been running for over 30 years. The conference also opened doors to several consulting opportunities. For example, a four-person team from Springfield College designed and implemented a program for the Ladies Professional Golf Association (Petitpas and Elliott, 1987). We traveled to a different tour stop each month during the professional golf season and provided transition and career development services to 37 of the golfers.

Second, in 1983, the United States Olympic Committee's Advisory Board on Sport Psychology published a document that outlined three types of sport psychology activities: clinical, educational, and research (United States Olympic Committee, 1983). Clinical interventions were defined as activities that assist athletes who exhibit severe emotional problems such as depression, panic, and interpersonal conflicts, and were carried out in a one-on-one basis. Educational interventions were said to be group activities that focused on teaching psychological skills, such as relaxation, imagery, and attention control to enhance athletes' sport performance. Research was not seen as a form of intervention, but as an important activity to enhance the work of both clinical and educational practitioners. Although these guidelines were developed to show the range of activities deemed necessary for the provision of comprehensive sport psychology services to Olympic athletes, they inadvertently spawned a turf war between professionals trained in psychology and those trained in the sport sciences. Even today, questions about appropriate training, practitioner competencies, and the use of the term sport psychologist still exist (Berger, 2010). As a person trained in psychology, I was frequently identified in the clinical category, even though my training in traditional counseling psychology had more in common with educational sport psychology. I will discuss this in more depth in the next section.

The third and fourth significant events were the development of the Association for the Advancement of Applied Sport Psychology (AAASP) and the Division of Sport and Exercise Psychology of the American Psychological Association (Division 47). These two organizations provided me with invaluable continuing education and numerous opportunities to network with many of the most renowned sport psychologists in the world. For example, Shane Murphy, former head of sport psychology services for the United States Olympic Committee (USOC), invited me to join Steve Danish, Dan Gould, Bob McKelvain, and others to develop a career assistance program for Olympic athletes. Shortly thereafter, I became involved in several USOC programs, including the Elite Coaches College, the 1990 Olympic Festival, and the Alcohol Education Seminar.

Over the last 20 years, I have had the good fortune to provide consulting services for a wide range of sport organizations, including the U.S. Ski Jumping and Nordic Combined Teams, the New England Blizzard of the American Basketball Association, the National Basketball Association, the Montreal Alouettes of the Canadian Football League, and the National Football League's Players Association. While I continue to enjoy working with elite and professional athletes, I have spent much of the last two decades focused on programs that promote positive youth development.

Presently, I direct Springfield College's Center for Youth Development and Research. The primary mission of the Center is to provide consulting services to organizations that use sport and physical activity as a vehicle to help young people acquire important life skills and prepare for the future. Working in sport-based youth development has been very rewarding and I have been fortunate to work on the planning and program development teams for a significant number of initiatives, including The First Tee's Life Skills and Mentoring Programs, the National Collegiate Athletic Association's Youth Education through Sports (YES) Program, the Montreal Alouettes' On Point Program, Pop Warner Football's Coach Education Seminars, the National Football League (NFL)/National Football Foundation's (NFF) Coaching Academy, the NFF's PLAY IT SMART Program, Academics in Motion's Project Rebound, and Springfield College's Leaders in Academics, Community Engagement, and Service project. Each of these initiatives uses sport and physical activity to create an environment where young people can learn about themselves, develop relationships with caring adult mentors, acquire important life skills, and find a valued place in a positive group.

Throughout my career, I have promoted athletic counseling as an approach to sport psychology consulting. As such, I felt a sense of pride when our Athletic Counseling program was selected to be the first program highlighted in the APA Division 47 (Exercise and Sport Psychology) Newsletter as a model training program. In the next section, I will outline my beliefs about an athletic counseling approach to sport and exercise psychology.

Defining athletic counseling

After the USOC's Advisory Board on Sport Psychology published in 1983 the controversial document that outlined three types of sport psychology activities: clinical, educational, and research, sport psychologists trained in psychology were typically classified as clinical and those trained in the sport sciences as educational.

Professionals trained in counseling psychology often found themselves misclassified as clinical specialists. Consider that traditional counseling psychology focuses on individuals' strengths and adaptive strategies across the life-span, a focus that has more in common with educational sport psychology (Petitpas *et al.*, 1995; Petitpas *et al.*, 1999).

Over the last several decades, differences between clinical and counseling psychologists have become less clear (Society of Counseling Psychology, 2011). Typically, both clinical and counseling psychologists are trained to provide counseling and psychotherapy, are eligible to hold licensure in every state in the United States as "licensed psychologist," and are able to practice independently as health care providers. However, traditional counseling psychologists are trained to take a psychoeducational and developmental perspective that emphasizes growth and enhancement in normal populations (Danish *et al.*, 1993).

The American Psychological Association's Division 17 (Counseling Psychology) website provides a history of the differences in the evolution of clinical and counseling psychology (Society of Counseling Psychology, 2011). The term clinical comes from the Greek word for bed, "kline," which refers to providing bedside care to ill patients. Counseling derives from the Latin word, "consulere," which means to advise or consult. Traditionally, clinical psychologists took a corrective approach to working with mental illness and learning disabilities, whereas counseling psychologists build on a person's existing strengths while providing career guidance. In 1951, the Counseling Psychology Division of APA changed from an exclusive focus on career issues, to an emphasis on identifying strengths to promote positive well-being throughout the life-span. This emphasis was reaffirmed at the Third National Conference for Counseling Psychology in 1987 (Weiner *et al.*, 2003).

Counseling psychologists focus on individual strengths, development, decision-making, and life-work planning across the life-span. This focus seems more consistent with the USOC's description of an educational rather than a clinical sport psychologist. From the beginning, the athletic counseling program adhered to Shertzer and Stone's description of counseling as "an interaction process which facilitates meaningful understanding of self and environment and results in the establishment and/or clarification of goals and values for future behavior" (1966, p. 26). It is interesting to note that the recent positive psychology movement has shown that interventions that build gratitude, and increase awareness of self positives and character strengths can increase happiness and decrease depression (Seligman and Csikszentmihalyi, 2000; Seligman *et al.*, 2005). Based on these descriptions, it is difficult to differentiate between positive psychology and traditional counseling psychology. Whether positive psychology is a new focus in psychology or simply an up-named version of traditional counseling psychology is still up for debate. However, I believe that there is considerable merit in conducting positive asset searches with athlete clients, building on their strengths, and assisting them in planning for future life transitions. I firmly believe in the mantra of positive youth development, "problem free does not mean prepared for the future"

(Pittman, 1991), and both positive and traditional counseling psychology strive to identify strengths and assist individuals in acquiring the skills necessary to function and prosper throughout the life span.

As sport psychology practice has evolved, there has been a shift from a focus on improving sport skills to a concern for the role of sport in human development and the use of sport to enhance personal competence (Danish *et al.*, 1993). As such, I believe that counseling interventions should be added to the traditional educational and clinical approaches resulting in a new model of sport psychology consultation that is concerned with athletes' well-being and development across sport, school, career, and personal domains. I named our graduate training program, Athletic Counseling, so that perspective students would understand this philosophy and approach to consulting with athletes and coaches.

My approach to sport psychology consulting

In general, I believe that the quality of the working relationship between the consultant and the athlete is the critical factor in sport psychology consultations. If I can create an empathetic relationship in which athletes believe that I understand what they are going through, they are more likely to take risks and attempt new behaviors. I believe that athletes are the experts on themselves and I make the assumption that when they are having difficulties, the first thing they do is to try to fix the problems themselves. If this does not work, they will typically go to their friends or family for assistance. If they still cannot resolve the situation, they might seek out a sport psychologist, athletic counselor, or some other type of helping professional. Ironically, most of the problem situations that I consult on are a result of the athlete's own attempts at "self-cure" that are no longer working. For example, a female basketball player who believes that her coach has something against her might simply avoid talking with or having as little contact as possible with the coach. Although this strategy may give her some immediate relief, the coach may view her as having a bad attitude and treat her accordingly.

My first goal as consultant is to strive to understand what the problem means to the athlete and how he or she has tried to correct it. I also try to learn what athletes hope to get out of their meetings with me. The key to understanding situations from the athlete's perspective is to be patient and to listen well. One of the common problems that I encounter when providing supervision to new graduate students is their attempt to provide quick solutions to their athletes' situations before they understand the situations from the athletes' perspectives. Consultants should never assume that they know what an athlete is thinking or feeling. Instead, they should verify their initial perceptions by using listening skills, such as asking appropriate questions, reflecting feelings, and paraphrasing the athletes' statements. I like the "Columbo approach" identified by Meichenbaum (1985) and believe that the more inquisitive I am about athletes' situations, the more explicit they become in explaining their unique experiences. This process of inquiry not only allows me to gain a better understanding of athletes' perceptions of the problem, but it often increases their self-understanding as well. As athletes explain the specifics of a situation to me, they often gain additional insight about themselves and their reactions.

I believe that encouragement is an important element in the consultant/athlete relationship. However, consultants who offer encouragement before rapport has been established with an athlete run the risk of "discounting" the athlete's feelings and impede the development of a working relationship. Therefore, I believe that it is critical to match or attend to athletes' present focus before attempting to encourage them or help them view a situation from a different perspective. Premature attempts at fixing problems or failure to attend to athletes' immediate concerns are likely to have a negative effect on the consultant/athlete relationship.

I find a lot of athletes are skeptical about the efficacy of sport psychology interventions. These athletes will question whether just talking about problems can really make any difference. Unfortunately, these doubts can become major distractions or restrict the amount of effort that athletes put into acquiring new skills or trying different strategies. Therefore, it is important to pay close attention to athletes' verbal and non-verbal communications, their failure to do "homework" assignments, or their reluctance to engage in activities during meetings. Because of the power differential that is often inherent in the consultant/athlete relationship, many athletes will go along with where consultants are leading them, even when they are skeptical or believe that something else is a more pressing concern. I believe that if I listen carefully with both my ears and my eyes, I can identify when athletes have doubts. In particular, I pay attention to athletes' use of "but," whether it is communicated verbally or non-verbally. Recognizing athletes' doubts helps me to keep the focus of the interaction on their agenda.

I have found that many athletes/clients go through a cognitive transition that begins with the thought, "maybe I can do this," and continues on until they have experienced the benefit of the new strategy often enough that they start to think "I know I can do it." However, I find that some athletes will run into difficulties that they did not anticipate, become discouraged, and stop trying the new strategy. Therefore, I think it is important to help athletes understand that the acquisition of skills does not often take place in a straight line from point "A" to point "B." Instead there are typically a series of learning plateaus or setbacks that need to be addressed before mastery takes place. I strive to provide enough information to help athletes avoid the types of surprises or disappointments that can impede skill acquisition and assist them in preparing for possible roadblocks. These roadblocks usually fall into one of four categories: (1) a lack of knowledge; (2) a lack of skills (3) hesitancy to take risks; or (4) a lack of social support (Danish *et al.*, 1993).

Finally, I believe that it is important to train for generalization. I strive to ensure that athletes not only can demonstrate the desired skills on the playing field, but they can also use the skills in other situations. The more success athletes have in using a skill or behavior in various situations, the greater the likelihood that their mastery level and self-efficacy will also increase.

Conclusion

I feel fortunate to have found sport psychology as a career. In looking back, I can state without question that the key to everything I have been able to accomplish is a direct result of the relationships that I have developed with colleagues, coaches, and athletes. In particular, I would like to recognize Britt Brewer, Steve Danish, Burt Giges, Shane Murphy, and Judy Van Raalte for all the support they have offered me over the years.

References

American Psychological Association (2008) A proficiency in sport psychology. Available at: www.apa.org/division47/sports_proficiency.html (accessed November 21, 2008).

Berger, B. (2010) Celebrating 25 years of AASP: looking back and looking at the present as we chart our future. Presidential address at the Annual Conference of the Association for Applied Sport Psychology, Providence, RI, October.

Danish, S. J., Petitpas, A. J. and Hale, B. D. (1993) Life development interventions for athletes: life skills through sports. *The Counseling Psychologist*, 21: 352–385.

Meichenbaum, D. (1985) *Stress Inoculation Training*. Elmford, NY: Pergamon Press.

Petitpas, A. J., Buntrock, C. L., Van Raalte, J. L. and Brewer, B. W. (1995) Counseling athletes: a new specialty in counselor education. *Counselor Education and Supervision*, 34: 212–219.

Petitpas, A. J., Danish, S. J. and Giges, B. (1999) The sport psychologist–athlete relationship: implications for training. *The Sport Psychologist*, 13: 344–357.

Petitpas, A. and Elliott, W. (1987) Preparing for future careers. Presentation at the Annual Sponsors' Meeting of the Ladies Professional Golf Association, Pine Isle, GA, November.

Pittman, K. J. (1991) *Promoting Youth Development: Strengthening the Role of Youth-Serving and Community Organizations*. Report prepared for the U.S. Department of Agriculture Extension Services. Washington, DC: Center for Youth Development and Policy Research.

Seligman, M. E. P. and Csikszentmihalyi, M. (2000) Positive psychology: an introduction. *American Psychologist*, 5(1): 5–14.

Seligman, M. E. P., Steen, T. A., Park, N. and Peterson, C. (2005) Positive psychology progress: empirical validation of interventions. *American Psychologist*, 60(5): 410–421.

Shertzer, B. and Stone, S. (1966) *Fundamentals of Counseling*. Boston: Houghton Mifflin.

Society of Counseling Psychology (2011) Counseling vs. clinical. Available at: www.div17.org/students_differences.html.

United States Olympic Committee (1983) USOC establishes guidelines for sport psychology services. *Journal of Sport Psychology*, 5: 4–7.

Weiner, I., Freedheim, D., Schinka, J. and Velicer, W. (2003) *Handbook of Psychology*, vols 1–12. Hoboken, NJ: John Wiley & Sons, Inc.

PART IV

Psychology

10

THE (SPORT) PSYCHOLOGIST IN SPITE OF HIMSELF

Mark B. Andersen

I chose this title because in the realm of sport and competition I am, like Molière's doctor in *Le Médecin Malgré Lui*, a fraud. I was never, by any stretch of anyone's imagination, a jock. I am ungainly and uncoordinated; I trip over something at least once a day. When I attempt to participate in hand–eye coordination sports, the results are near Chaplinesque. I am also gay and, therefore, unmanly in the über-manly arena of homophobic male sport (especially in the 1960s during my teenage years). So, with all this stuff working against me, how did I grow up to be a practitioner and academic working in applied psychology and sport? It's a long story.

The early years

I grew up in the 1950s and 1960s near San Francisco. The Bay Area was a center for many radical movements and protest demonstrations (the anti-Vietnam War protests, the free speech movement, the civil rights campaign, the Black Panthers), and I was immersed in an atmosphere of righting wrongs. One of the injustices (albeit a minor one in the grand scheme of what was happening in the 1960s) I felt at the daily personal level was physical education (PE) classes. For most of each school year, PE was 45 minutes of humiliation and failure. Besides being a klutz, I am also congenitally incapable of determining which directions left and right are if I have to choose quickly (give me 5 seconds to think about it, and I can usually get it correct). So on a basketball court when the team leader would yell at me, "Go right!" at least 50 percent of the time I would get it wrong – more humiliation. In high school, I had some respite because I was on the swim team (no hand–eye, left–right issues there) and did not have to attend PE classes during the swim season.

By my senior year in high school, my uncoordinated best friends and I had had enough, and, in the spirit of the times, we lodged a protest with our PE teacher.

We explained to him our plight and our miseries, and suggested that he should let us run around the track to get some exercise. To our relief and surprise, he said, "OK." I think he was happy just to get rid of us. I believe the *Zeitgeist* in the 1960s of righting wrongs, of protest, and of trying to fix things became internalised and, eventually, part of my character.

Intimate encounters with mental illness

My first experiences with psychopathology and the profession of psychology stemmed from two sources. My mother had repeated bouts of major depression during the last 30+ years of her life. For a teenager, watching my Mom descend into her private hell over and over again was both confusing and terrifying. I know I developed a Winnicott-like (1971) *caretaker self*, where the child subjugates his needs and focuses on attempting to take care of a parent's distress. After years of study and psychotherapy, I have come to see my achievements as having their roots in trying to make my mother happy through my accomplishments. This unconscious tactic, of course, did not work, but my caretaker self is still operating years after her death. I watch that caretaker pop up again and again, even now, with my clients and my students in my desire to fix them and save them. With such salvation needs, caretaking, and mental illness in my family, it is no surprise I became a psychologist.

My second source was my best friend's father. He was a calm, gentle, rational, and compassionate man, and he was also a psychologist. In my confusing teenage (*confusing* and *teenage* seem redundant) years when my Mom's depression bouts were discombobulating me, I turned to this man to help me understand. His explanations of depression and his empathy soothed a lot of my anxieties, and I am sure, at some unconscious level, I was saying to myself, "I want to be like him." But psychology was not my first choice when I entered university.

From foreign languages to internal landscapes

When I was 17, I left home to study in Sweden for over a year. When I turned 18 in Stockholm, I registered for the draft at the US Embassy. Hồ Chí Minh had recently died, but the war in Vietnam was still raging, and I was thinking that I might have to stay in Sweden because my draft lottery number meant that I would be called up to serve in the military when I came home unless I could secure a university enrolment deferral. The war was counter to all my values, but probably most of all, I did not want to die. It all turned out well; I got my student deferment, and by the time I completed my bachelor degree, there was no more draft.

I had studied French and German in high school and then French, German, and Swedish in both Sweden and at the University of California (at the Davis and Berkeley campuses). I was planning for a (vague) career in languages, maybe a translator, maybe a world tour guide, maybe an airline steward on international flights. While I was studying languages at UC, I started taking psychology subjects and fell in love with the area and graduated with a BA degree in psychology in

1973. In my undergraduate days, my heroes became (in chronological birth order) Buddha, Darwin, Nietzsche, and Freud. It is through those men's work, and the people who followed after them, that I understand and interpret my world. My love affair with them continues to this day. My other love affair with language is also still with me. My psychotherapy clients, my students, and I pay close attention to the language we use and how language can both illuminate and conceal and also help us generate potent metaphoric images of our internal landscapes that lead to understanding and even healing.

The ski and beach bum years

In the USA there is almost nothing one can do with a BA in psychology, so after a year of being a ski bum I went to San Diego State University for my Master's degree in psychology. My two-year degree took me four years to complete because I was living at the beach, working on my tan, and gleefully plunging myself into the sex, drugs, and discos of the gay scene in the 1970s. I occasionally feel nostalgia for that pre-HIV era.

At university, I started clinical training with coursework and placements. In my first placement I was thrown in at the deep end with a position in the locked psychiatric ward at the San Diego Veterans Administration Hospital. I was mainly helping with psychometric testing but also listening to stories the vets told as we were doing tests. My anxieties about being on a locked ward, with patients who were potentially violent, slowly ebbed and were replaced with empathy and sadness, especially for those vets who were seriously psychologically and physically damaged by the war in Vietnam. I often thought, "There but for the grace of God, go I."

I was planning on teaching at the community college level (equivalent to the first two years of university in the USA) after my Master's degree, but could not land any full-time jobs. After a few years of being a ski bum again, I applied and was accepted into the psychology PhD program at the University of Arizona (U of A).

Going out to play

Despite what I wrote at the start of this chapter about sport and PE, I grew up in a physically active family. We downhill and cross-country skied, sailed, hiked, and swam – all quite suited to not drawing much on hand–eye coordination. Some of the fondest memories of my adolescence and young adulthood center on these activities. Before applying for doctoral programs, I asked myself what I really wanted from such a degree, and the answer that kept coming back was, "When I go to work, I want it to feel like I am going out to play." A career in sport psychology seemed to fit the bill perfectly, and U of A also fit well because I could get my degree in psychology, but I had to also have a doctoral minor (coursework equivalent of a Master's degree without the thesis) in another area, and I could complete the minor in the exercise science department. And Jean Williams was there.

When my psychology students discuss the clients they are seeing in our group supervision classes, some will occasionally say to me, "When I was talking to the athlete about staying in present time, the words coming out of my mouth were yours. I had turned into a mini-Mark." Laughter usually follows, and I often say, "Exactly! That is the process, but those words that you think are mine don't really belong just to me. They are also the words of my mentors. We are historical beings. I have the voices of my mentors in my head, and I consult with them all the time. When I talk with you, you are also talking to my professional ancestors, my academic mentors, and my therapists. That's what we do. We internalise our mentors, and eventually they become us. Same thing happens in therapy with your clients. They take you in as a model of compassion, care, and rational living for them to consult with in their real worlds." Jean's voice is still in my head 30 years after I first met her.

I completed my clinical internship at the Arizona State Prison Complex in Tucson (a complex of prison "campuses" ranging from minimal to maximal security). I love telling my new students a story that begins with, "When I was in prison for 14 months…" and watch their jaws drop before I add, "as a clinical intern." I learned so much about Axis II disorders (e.g., antisocial personality disorder; American Psychiatric Association, 2000) and brain damage (Axis III disorders; lots of inmates with traumatic brain injuries from blows to their heads or substance abuse) that I think I gained more knowledge in prison than I did working with athletes.

Out in the real world

When I was still a doctoral student, I attended the inaugural Association for the Advancement of Applied Sport Psychology conference in 1986. The strongest memory I have of that time was what amounted to a yelling match between clinical/counselling psychologists and exercise science sport psychology practitioners. The argument was around clinicians not knowing enough about sport and over-pathologising athlete concerns and exercise science-trained sport psychology practitioners not knowing what they were doing working with psychological material. The argument is still around in various forms. I remember thinking, "Here are a bunch of trained academics and practitioners regressing to a schoolyard fight." I also remember thinking, "Cool, I am on the right track. I am being both psychology and exercise science trained. I am going to become one of the most well-rounded new sport psychologists." Nice fantasy.

I decided that I wanted to be both an academic and a practitioner, and I fantasised about a job in higher education in a psychology or exercise science department and then working with athletes and teams at that university or college. And then I ran into a problem. As Robin Vealey once explained to me when I was rejected for a position at her school, "Mark, I think you have two problems. The reason my university did not want you is because your degree is in psychology, not exercise science, and I would bet that the trouble you are having finding jobs in psychology departments is because you are mainly interested in sport, which for most psych departments is really 'fringe' psychology." Those words were not exactly what she said, but they capture the message.

Since receiving my doctorate, I had had five different jobs in six years with no tenure-track positions in sight, but there was a two-year period where I held down the position of sport psychologist for the intercollegiate athletics department at Arizona State University (ASU). During these two years, I also completed post-doctoral training in psychodynamic psychotherapy, seeing clients and receiving supervision outside the sport setting. When my Neo-Freudian supervisor first took me on, she said, "Here's this book. It was what I started with in my psychodynamic training, and I think you should too." The book was Basch's (1980) *Doing Psychotherapy*. About a decade later, the first book I published was *Doing Sport Psychology* (Andersen, 2000), and it owed its structure and presentation to Basch's work. I have never met Basch, but he is one of the biblio-mentors in my head. Psychodynamic models and concepts began to emerge in my published work as a *leitmotif* in the 1990s (e.g., Andersen and Williams-Rice, 1996), and they have been recurrent themes ever since (e.g., Andersen, 2010).

At ASU I met two doctoral students in psychology, and I became the supervisor for their placements with the tennis and cross-country teams. They have gone on to become internationally recognised and highly respected academics and practitioners in sport and rehabilitation psychology. When I was first introduced to Judy Van Raalte and Britton Brewer, my impression was that they were extremely polite, and even deferent, to me. Britt asked, "What should we call you? Dr. Andersen? Or just 'Mark'?" Feeling somewhat uncomfortable with their deference, I replied in a flippant manner (and with a reference to Tennessee Williams), "Why don't you just call me Big Daddy?" And they did. Every year since we met, I get a card from them on Father's Day. I love that Oedipal story. That first meeting was the beginning of a life-long friendship and collaboration. They were, and still are, central figures in my personal and professional development.

My position at ASU was eliminated during some major funding cuts and the arrival of a new director who did not have the interest in funding a psychologist that the previous director had. In retrospect, losing the ASU job was probably a good thing. At times during semesters, I would have 35+ one-on-one sessions for weeks, plus going to practices, group sessions, committee meetings, and seeing my three to four weekly clients in psychodynamic therapy. If I had continued that way, I probably would have burnt out. After I lost the job I went to Kuala Lumpur to work with the Malaysian National Badminton Team. There's another long story that I won't go into here. After Malaysia I bounced around one-year jobs here and there until I landed my current position in Australia, and I have been here at the same university for over 18 years. Every day is a new personal best for me in terms of length of time in one job.

Working down under

The job at Victoria University was ideal for me. Besides research, one of my main tasks is to be the program coordinator of our Master of Applied Psychology (Sport) degree. I get to oversee the training, education, and supervision of many of Australia's future sport psychologists. In Australia, sport psychologists are trained within psychology departments, not exercise science. One can be registered (licensed, chartered) as a psychologist with a Master's degree in applied psychology. In 1994, I had finally found a position that was a near-perfect fit with my tertiary education, and I get to teach in both the psychology and the exercise science departments.

In Australia, sport psychologists are trained as psychologists first, and then as psychologists who have expertise in sport and exercise settings second. The title "sport and exercise psychologist" is protected by law in Australia. Some of our students stay in sport settings; others go on to careers outside of sport. When they leave us, they are equipped to work in many health, exercise, and sport settings. I did not set up the training model for sport psychologists in Australia, but I have been pleased to be its caretaker for the last 18 years.

When I first arrived in Australia, I worked with divers and baseball players, but I no longer do that bread-and-butter type of sport psychology work. I think I am in the Eriksonian stage of generativity versus stagnation, and I am negotiating that challenge by helping the next generation of sport psychologists find their ways, or find their feet, or travel along their paths (pick a metaphor). In my private practice, I have moved far away from sport. I never have really thought of myself as a "sport psychologist," hence the parenthetical (sport) in the title of this chapter.

The central issue: relationships

It seems that the sport psychology profession has been somewhat stuck in a medical and unidirectional model of athlete care. When sport psychologists say that they work only with performance enhancement, such statements sound like surgeons saying they repair and reconstruct only elbows and shoulders. The exchange of knowledge and treatment flows from the professional to the patient (and to just one aspect of that patient). I think the emphasis on performance enhancement and teaching mental skills to athletes (narrow, unidirectional) has severely limited the field's growth (see Andersen, 2009).

Much of my writing efforts and my teaching future psychologists have to do with relatedness. Freud discovered that it was the quality and exploration of the therapist–client relationship that fueled change. A core feature of Buddhist philosophy is *interrelatedness* and that "to be is to be related." Freud and the former Prince Siddhartha are frequent visitors in our classrooms and supervision sessions with students. We explore their clients' transferences to them and their own counter-transferences to their clients. We examine the transference–counter-transference configurations that are happening between me and them. Sometimes

I am the benevolent Big Daddy; other times I may be the fantasised vengeful father who will punish the student for transgressions. Occasionally, I have erotic counter-transferences to intelligent and handsome male students, and I discuss many of our relational responses with my students with curiosity and fascination that such phenomena occur and what these responses have to tell us about human relationships (and the human condition) in supervision, in treatment, and in life.

On the Buddhist side, my students and I often explore what it is to be mindfully present when interacting with clients and how they and I should make a goal of being as mindful as possible in supervision. Of course, we continually fail at the job of "staying in the room" during supervision, but that is OK, and it is just more data for the supervision process: Why did I leave the room? What hooked me and drew me out of present time? Mindfulness is one of the Eightfold Paths of the Fourth Noble Truth of Buddhism, and it irritates me that it has entered sport psychology as a means to a performance enhancement end (e.g., Gardner and Moore, 2007). Its use to that end smacks of what Trungpa (1973) called "spiritual materialism" (i.e., acquiring spiritual practices for personal or material gain). My irritation is a harsh judgment and antithetical to being mindful, so when it arrives on the scene and hooks me, I breathe and watch the irritation rise and fall and eventually pass away. Like all our other judgments, it is empty.

Mindfulness is not really a "technique" to improve performance. It is a state of being wherein we can connect with ourselves, the environment, and others. When a student is mindfully present with an athlete or a supervisor, then there can be attunement with the other and the ultimate relatedness of *resonance* between two people. This chapter is too short for me to go into how mindfulness works, but readers can check out Andersen (2012). Psychodynamic theory and Buddhist philosophy are the lenses through which I understand my world and my interrelatedness with my clients, my students, my partner, my friends, and my family. For readers interested in the marriage of psychodynamic therapy and Buddhism, I highly recommend Epstein's (1995) book *Thoughts Without a Thinker*. It ranks up there with Basch's (1980) work as having a huge influence on my professional life and my world-view.

I often talk to my students about how the personal and professional selves, at the beginning of a career, may seem disparate (e.g., there is me, and then there is "me" as a sport psychologist) and how, over time, the personal and the professional identities begin to coalesce, and how, with mindful practice, these ideas about self begin to dissolve into no-self (in the Pāli language of Buddhist scriptures *anatta*) and liberation from clinging to a false self (caretaker self, sport psychologist self; see Andersen and Mannion, 2011).

Parting glances: on being a gay (sport) psychologist

In my classroom graduate seminars that focus on working with gay and lesbian athletes, my students almost never ask me about my experiences despite them knowing that I am gay. When I ask them about why they were reluctant to question the "expert" sitting in the room, their stated reasons include things such as, "I didn't want to offend you" or "I didn't want to pry." It is a protective, and even anxious, stance that I appreciate and understand. I usually respond with, "There is little you could ask me that would offend or embarrass me, and with my narcissism, I can talk about myself for ages. So, fire away." I then answer their questions, but usually add at some point, "I think of being gay as a *gift* for me as a psychologist. I'm a white male, and in our society I am at the top of the food chain, but add the adjective *gay*, and I move way down the pecking order. I think straight white males in our profession are often at a disadvantage when it comes to understanding prejudice, discrimination, and hate. Most of them have not experienced what it is like to be discriminated against, what it is like to have violence perpetrated upon them because of who they are, or what it is like to lose a job because of whom they love. From my experiences as a gay man, I think I can relate to many women and their struggles with sexism, discrimination, and inequality. I think I can understand marginalised people, and I know what it is like to be in a closet. That said, we all have our own closets. There are depression closets, and anxiety closets, and I-am-a-fraud closets, and the big closet that hides the emptiness and pain of feeling unworthy of love. Also, we are all racists; we are all sexists; we are all homophobes. I am a homophobe. Your job, and my job here in your training as future psychologists, is to examine our racism, sexism, homophobia, and a whole host of other *isms* and see if we can reduce their parts per million to something manageable, human, and humane."

I think the academic and professional fields of sport psychology are deeply homophobic, especially for gay men. I find it intriguing that we have loads of internationally known out lesbians in our field, but out gay men in our profession are rare. As a brief exercise, count all the internationally known gay male sport psychologists you can think of. If you come up with more than two names, please let me know.

References

American Psychiatric Association (2000) *Diagnostic and Statistical Manual of Mental Disorders IV*, text rev. Washington, DC: Author.

Andersen, M. B. (2000) *Doing Sport Psychology*. Champaign, IL: Human Kinetics.

——(2009) Performance enhancement as a bad start and a dead end: a parenthetical comment on Mellalieu and Lane. *The Sport and Exercise Scientist*, 20: 12–14.

——(2010) Psychodynamic models of therapy, in S. J. Hanrahan and M. B. Andersen (eds) *Routledge Handbook of Applied Sport Psychology: A Comprehensive Guide for Students and Practitioners*. London: Routledge, pp. 160–167.

——(2012) Supervision and mindfulness in sport and performance psychology, in S. M. Murphy (ed.) *Oxford Handbook of Sport and Performance Psychology*. New York: Oxford University Press, pp. 725–737.

Andersen, M. B. and Mannion, J. (2011) If you meet the Buddha on the football field – tackle him!, in D. Gilbourne and M. B. Andersen (eds) *Critical Essays in Applied Sport Psychology*. Champaign, IL: Human Kinetics, pp. 173–192.

Andersen, M. B. and Williams-Rice, B. T. (1996) Supervision in the education and training of sport psychology service providers. *The Sport Psychologist*, 10: 278–290.

Basch, F. M. (1980) *Doing Psychotherapy*. New York: Basic Books.

Epstein, M. (1995) *Thoughts Without a Thinker: Psychotherapy from a Buddhist Perspective*. New York: Basic Books.

Gardner, F. E. and Moore, Z. E. (2007) *The Psychology of Enhancing Human Performance: The Mindfulness-Acceptance-Commitment Approach*. New York: Springer.

Trungpa, C. (1973) *Cutting Through Spiritual Materialism*. Berkeley, CA: Shambala.

Winnicott, D. W. (1971) *Playing and Reality*. London: Routledge.

11

ADVENTURES IN COGNITIVE SPORT PSYCHOLOGY

From theory to practice...and back again

Aidan Moran

We shall not cease from exploration. And the end of all our exploring will be to arrive where we started and to know the place for the first time.

(T. S. Eliot, 1943)

Introduction: accepting the challenge

When I received an invitation to write a personal account of my applied work in sport psychology in Ireland, I experienced a variety of contrasting emotions. On the one hand, I felt honoured and flattered to have been given the opportunity to add my voice to a chorus of international contributors in sharing reminiscences of experiences in applied sport psychology. On the other hand, I felt daunted by this reflective exercise for three main reasons. First, like some other authors in this book, I don't regard myself as a sport psychologist at all. Moreover, since I don't have any formal qualifications in sport psychology, how can I talk with any degree of credibility about becoming something that I'm not trained to be? In an attempt to sidestep this dilemma, I'd like to focus on what I *am* rather than on what I am not. In this regard, I see myself as a cognitive psychology researcher who loves playing sport (especially, competitive tennis at a club level and recreational golf) and who believes that this domain offers psychologists a fascinating natural laboratory in which to study how the mind works. It is precisely this theme of exploring cognition in action in skilled performance that has dominated my research activities for over two decades.

The second daunting challenge in writing this chapter concerns the question of how to make sense of the past without distorting it. Put simply, how can I provide a narrative thread for distant events that seemed rather accidental and disconnected at the time? Fortunately, I keep a diary of my consultancy experiences so I hope that by checking relevant facts, the threat of a significant 'egocentric bias' (i.e., a tendency to recall past events in a self-serving manner) will be diminished. Nevertheless, it's important to clarify that I never set out with the intention of doing *any* applied sport psychology work in my career. It just happened – often rather reluctantly – in response to requests from athletes, teams and sport organizations in Ireland in the early 1990s for information and advice about mental aspects of sport. In responding to these requests, my colleagues and I displayed a mixture of unaccredited expertise, enthusiasm, naivety and, above all, a spirit of adventure. Unwittingly, we became the first generation of sport psychologists in the country (for a more detailed account of sport psychology in Ireland in that era, see Kremer *et al.*, 1998).

The final challenge in writing this chapter is editorial in nature. Given the word-length constraints of the present chapter, which aspects of my consultancy experience should I include and which ones should I omit? In addressing this question, I have tried to provide examples of applied work that was *memorable* in some way – either because it was enjoyable and successful or simply because it was not. An important feature of the three experiences that I've selected, however, is that they have been documented in public. Hopefully, this fact should help to allay any anxiety about the danger of breaching client confidentiality.

To summarize, undaunted by the preceding challenges, the present chapter will describe some of my adventures in applied sport psychology over the past two decades. By recounting these experiences, I hope to 'arrive at where we started' (see T. S. Eliot's phrase above) in the early days of sport psychology in Ireland.

My introduction to cognitive psychology

Having done well academically at secondary school under the tutelage of the Christian Brothers in Oatlands College, Mt Merrion, Co. Dublin, I gained a scholarship in 1974 to study psychology at University College Dublin (UCD). I thoroughly enjoyed my undergraduate (BA, 1977) and postgraduate (MA, 1978) years there and was especially captivated by the courses on perception and cognitive psychology that were taught by Professor Michael Nolan (Department of Psychology). After my Master's degree, between 1978 and 1979, I worked as a research psychologist with FÁS, the Irish national occupational training organization, based in Dublin. This research was mainly psychometric in nature and involved validating aptitude tests for use in Irish contexts. Fortuitously, the psychometric training that I received at this time helped me to produce my first publication in a peer-reviewed journal (Moran, 1982). In September 1979, I accepted my first lecturing position – an appointment to the academic staff of the recently established Department of Psychology in the National University of Ireland, Galway (NUIG), to teach cognitive psychology. While engaged in full-time teaching and research there (between 1979 and 1985), I completed my PhD research (1984) on the relationship between cognitive style and problem solving in electronic fault diagnosis. My supervisor was Professor Martin McHugh, a wise and gifted methodologist and statistician, who was Head of the Department of

Psychology in NUIG. I was delighted that the External Examiner of my PhD thesis was Donald Broadbent (University of Oxford), the eminent British experimental psychologist whose research on attention had a major influence on modern cognitive psychology. Getting his stamp of approval on my research meant a lot to me. After six wonderful years in Galway, I returned to UCD in 1985 as a Lecturer in Cognitive Psychology and Director of the university's Psychology Research Laboratory.

From mental practice research to mental advice

In teaching cognitive psychology in UCD in the late 1980s, I became fascinated by two topics: mental imagery (our cognitive capacity to simulate sensations, actions and other types of experience), and attention (or the ability to focus on what is most important in any situation while ignoring distractions). Unfortunately, when I taught these topics using the standard cognitive textbooks of the day, I soon discovered – usually from a sea of glazed expressions in class – that they were too arid and abstract for my students' tastes. Searching for a more dynamic way to present research on imagery and attention, I began to explore what was known about these topics in the domain of competitive sport. Soon I became intrigued by 'mental practice' or the systematic use of imagery to 'see' and 'feel' actions in one's imagination without engaging in the actual physical movements involved. As a keen tennis player and recreational golfer, I'd heard a lot about visualization in sport but unfortunately, the cognitive textbooks had little or nothing to say about this topic. Parenthetically, little seems to have changed because a search of the subject indices of contemporary textbooks of cognitive psychology for terms like 'sport' or 'motor imagery' elicits little or no material (a problem discussed in Moran, 2012; Moran et al., 2012). Nevertheless, my curiosity about mental imagery in sport, and its relationship to attention, had begun to take root. This burgeoning research interest had three important consequences for my career.

To begin with, it encouraged me to supervise a myriad of final-year Psychology students' experimental studies of mental practice in golf, tennis, rugby, soccer and Gaelic Games. Furthermore, since nobody else was doing this kind of imagery research in Ireland at the time, my lab in UCD soon became the mental practice capital of the country (imagine that!). Not surprisingly, my first conference abstract in sport psychology (a paper presented at the 8th European Congress in Cologne in 1991) examined issues raised by the attempt to measure mental imagery skills in athletes. I revised this paper and published it in the *Journal of Sport Behaviour* (Moran, 1993). A second consequence of my research on mental imagery and mental practice was that it led to requests from members of the Irish sporting community for advice on psychological techniques that could improve athletic performance. For example, in 1989, I was invited to present a seminar on mental practice for the Olympic Council of Ireland. Similar invitations followed and soon I was inundated with requests to give lectures on mental imagery and other aspects of sport psychology to competitive performers in golf, tennis, soccer, hockey, rugby, and

Gaelic Games throughout the country. Through such lectures, which were often conducted in collaboration with UCD psychology graduate students such as Eric Brady (who later became President of the Psychological Society of Ireland, 2012–2013) and Betty Cody, I became aware of other colleagues engaged in similar activities around the country in the early 1990s. For example, in Northern Ireland, psychology researchers such as John Kremer (from the School of Psychology, Queen's University, Belfast; QUB) – a great friend from whom I have learned a lot as we continue to collaborate together in writing books and journal articles – Craig Mahoney (also of QUB) and Deirdre Scully (then of University of Ulster) had developed a system of workshops and individual consultancy services in sport psychology for a variety of individual athletes, teams and sports organizations. To illustrate, in Gaelic football, John advised the successful Tyrone team for many years and Craig was the psychologist who helped Derry to claim an All-Ireland football title in 1993. In addition, John Kremer and Deirdre Scully made important theoretical contributions to the field internationally. For example, their seminal book, *Psychology in Sport* (Kremer and Scully, 1994) – note the clever and precise phrasing of the title – was the first major attempt to evaluate research in sport psychology from the theoretical and methodological perspectives of mainstream psychology. Shortly afterwards, Scully and Hume (1995) investigated the attitudes to sport psychology of elite athletes and coaches in Ireland at the time. Perhaps most significantly from an applied perspective, Kremer and Scully (1998) developed an innovative model for the delivery of sport psychology services to athletes and coaches. Briefly, this new model identified the *coach* rather than the athlete as the primary target for psychological education. Based on this model, Kremer and Scully postulated that the role of sport psychologist should change from that of a medical expert to that of a management consultant whose ultimate goal was not to nurture dependence but to support the athlete to the point where the services of a sport psychologist should become less and less significant. Given such developments, it is notable that in Ireland in the early 1990s, sport psychology not only had a strong theoretical base in mainstream psychology in University College, Dublin, and Queen's University, Belfast, but also an explicit awareness of the importance of having a clear conceptual rationale for the delivery of its services. Looking back, this focus meant that in some ways, applied sport psychology in Ireland was considerably ahead of its time. The third career consequence of my imagery studies in the early 1990s was that it led me to collaborate productively with Jim Driskell (Florida Maxima Corporation) and his colleague, Carolyn Copper (then working with the US Government), in a meta-analysis on the effects of mental practice on skilled performance. Jim's invitation to work on this project had come about through a mutual friend – the late Brian Mullen, a prolific meta-analysis researcher from Syracuse University, New York, who died unexpectedly in 2006. We published our meta-analytic review paper in the *Journal of Applied Psychology* (Driskell *et al.*, 1994). This paper, which showed that mental practice has a significant effect on the learning and performance of a range of skills, attracted a great deal of interest from researchers around the world (e.g., it has been cited over

570 times to date, according to Google Scholar). Later in 2004, I obtained a Fulbright Scholarship to attend the First International Summer Institute of Cognitive Science in SUNY, Buffalo, New York, and to visit both Robert Singer (University of Florida) and Shane Murphy (US Olympic Committee, Colorado Springs) to conduct research on imagery and attentional processes in athletes. The summer school was demanding (with seven hours of classes per weekday for about a month) but exhilarating as it enabled me to attend lectures by many of the world's leading neuroscientists such as Stephen Kosslyn (Stanford University), the renowned imagery researcher. Equally stimulating and productive were my visits to the University of Florida and the USOC Training Centre in Colorado – due mainly to the exceptional hospitality of my hosts, Bob Singer and Shane Murphy, respectively. While at the University of Florida, I wrote the first draft of my book, *The Psychology of Concentration in Sport Performers: A Cognitive Analysis* (Moran, 1996) and presented a paper at the NASPSPA conference in Clearwater Springs – where I met Mark Williams (Liverpool John Moores University), with whom I have collaborated on many occasions. Bob Singer also introduced me to his protégé, Chris Janelle, who has become renowned for his research on the relationship between attention, emotion and skilled performance. In Colorado Springs, I was delighted to meet Sean McCann (Head of the Sport Psychology Department at the USOC) who gave me valuable insights into the way in which some of the world's leading athletes use psychological techniques such as mental imagery to enhance their performance.

The consultancy years: three memorable experiences

Most of my consultancy work in applied sport psychology was conducted between 1990 and 2005. During that period, I presented numerous lectures, seminars and workshops to elite athletes and coaches in sports like golf, tennis, soccer, rugby, hockey, rowing, Gaelic football and hurling. I also presented seminars at continuing professional development meetings for rugby referees and cricket umpires. As most of these sessions were single events (usually either half-day or evening presentations), however, their impact is difficult to evaluate. Nevertheless, at a personal level, three consultancy experiences stand out from this era – two involving teams (namely, the Irish Olympic Squad and Mayo Gaelic football squad), and one involving an individual athlete (the golfer, Pádraig Harrington). In the following summary, I'll try to explain either what I enjoyed about or learned from each of these experiences.

First, in October 1993, I accepted an invitation from the Olympic Council of Ireland (OCI) to become the honorary Official Psychologist to the Irish squad in preparation for the 1996 Olympic Games in Atlanta. This position had become vacant because my predecessor, Felicity Heathcote, had moved abroad. I quickly decided that my role needed to be expanded because I felt that it was neither feasible nor desirable for one psychologist to attempt to deliver mental skills training services to *all* OCI athletes, coaches and managers. Accordingly, I invited various sport psychology colleagues from around the country to form a consultancy panel for this purpose. Happily, these colleagues responded enthusiastically to this invitation and so our initial OCI sport psychology panel was born. It comprised Eric Brady (UCD), Betty Cody (UCD), John Kremer (QUB), Craig Mahoney (QUB), Lucy Moore (St John of God Services, Dublin), Deirdre Scully (University of Ulster) and P. J. Smyth (University of Limerick). Following an inaugural meeting of this panel in UCD in February 1994, we organized a day-long series of workshops on mental skills training for Olympic Council athletes, coaches/managers and administrators in UCD in May 1994. The outcome was decidedly mixed. On the one hand, the good news was that these workshops were very well attended and received excellent feedback from participants. However, on the other hand, the bad news was that only a handful of *athletes* actually attended them! Later, we discovered that our workshops had not been advertised adequately to the athletes concerned. A further problem was also evident. Specifically, the majority of the athletes in the Olympic squad were committed to training and competing abroad for most of the year, thereby making it extremely difficult for us to organize group psychology sessions for them in Dublin. Such logistical difficulties hampered the progress and efficacy of our fledgling OCI sport psychology panel. Despite such obstacles, however, our panel meetings proved very useful and enjoyable for another reason. Serendipitously, they enabled us, as psychologists from different parts of Ireland, to create a professional identity, forge enduring friendships and to exchange ideas about developing applied sport psychology in the country. Consequently, we continued to meet regularly for several years even though our direct contact with Olympic athletes was negligible.

Subsequently, our group expanded with the arrival of two new psychologists – Niamh Fitzpatrick (who advised the Wexford hurling team to All-Ireland success in 1996 and who succeeded me in the role of Official Psychologist to the Irish Olympic squad from 2004 to the present day) and my friend and colleague Tadhg MacIntyre (whose PhD thesis on motor imagery I supervised and with whom I have collaborated extensively). Subsequently, in 1998, the OCI panel blended into the psychology support network of the Irish Sports Council's 'carding' scheme for elite athletes. Since 2009, however, the Council's medical and sport science (including psychology) support services have been provided by the Irish Institute of Sport.

My second memorable sport psychology consultancy experience arose from my work with a young amateur Irish golfer: Pádraig Harrington. In 1993, aged just 22, Pádraig contacted me for advice about how to improve his concentration skills. He was extremely bright, inquisitive and dedicated and was especially fascinated by the psychological aspects of golf. We worked together regularly for the next three years (1993–1996) as he made the transition from a glittering amateur career (in which he won many national titles and represented Great Britain and Ireland in the Walker Cup on three occasions) to the professional ranks (which he joined in 1995). Unusually for many athletes I have advised, Pádraig insisted on acknowledging my assistance publicly (e.g., after he had won his first professional title, the Spanish

Open, in 1996; see Norman, 1996). As his professional career blossomed, however, it became clear to both of us that in order to make further improvements in his mental skills, he needed to obtain help from a specialist golf psychologist on the professional tour, which is how he came to work with Dr Bob Rotella. Subsequently, Pádraig became one of Bob's most famous clients as a result of winning three Major tournaments – the 2007 and 2008 Open Championships and the 2008 USPGA Championship. I enjoyed working with Pádraig not only because he was meticulous in reading the psychology material that I gave him but also because he was not afraid to challenge me with insightful questions (e.g., why do pre-shot routines lose their effectiveness over time and how can they be kept fresh?). To this day, one of my most treasured possessions is a crystal bowl that he presented to me after one of his last victories as an amateur golfer.

My third applied psychology experience concerned a bittersweet adventure with Mayo Gaelic football team in 2004 in their quest to win the All-Ireland championship – something that the county had not achieved since 1951. By way of background, in early May 2004, I received an invitation from John Maughan, the manager of the Mayo football team, to give a talk to his squad before the championship season began. My talk was well received by the players and management and led to a lengthy question-and-answer session. After that, I was asked to work with the team throughout the championship season. Over the next four months (June to September 2004), I advised John and his co-selectors and travelled regularly to Mayo to attend squad training sessions. Typically, at these sessions I gave short presentations to the management team and playing squad and also made myself available for individual consultations, if required. The feedback that I received was encouraging and as the championship season unfolded, Mayo began to develop a significant momentum. After the team had won the Connacht Championship, they defeated Tyrone (one of the favourites for the All-Ireland title) in the quarter-finals. Then, in the next round in late August, they defeated Fermanagh to reach the final against Kerry who are by far the most successful team in the history of the competition which dates back to 1887. Unfortunately, there was no fairytale ending for Mayo as Kerry performed brilliantly in the final to win the match emphatically. Although I was very disappointed with this result, I had happy memories of the adventure with Mayo during that summer. In retrospect, the most valuable lesson that I gained from this applied work was the importance of working closely with the management team of a squad before engaging in any psychological skills training with the players. Clearly, this insight supported the model of sport psychology delivery developed by Kremer and Scully (1998).

Conclusions

In this chapter, I have described the background to, and some outcomes of, my adventures with various colleagues in using psychology to help athletes and coaches in Ireland to do their best when it matters most. Through these adventures, I learned the wisdom of Lewin's famous aphorism: 'there is nothing so practical as a good theory' (1951, p. 169). Typically, my most enjoyable and successful consultancy experiences occurred when my colleagues and I were able to persuade our clients to go beyond a 'quick fix' mentality and to reflect more deeply on what they were trying to achieve by exploring mental aspects of sport performance far away from the immediate pressures of competition. Clearly, to facilitate this reflection, a special kind of guidance from psychologists is required – one that is not only evidence-based (i.e., derived from scientific psychological principles) but also *experiential* (i.e., forged from our discovery of what works best in real-life competitive sport). Therefore, since the late 1990s, my colleagues and I have tried to condense the lessons we have learned from our applied work in practical books (e.g., Kremer and Moran, 2013) and CDs (e.g., Moran, 2009). Put simply, these resources offer people practical tips on using psychology effectively in sport. In this way, we have gone from theory to practice...and back again.

Acknowledgements

I would like to acknowledge with gratitude the helpful feedback received from John Kremer on an earlier draft of this chapter.

References

Driskell, J. E., Copper, C. and Moran, A. (1994) Does mental practice enhance performance? *Journal of Applied Psychology*, 79(4): 481–492.

Eliot, T. S. (1943) *Four Quartets*. New York: Harcourt, Brace, and Company.

Kremer, J. and Moran, A. (2013) *Pure Sport: Practical Sport Psychology*, 2nd edn. London: Routledge.

Kremer, J., Moran, A. and Scully, D. (eds) (1998) Sport and exercise psychology in Ireland. Special Issue, *Irish Journal of Psychology*, 19(4).

Kremer, J. and Scully, D. (1994) *Psychology in Sport*. London: Taylor & Francis.

——(1998) What applied sport psychologists often don't do: on empowerment and independence, in H. Steinberg, I. Cockerill and A. Dewey (eds) *What Sport Psychologists Do*. Leicester: The British Psychological Society (Sport and Exercise Psychology Section), pp. 21–27.

Lewin, K. (1951) Problems of research in social psychology, in D. Cartwright (ed.) *Field Theory in Social Science: Selected Theoretical Papers*. New York: Harper & Row, pp. 155–169.

Moran, A. (1982) Achievement motivation of Irish apprentices: item analysis, reliability and validity of Smith's, 1973, Quick Measure of Achievement Motivation. *Irish Journal of Psychology*, 5: 147–165.

——(1993) Conceptual and methodological issues in the measurement of mental imagery skills in athletes. *Journal of Sport Behaviour*, 16: 156–170.

——(1996) *The Psychology of Concentration in Sport Performers: A Cognitive Analysis*. Hove: Psychology Press.

——(2009) *Learn to Win at Golf*. MindCool Productions. Available at: www.mindcool.com/productdetails/19/learn-to-win-at-golf.aspx.

——(2012) Thinking in action: some insights from cognitive sport psychology. *Thinking Skills and Creativity*, 7: 85–92.

Moran, A., Guillot, A., MacIntyre, T. and Collet, C. (2012) Re-imagining motor imagery: building bridges between cognitive neuroscience and sport psychology. *British Journal of Psychology*, 103: 224–247.

Norman, E. (1996) It's heaven for Harrington. *Irish Independent* (Sports Supplement), 13 May, p. 10.

Scully, D. and Hume, A. (1995) Sport psychology: status, knowledge and use among elite level coaches and performers in Ireland. *Irish Journal of Psychology*, 16: 52–66.

12

SPORTING SUCCESS

'You do know you won't come out of your Master's and get a job with Manchester United, don't you?'

Rebecca Symes

This was one of the last things that was said to me when I was interviewed for my Master's degree in Sport and Exercise Psychology. Thankfully, I was aware of that! However, I had made it very clear during the interview that my focus was on the applied side and that I wanted to become a full-time consultant, so perhaps that comment was fair enough.

I have always liked sport and played for many school teams. However, unlike my older brother, I wasn't what you would call fanatical about sport. I liked it, I enjoyed playing it but I also had many other interests as well and going into a career in sport certainly wasn't anywhere on my radar for the majority of my teenage years. When I was a kid, all I wanted to do was be a teacher and then when I was 16 I wrote on my record of achievement that I wanted to be an accountant (thankfully that idea didn't last long!).

Up to 16 I had been at a state school, which I loved, but I changed and went to a public school for sixth form and it was here that sport took on a whole new meaning. It was a major part of the curriculum and was on the agenda five days out of six and my interest in it shot up; but I still didn't really think about it as a career option. I was, however, pretty clear that I wanted to do a psychology degree. I had always been interested in people and when I got a holiday job working in the Customer Services team at a large high street bank when I was 16, I was always fascinated by the dynamics. As a group of staff, the social side was brilliant; everyone was friends, regularly socialized together and had a laugh but inside of work the morale in the office was very low, people were overworked, stressed and generally demotivated. This really fueled my interest in understanding more about people and the environment.

I went on to complete a psychology degree (BSc) but there was never a mention of sport psychology; it was heavily focused on developmental, social, biological, cognitive and clinical aspects of psychology – something that I am now grateful for.

I knew that I wanted to become a Chartered Psychologist but I wasn't sure in which division, as occupational, clinical and educational all interested me.

A light-bulb moment

Post university I decided to take a year out where I would get a job in London, enjoy having some freedom and money in my pocket and use that time to really think about where I wanted my career to go. I got a job working for a business research consultancy and was also involved as a volunteer for a local charity.

One of the fundraising events I attended was the charity's annual ball in 2005 and it was here that I met Alan Butcher, who at the time was the Head Coach of Surrey County Cricket Club. Through a chance conversation with him, my career in sport psychology began. We were talking about my love of sport, having done a psychology degree and my desire to become a chartered psychologist, and he simply said to me 'Have you ever thought about combining the two?' And that was it. A light-bulb moment, so obvious. Why had I never thought about it? In simple terms I don't think I was really aware that sport psychology was a profession. At the time, the BPS didn't have their sport psychology training routes up and running, and having come from a pure psychology background, I had never heard of BASES. Alan kindly offered to put me in touch with the psychologist at Surrey CCC, Amanda Owens, and after meeting with her the following week I knew this was definitely the route I wanted to go down. From there it all seemed to happen quite quickly; I found out about BASES, Amanda agreed to be my supervisor and I applied for a Master's degree.

What does the athlete need? No idea, I'm not listening

When I started my Master's there were eight of us on the course and I was surprised at two things. First, that not everyone wanted to go into the applied side and second, of those of us who did, not everyone had started their supervised experience. I thought it was normal to do your first year of supervision in conjunction with your Master's, evidently not. However, if it's still possible, that would be my recommendation since I gained great benefits from learning the theory and putting it into practice at the same time. I was also lucky enough to be part of a group supervision, and again I would recommend this where possible as I got so much out of going through the process with other people and learning and sharing experiences with them. It's great to know that all the thoughts, worries, anxieties and concerns you have in your early days are completely normal!

I started my Master's in the September and did my first piece of consulting in the December – I hasten to add that it was terrible, and I was amazed when the athlete wanted another session. I was offering my services for free so that might have been part of it! This session was with an international swimmer, who was the daughter of a family friend. The reason I say it was terrible was because I had such a fixed view going into the session of what I was going to do. I had learnt about goal setting, so was comfortable with that, hence we had a goal-setting session – was this what she needed? Who knows! I don't think I listened long enough to find out. I still cringe when I think about it now. My second piece of applied work was a couple of months later, this time with a physiology Master's student, who was also an international laser sailor. I was far more relaxed in these sessions compared to the swimmer; however, I talked a lot and would imagine the percentage of me talking to him talking was about 60–40 percent. Both of these examples are classic in the early days of consulting, when the need to be in control is highest. My third and noteworthy piece of consulting during this time came in the April, when I offered to run a session with the cricket team I played for on setting our vision for the season. The session was alright, nothing special, and the biggest thing I learnt was not to consult with teams you are directly involved with. One of the benefits of a consultant is that you are usually independent. I wasn't and I therefore found it really difficult to facilitate without wanting to have my say. I had also planned far too much for the time we had available so was stuck in the session as to whether to move things on or stay with the moment. We got the desired outcome from the workshop but it was far from ideal.

These three pieces of consulting taught me a lot and also represent a journey highlighting some of the changes that have occured in my consulting over time. These are: (1) less need to be in control and more comfortable with allowing the client to lead; (2) allowing and enabling through effective questioning of the client to have a greater percentage of 'air time'; and (3) being comfortable with being in the moment and not thinking about what I am going to say next. As an aside, I intentionally used the word 'client' as opposed to athlete because although I went through the majority of my Master's thinking a sport psychologist works with athletes, and of course they do, they equally also work with coaches, performance directors, parents, physios and the like. In my view, these aforementioned areas develop with experience and confidence in your own skills as a practitioner, and while in the early days, those 'difficulties' can create some anxiety around consulting, without them I would not be the practitioner I am now.

Sporting Success

It was during the summer of my Master's degree that I set up Sporting Success. Over the past eight months it had become clear to me that one of the ways to become an applied practitioner was to set up your own consultancy, although it did seem a rarity. The majority of people seemed to be based at academic institutions while fitting consultancy around their university commitments. While I was aware of the EIS and their employment of psychologists, I wasn't anywhere near ready to take on a role with them and I don't recall there being any internships available. Equally, there was something in me that really made me want to give it a go on my own, to see if I could make it. So I opened a business bank account, registered a website domain and set up an email address. Simple really. Now I just needed some clients.

That summer when I wasn't working on my dissertation, I was really pro-active about establishing myself. I was also working two days a week with a business research consultancy since I had experience in this field and it enabled me to have some form of regular income. The offices were in London and one lunchtime I was walking through Trafalgar Square where there happened to be a sports exhibition, so I started talking to one of the guys working there. I found out what the exhibition was all about and told him about the consultancy I had just set up. It turned out this guy was a coach and the athletics development officer for Kent. So I gave him my business card and went on my way all excited – so much so that I had completely forgotten to ask his name, so when my phone went a couple of weeks later and he said 'Hi, it's Pete,' I was racking my brains to think who Pete was! He asked if I would go and deliver some sport psychology workshops at a county athletics squad day and that was the start of my work in athletics and the real start of Sporting Success. Off the back of that, a number of opportunities then arose through recommendations and word of mouth and things seemed to go from strength to strength.

An eclectic approach

When I first started out, my consulting approach would have fallen into the cognitive-behavioural field. I think this is probably true of most practitioners as this approach gives a good framework for structuring conversations, which is especially helpful when you're inexperienced. As my consulting experience gained momentum and I undertook some counseling training as well as experienced counseling for myself, my approach moved more towards a humanistic one and now I would describe my approach as eclectic. The benefit for me of the eclectic approach is that it enables me to draw on the most relevant aspects of a particular philosophy. That choice of philosophy might differ depending on many factors including who the client is, their age, the environment in which I am working, and the presenting issues. For example, when working with a specific issue in time-bound conditions, the cognitive-behavioural approach can often be the most appropriate as it lends itself to being used in time-limited conditions. Yet when working with clients over a longer period of time, I would be more guided by humanistic principles and look to develop the individual as a whole and not just focus on one issue. As part of this, the relationship between my client and me becomes very important. I therefore adapt my approach based on what I feel will be the most effective in any given situation, and I do find that the different approaches can be complementary.

I mentioned earlier that I am grateful to my background in pure psychology and I have to say that I am pleased at the recent developments in the field of psychology in the UK whereby the title of 'psychologist' has become a protected one and the path to becoming a Sport Psychologist is to gain a degree in psychology first. I would estimate that in approximately 80 percent of the work that I do I am drawing on pure psychological knowledge and in the other 20 percent it is specific sport psychology knowledge.

Many of the areas I deal with are to do with confidence and self-esteem, understanding identity, managing relationships, dealing with success and failure, managing expectations, and so on, and these all have underpinning psychological components which relate more to the fields of pure psychology. Of course, these have to be understood within the context of a sporting environment since that is the arena in which they manifest themselves, but without the core underpinning psychological knowledge I believe I would not be as effective. In essence, a sport psychologist deals with psychological issues experienced by athletes and it is therefore vital they have the appropriate psychological training. It is worth pointing out that the underpinning knowledge is what guides my approach and lines of questioning but I rarely tell athletes about it, hence the real skill of an applied practitioner is being able to translate the theory into practice.

Current reality

Bringing things up to date, at the current time I have two key contracts within cricket and paralympic archery, regularly do work within athletics and pro Mixed Martial Arts (MMA) and have private clients across swimming, triathalon and football. For interest, other sports I have worked in have also included gymnastics, laser sailing, golf, hockey, darts, rifle shooting, air-pistol shooting and kickboxing. In my opinion, it is not important that you know the ins and outs of a sport prior to working in it, however, it is important that you are open and honest about that and take time to find out as much about the sport and the psychological demands as quickly as possible. Often knowing nothing about the sport can be an advantage since you don't go in with any preconceived ideas and it can help to build rapport with athletes since they are able to share their knowledge with you. About 95 percent of my time is spent working directly in sport, and for the other 5 percent of the time, I work as an associate for K2, helping the corporate world to prepare and perform like elite athletes.

On the cricket front, I have been working with Surrey CCC Academy since 2007 and also work with the ECB on some of their England development programmes. As mentioned, it was through Surrey CCC that I started on this career route in the first place and in October 2007 my supervisor decided to move on to other opportunities and recommended that I take over the role. You could say that this was lucky for me and in many ways it was but equally it was up to me: (1) to demonstrate to Surrey that I could do the role; and (2) to move the role forwards and maintain the contract year on year. My experience over the past five years has taught me many things, and I think reflecting on it here there are three key areas worthy of note. First, it taught me about working in a multi-disciplinary environment with coaches and other support staff (e.g., physios; strength and conditioning coaches). Second, it confirmed to me that it is important to see players all year round (not just at winter training), and, third, that in order to be as effective as possible, you need to understand a player in the context of their whole lives and not just in relation to their cricket. This has meant building up relationships with their parents and their schools which has been invaluable in order to help them not only with their cricket directly but also with their well-being which indirectly impacts upon their cricket.

Working in a multidisciplinary way is very important since none of the areas of coaching, psychology, strength and conditioning, physiotherapy, etc., are stand-alone. There is a knock-on effect of all areas onto each other and therefore coaches and practitioners have to be regularly communicating to ensure they are all on the same page, although this isn't always as easy as it sounds. This is also very important when a player is additionally on an England programme and therefore spends time away from the county.

When I was originally agreeing my role with Surrey, it was clear to me that I needed to have a role all year round and not just in the winter, as is the case with some other county cricket psychologists (for a variety of reasons). My rationale is that the relationship I have with the players is one of the factors that is key to me being effective and if I see players just in the winter and then don't see them for six months, it interrupts those relationships. Also observations are a key part of a psychologist's role and being able to see first-hand players performing in competitive matches, reacting to pressure situations and interacting with teammates/coaches, enable you to build up a bank of knowledge about players. This is useful to then be able to use during sessions with the players, ideally during the season to ensure continuity (cricket lends itself to this being a more viable option compared to other sports). Being present also gives an opportunity to see if the things you have been working on with the players in the winter (e.g., pre-performance routines) are being put into practice and enables you to assist and support coaches during what can sometimes be a hectic time for them. Finally, having a consistent presence helps to promote the role of a psychologist in performance enhancement rather than simply as a problem fixer ('oh, look, the psychologist has turned up, who's got the problem this time?').

With respect to Paralympic archery, I have been working with the GB squad since 2010 and this opportunity arose through a recommendation for me to go for an interview. My main role is to provide psychological support to the archers, which involves working on areas such as mental preparation for competition, pre-shot/shot routines, performing under pressure, controlling emotions, building confidence, managing relationships, and dealing with distractions, to name a few. I work with the archers through one-to-one sessions, group meetings and also practically on the shooting line. Naturally over the past two years the focus has been on building up to the Paralympic Games in London in 2012. Linked to this, I also have a role in the development of the coaching/support team to ensure we are operating as effectively as possible to enable us to provide the best support to the archers come Games time.

This role was my first within disability sport and there are a few things to be aware of when working in this environment. First, you need to have an understanding of the athlete's medical condition, as, for example, it's no good going through an in-depth visualisation routine with someone only to later find out they haven't got any sensations in a particular part of their body. Also it's useful to know whether someone has a congenital disability or if they have acquired a disability (e.g., through an injury/accident) as this could potentially have a bearing on their psychological well-being. Importantly though, it's about focusing on their abilities, not their disabilities. Aside from that, in direct relation to the athletes, it's no different from working with able-bodied athletes, however, as a member of staff you have to appreciate that although your primary role is a psychologist, you also have a role to play in helping out where possible, such as lifting and shifting of kit and, specific to archery, being an agent (scoring and collecting the archers' arrows in competition).

It might not be a bed of roses all the time but it's worth it

I absolutely love having my own consultancy and working full-time as an applied practitioner. I have worked in a range of sports, with a range of different athletes, been on some great (but very hard work) trips such as the Archery World Championships in Italy, pre-season cricket tours to South Africa and the London 2012 Paralympic Games. There are many advantages to having your own business, such as being able to negotiate contracts directly with sporting organisations, being able to choose (in some respect) the work you take on and having influence over the psychology pathway within a particular club or sport. However, it isn't all a bed of roses. Working in sport itself is very hard work, it can be unsociable hours and it certainly doesn't fit into a typical 9–5 day. It can also be quite full on and constant, especially when working for yourself. If you work an evening or a weekend, for example, there is no one there to give you a day off in lieu. Of course, it's up to you to do this for yourself, but the reality present is that if you don't work, you don't get paid, so the tendency from my own experience can be to work a lot! Linked to this, the financial situation can be unstable from month to month and that is where being able to gain contracts is very valuable since they enable you to have a regular source of income. There is also a lot of travelling and time away from home, which doesn't suit everyone. It can be lonely at times and I certainly found that in the beginning. Consequently, one of the things that has been most important to me over the past five years has been building up my own support network and getting to know other sport psychologists so that we can share best practice and engage in group supervision. You also have to be very pro-active. Opportunities rarely drop on your doorstep and even if they do, you have to work very hard to ensure they come to fruition. I speak with a lot of students who contact me for advice and being pro-active is one of the things I regularly say. I do believe that there are opportunities out there for sport psychologists but you have to be prepared to seek them out, build relationships, be patient and to a certain extent make sacrifices in your own life. But, in my view, this is all worth it to be able to do a job that you love.

13

SWEET DREAMS ARE MADE OF THESE

My journey to 2012

Sarah Cecil

Sport has always served me well. I moved every four years as a child and went to up to six schools in four different countries. Throughout my childhood, sport was my constant companion and also a way of making new friends and settling into new environments. I never reached international status in any sport but was in most school and university teams. My sporting experiences ranged from feeling sea sick while canoeing in the Bristol Channel, being an Austrian Hockey champion (there were only eight teams!), to playing a Dutch sport (Korfball) at the Home of Golf. I had never considered sport as a career choice and I came across the idea of sport psychology serendipitously. Owing to my love of the sea and the openness of St Andrews University to the International Baccalaureate, I ended up studying in the only university city without a nightclub. In my final year of a BSc in Psychology I was contemplating career choices. I was not tempted by the banking and accountancy milk round that many of my friends chose. I was initially intrigued by the idea of being a barrister but following a mini-pupillage in London, I knew that was not for me. A chance conversation with someone in my psychology class led me to explore the idea of an MSc in Sport Psychology. In a break between lectures, Paul (who went on to be the first man to canoe from Ulan Bator to the Pacific) suggested that I might be interested in an MSc at Exeter University that he was looking into. To this day I do not know why he mentioned this to me, but at a wedding of a mutual friend over 10 years later I did thank him. Following this conversation, I started to explore different MSc options and after a conversation with Ken Fox when he was up in St Andrews to viva a PhD, I opted for Exeter.

Before I knew it, I had swapped the gowns of St Andrews for the tracksuits of St Lukes. Following the first taught part of the MSc, I returned to London and collected data for my dissertation at St Mary's University College. I knew quite clearly that I wanted to work as an applied sport psychologist, that I did not want to do a PhD and that I wanted to get as much hands-on experience as possible. I did a variety of jobs while I wrote up my thesis, including working as a secretary at Kingston Sewage Plant, temping at International Management Group (IMG), doing sports massage and working for an events company.

Throughout this time, regardless of what other work I was doing, I set myself the goal of doing one thing a day to help me become a sport psychologist. I also enrolled in BASES supervision with Geoff Lovell at Roehampton University. I completed my thesis, a case study on an international rugby player rehabilitating from an ACL injury, while also doing *ad hoc* work for St Mary's College. In the Autumn of 1998, I covered for Sally May while she was on honeymoon and this led to ongoing visiting lecturer work at St Mary's. In March 1999, I organised a two-month internship at IMG, specifically at Bollettieri's Tennis Academy and Leadbetter's Golf Academy. This was an invaluable experience at this stage in my training as I was able to build and develop my basic mental skills while also honing my ability to build relationships with coaches. In September 1999, I was hired by St Mary's as a lecturer and started a six-year stint there. Throughout my time at St Mary's, I continued to focus on developing myself as an applied sport psychologist and in early 2000 started working with the British Canoe Union. I completed my BASES supervision in September 2000 and became accredited shortly after that.

Alongside my BASES accreditation I had started to do some training in Cognitive Behavioural Therapy (CBT) at the Oxford Cognitive Therapy Center. This played a major part in the evolution of my consulting philosophy. My six years as a lecturer provided a very solid research-based platform on which my applied practice was built. Over time, the amount of applied work I did grew.

A lot of my early practice was based on mental skills, but I quickly integrated CBT into my work. One of the skills which has proved invaluable is Socratic questioning, and the training I did in this continues to be beneficial. A lot of what I used in the early years can be found in the book *Mind Over Mood* (Padesky and Greenberger, 1995) and I can only begin to imagine how many 'hot-cross buns' I drew to illustrate the links between thoughts, emotions, behaviours and physiology. I remember at the time being frustrated that there was limited reference to CBT in the sport psychology literature. References to cognitive-behavioural approaches were abundant but it was hard to find referenced work about CBT applications.

In 2001, I secured contracts with both British Shooting and United Kingdom Athletics (UKA). The initial focus of my work with both these NGBs was individual work, based on CBT supported by effective goal setting, briefing and debriefing and a lot of work on pre-performance routines. I travelled extensively with British Shooting and this is when I began to learn my in-competition performance psychology. In British Shooting, I was immersed in the sport and interacted increasingly with the coaches, multidisciplinary support team and the performance director while maintaining my main focus on individual support. For UKA, my role was less immersed and more centred on individual support for development athletes.

Initially in my practice and certainly as part of my BASES accreditation, I would gain evaluation of my work from asking athletes to complete formal evaluation forms. As time developed, this became less formal. Though it may seem crude, initially my feedback was based on maintaining clients or contracts with the NGBs. In time, feedback was gained from evaluation of objectives and this became more formalised once I joined the English Institute of Sport (EIS). As well as feedback, I started to do an increasing amount of reflective feedback and also peer supervision, both with sport psychology colleagues and clinical psychology friends. Before I joined the EIS in the autumn of 2005, the next development was the integration of mindfulness into my practice. I once again returned to the OCTC for training in this. During this period I was actively involved in the British Psychology Society and in the evolving Division of Sport and Exercise Psychology. I became chartered in 2005 and have been an active member of the Division in terms of accreditation of Master's programmes and am also both a supervisor and accreditor for candidates doing Stage 2 of the programme.

In 2005, I left lecturing and took up a full-time role with the EIS as the London Lead for Sport Psychology. As I sit here, 50 days from the start of the London 2012 Olympics, I can reflect on how my role and practice have evolved. I have adapted my approach to include Acceptance & Commitment Therapy (ACT), mindfulness, solution-focused therapy, Jungian psychometrics (Insights Discovery), positive psychology, pressure training and neuropsychology. Underlying this is my belief that it is the perception of a situation, not the situation itself, that influences performance. I have worked in five sports (athletics, canoeing, fencing, shooting and women's rugby) across Olympic and Paralympic programmes. The biggest influences on my development have been my fellow EIS colleagues who have taught me an immeasurable and invaluable amount of performance psychology. As I write this piece about my approach and how I work, I am conscious that it is not 'my' approach but something that has grown as a product of all those who have had an input into my practice over the years. Many thanks are required.

My approach is built around the aim of preparing athletes and coaches to be able to train to perform at their optimum when they need to. This is a complex aim and I break it down into three interacting cogs: (1) knowing yourself; (2) stretching yourself; and (3) coping. Neuropsychological advances in the past 10 years have been a major influence on my work, and an understanding of how the brain works forms a large part of how I help athletes and coaches understand themselves more clearly. This may include understanding elements such as the impact of perceived unfairness on the brain; how the brain reacts to threat to ego in a similar fashion to physical threat; that self-control is like a muscle, or the impact of mindfulness/ meditation on the size of the Insula. Since 2007, I have also utilised the Insights Discovery psychometric as part of self-awareness and self-regulation promotion and have used it extensively for coach–athlete relationships and team dynamics.

In terms of 'stretching yourself', this has led to education on being value-driven as well as goal-driven and also a lot of work on the environment that athletes and coaches are in. The importance of this was clearly apparent at Bollettieri's Tennis Academy in the fortnightly competitions which were held there. When I was there in 1999, there were 10 graded groups. Every two weeks a competition was held within each group and the loser of that competition had to play off against the winner from the group below. This could lead to relegation to a lower graded group, regardless of age. This meant a lot of tears, a lot of pressure and the possibility of a 15-year-old being in the same group as a 10-year-old. From my perspective this fortnightly play-off was a key environmental factor in the success of Bolletierri's. This has translated into my practice through the idea of helping coaches and athletes expose themselves to uncomfortable situations. Within the EIS, we have a pressure training tool which encapsulates how this can be devised in order for athletes to choose to approach rather than avoid fearful or uncomfortable situations.

In terms of helping athletes and coaches cope, there are two elements, first, is education and implementation of mental toughness/resilience plans or programmes. More recently my work in this has been inspired by the work that Seligman has done with the US Marines. The resilience programme done by Seligman is focused on self-awareness, self-regulation, optimism, mental agility, character strengths and connection. This programme fits well with the cornerstones of my philosophy of ACT, positive psychology, mindfulness and understanding of self. The second part is effective reflection and logical debriefing to ensure that the individuals continue to learn and hopefully to learn more quickly than their opponents.

In all my work, when possible, I aim to build a collaborative relationship with the coach. Within the EIS we have a coach-driven, psychologist-led model and thus an increasing amount of my time is spent with coaches. This has certainly evolved from when I first started working predominantly in a one-to-one fashion. My starting point to building a collaborative relationship with a coach is an acknowledgement that I could not do their job, so I start from a perspective of respect. I try to be mindful of this aim as often within the current drive towards accountability, it is easy to be distracted by my objectives and organisation objectives. I take care not to be driven by achieving these at the expense of appreciating the skills of others. My aim is not to be a teacher but part of a team searching for performance solutions.

As well as coaches, I aim to build effective relationships with the Multidisciplinary Team, the Performance Directors and more recently due to the Home Games in London I am also interacting with the NGB media teams and also the family and friends of the athletes.

The London Olympics has shaped my career as a full-time practitioner. I started my EIS job two months after the bid was won and the Home Games has been a guiding light especially since the end of the Beijing Games. My role within the EIS has changed such that since September 2009, I have taken on an increased leadership role and now technically manage six other psychologists. After Beijing, my role also changed in terms of sports as I initially split my time between working with British Fencing and UK Athletics. In the last year before the Games, my role changed again as I started to work solely for UKA across both the Olympic and Paralympic programmes.

It is worthwhile reflecting on the impact that changes in funding, NGB management and my role have had on me as a practitioner and as a person. The uncertain nature of applied roles in sport has meant that I have had to accept the insecurity that comes with this job. I have managed this by applying many of the techniques I teach to athletes to myself. I regularly remind myself that it is my choice, to view situations as opportunities and also to know how I will judge my success.

My work with Paralympic sport had been limited until I travelled with the UKA Disability Team to the World Championships in New Zealand in January 2011. As the focus of this team was performance, as was illustrated by winning medals at the World Championships being the singular criterion for staying on podium funding, my immersion in Paralympics sport may have taken a slightly different route to other practitioners. In terms of exploring disability, I very much left this in the hands of the athlete to disclose if and when they thought it was appropriate. This may have also been influenced by my initial focus being on staff team dynamics and also the bulk of my work starting at a major championship. In terms of working at a major championship, the model within the EIS is that performance psychologists play a 'helicopter role' which involves the ability to have objective distance and incorporates when necessary social support, crisis management, acting as a barometer and providing clean feedback and looking for 1 per cent performance changes. Though I had not travelled with a team for a number of years, I found it easy to adapt into this role as at heart I enjoy the intensity of the competitive environment. When I travel with this team, I always agree the terms of engagement with the Head Coach before we travel.

The potential unique demands and opportunities of a Home Games have led me to be involved in a number of initiatives within the EIS, UKA and the British Olympic Association (BOA). The largest of these is the First Games Home Games project which, alongside other EIS colleagues and the BOA, has led to the production of over 20 bespoke films targeting specific psychological challenges for first-time Olympians, multi-Olympians and first-time Home Olympians. Other initiatives have included programmes to deal with distractions, education on what actually constitutes home advantage and a series of workshops and booklets for the friends and families of athletes to ensure they know how to support their athletes effectively. A part of this work has been collaboration with the EIS Performance Lifestyle (PL) advisors. Indeed, the collaborative relationship with fellow EIS colleagues is a key part of my delivery of effective performance psychology. As an example, the PL advisor's role is to provide support on careers, education, finance, etc., for athletes. I have always worked closely with the PL advisors and find it effective to provide coherent support for the athletes in all elements of their life alongside their coaches. There is no doubt that excellent teamwork is needed to help athletes perform to their best and knowing what they go home to is a key part of this work.

As previously mentioned, technical management of six psychologists is a major part of my work. In helping to train and develop young practitioners within the EIS, we have taken a coaching/mentoring approach. I have had line management training as part of my initial role within the EIS and have also been involved in the

UK Sport Fast Track Practitioner programme. A strong part of training young practitioners has been selecting the right psychologists at the start. Most of the practitioners are either already qualified or working towards British Psychology chartered status. Within the EIS we are concerned about picking practitioners on their character. To expand alongside academic and professional qualifications the ability to build effective relationships, convey messages, influence others and have the ability to be present and objective at competitions are all part of the mercurial skills we are looking for. And, as such, these are also the skills we are looking to develop along with the skills to deal with the pressures of the environment. Though personality is important, I am also keen for practitioners to understand the distinction between themselves and themselves as a psychologist and to work hard to find the balance between personal disclosure, genuineness and effectiveness. A difficult trio of a balancing act.

In writing this piece I hope I have shared some insight into my own development, the different careers and roles I have had as a sport psychologist alongside the varied demands and challenges of my current day job. I feel I have had a good balance between the science and art of sport psychology in my development. The result is that I feel comfortable providing both proactive and reactive psychological support.

As I sit here, having watched athletes complete their Olympic journey in what has been an incredible Home Olympics and prepare to be part of the Paralympic GB support team in a Home Games, I reflect on what a journey I have been on. As a 12-year-old, I got to hold the GB Hockey Men's Bronze Medal and meet the man who had won it, now a few years later Olympic fever still burns strong in me, as does the fascination with understanding all the components that contribute to delivering on the biggest stage.

Reference

Padesky, C. A. and Greenberger, D. (1995) *Mind over Mood*. New York: The Guildford Press.

PART V

Clinical Psychology

14

FROM CLINICAL SCIENCE TO SPORT RESEARCH AND INTERVENTION

Ronald E. Smith

There was no recognized subdiscipline of sport psychology when I received my training in clinical psychology in the late 1960s. Not until I read an article by Tom Tutko and Bruce Ogilvie was I aware that clinical psychologists were working with athletes and teams. I, however, was committed to a career in academia and never considered such practical work as an option. In the early years of my career, my major focus was on the study of anxiety's effects on behavior and on the development and assessment of cognitive-behavioral treatment techniques for anxiety reduction. Through quite serendipitous paths, my interest in stress and stress management led me into a program of basic and applied research in sport. These extensions took two directions, namely, youth sports and sport performance enhancement. I'll describe each of these in turn.

Youth sports: coaching the coaches (and parents)

When I attended the University of Washington's football and basketball games in the early 1970s, I often sat with Earl Hunt, a prominent cognitive psychologist. Hunt was also a youth sport coach who preferred soccer because at that point in time, he said, "American parents didn't know enough about the sport to get in the way and cause problems." On one occasion, we were discussing the controversy about the role of adults in youth sports. It was becoming increasingly recognized that coaches and parents could create considerable stress for young athletes. Like Hunt, I had done a considerable amount of coaching as a playground and social center director while in college, and we decided that we knew enough as psychologists to write a book for youth sport coaches, showing them how to employ principles such as positive versus aversive behavior control to create a positive youth sport environment that would enhance psychosocial development and sport enjoyment. For Hunt, a leading researcher on artificial intelligence, this was a welcome foray into a different topic. For me, it was the dawning realization that the sport environment is a wonderful natural laboratory to study almost any psychological phenomenon, including my own interest in stress.

As we started meeting to plan the content of the book, Hunt and I began to realize that we were, in reality, putting forth interesting hypotheses that had never been tested in the youth sport environment. We shelved the book at that point and, in collaboration with Frank Smoll from our Kinesiology Department, wrote a grant proposal to the National Institute of Mental Health to study the effects of coaching behaviors on young athletes. As is the case with all of my clinical science research, the grant had two phases in which basic research results from phase 1 were to be used to develop and test an intervention at phase 2. The proposal was funded in 1975 and so began a line of research and intervention that extends to the current day. As for the book, after more than 30 years, it has finally been written (Smith and Smoll, 2012). We think the book is much better than it would have been had we written it in 1975 based on our intuitions, for the principles and behavioral guidelines now have a solid scientific basis based on more than 30 years of research (see Smith and Smoll, 2011, for a summary).

When we began our Youth Enrichment in Sports project, we found that no one had studied coaching behaviors in the natural environment in the manner we wanted to. To study coaching behaviors, we developed the Coaching Behavior Assessment System (CBAS), a 12-category behavioral assessment instrument that we used to code specific behaviors during practices and games. We found that during an average baseball, soccer, or basketball game, coaches engaged in more than 200 codable behaviors. By observing coaches over four to five games, we could develop a behavioral profile consisting of more than 1,000 coaching behaviors. In our first study, we coded 57,213 behaviors of 51 youth baseball coaches over 210 games. After the season, we individually visited and collected data from 542 of the athletes who had played for the coaches. We asked the players to rate how frequently their coaches had engaged in the 12 behaviors, their attitudes toward the coach, their teammates, and their experience, and we obtained measures of self-esteem and anxiety. Using the same rating scales completed by the athletes, we also asked coaches how frequently they engaged in the coaching behaviors. When the coaches' and athletes' ratings were correlated with the actual behavior profiles, the athletes were far more accurate perceivers. For the most part, coaches were blissfully unaware of what they were doing. The implication, of course, was that coaches would have to be trained to self-monitor their behavior in order to bring about behavior change.

In this basic research phase, clear-cut relations emerged between behaviors (both observed and athlete-perceived) and the outcome variables. Not unexpectedly, we found strong support for a positive approach featuring prominent use of encouragement, positive reinforcement, and sound technical instruction delivered in an encouraging manner, and negative relations for punitive and regimenting behaviors. The coaching behaviors had an especially profound effect on athletes who were low in self-esteem, and such athletes showed increases in self-esteem after playing for positive coaches. We now felt that we had enough solid data to develop an intervention in which we share with coaches a set of empirically-based behavioral guidelines

We entered this phase of our work with guarded expectations. Could we really hope to change coaches' behaviors with a simple coaching clinic that lasted only a few hours? In our favor, we had a set of specific guidelines that would be easy for coaches to incorporate into their coaching style with the expectation that they would yield positive results. We also attacked the professional model notion that winning is everything, promoting instead a definition of success as giving maximum effort, striving for improvement, personal development, and enjoying the activity for its own sake. We told coaches that, based on our research results, if they were successful in creating a positive, encouraging, and enjoyable environment and one that reduced fear of failure, good things would happen. In essence, we were, in the terms of achievement goal theory that was to develop years later, promoting the principles of a mastery (task) climate as opposed to an ego climate. Over the years, the name of the intervention changed from Coach Effectiveness Training to its current name, Mastery Approach to Coaching.

To our relief, coaches were highly receptive to our message, given that we had the data to support it. We also gave them tools to monitor their own behavior and to measure the extent to which they were adhering to the guidelines. Over the years, a series of experimental trials of the intervention has shown strong positive results on both coaches and the athletes who play for them. To summarize these studies, we and other investigators have shown that coaches who have been trained do indeed adopt the behavioral guidelines and exhibit positive behavior change. Compared with control groups, children who play for trained coaches (1) describe their sport environment as a mastery motivational climate as opposed to an ego environment; (2) enjoy their relations with their coach and teammates more; (3) show increases in self-esteem over the course of the season; (4) exhibit significant reductions in performance anxiety; (5) show increases in a mastery achievement goal orientation and a decrease in ego goal orientation scores; and (6) are five times less likely to drop out of sports the following season. Moreover, motivational climate has proven to be far more important than won–lost records in influencing positive attitudes toward coaches, a fact that helps make coaches more receptive to our guidelines (Cumming *et al.*, 2007). Over the years, more than 500 coach workshops have been conducted by my colleague Frank Smoll, exposing over 27,000 coaches to Mastery Approach principles.

The Youth Enrichment in Sports program has recently been expanded to include a companion program for parents called the Mastery Approach to Sport Parenting. To facilitate dissemination, we have written a parent book (Smoll and Smith, 2012) and put both the coach and parent interventions on DVDs. The interested reader can view portions of the coach and parent interventions as well as abstracts of the supporting research on the Youth Enrichment in Sports website (www.Y-E-Sports.com).

Performance enhancement through psychological skills training

As I began my academic career at the University of Washington in the early 1970s, I began to build on previous behavior therapy interventions and developed a brief (six-session) stress management training intervention called Cognitive-Affective Stress Management Training that allowed people to develop and rehearse stress-reducing coping skills such as relaxation, cognitive restructuring, and self-instructions that they could apply in stressful situations. In one efficacy study, we applied the intervention to test-anxious college students. The intervention proved to be highly effective in reducing test anxiety and increasing academic performance. About a month after the conclusion of the study, I received a call from Don James, the Washington football coach. He told me that one of his athletes of great ability who consistently performed below expectations in games because of high anxiety had suddenly shown dramatic improvement in his performance. When queried about his improvement, the athlete told the coaches that he was applying stress reduction skills he had learned in a psychology experiment. James told me he had other "Wednesday All-Americans" who choked during competition and asked if I'd be willing to work with these athletes, assuring me that I would have the ability to collect whatever data I wanted to. Thus began my work in performance enhancement in sports. In 1979, I presented a workshop on stress management training and its outcomes at the World Congress of Sport Psychology (Smith, 1980). Combined with the seminal work of Robert Nideffer and Michael Mahoney, the workshop helped generate interest in psychological skills training among the many attendees from sport science departments. Such interest played a role in the development of a subdiscipline of applied sport psychology that grew rapidly during the 1980s and gained organizational status with the founding of the Association for the Advancement of Applied Sport Psychology and, somewhat later, the American Psychological Association's Division of Exercise and Sport Psychology.

My career took an unexpected direction when Karl Keuhl became Director of Player Development for the Oakland Athletics. Kuehl was convinced that psychological factors were critical determinants of both athlete and organizational success, and he viewed my work as relevant to both staff and athlete development. He invited me and my colleague Daniel Landers of Arizona State University to Spring training in 1985 and we did a workshop for the managers and coaching staff (basically, an extension of the coach intervention we were doing with youth coaches). I also did a stress management workshop for the athletes.

I thought my consultation in professional baseball was over, especially after the A's hired a full-time person to fill that role. However, the following year, I received a call from Fred Stanley, one of the A's coaches who had been at our workshops the year before. Stanley had recently taken a job as minor league field director for the Houston Astros organization. Stanley offered me a full-time job as sport psychologist for the Astros, but I was not interested in leaving my university position. As an alternative, I asked him if the Astros had anyone in their organization whom I could train and supervise to do the work. I thought a "baseball man" from within would be ideal and would also have more credibility. Stanley identified one of his minor league managers, Jim Johnson, as a person who had a Master's degree in counseling and guidance. Johnson enthusiastically agreed to the arrangement, and I trained him during the offseason as I would one of my clinical or sport psychology graduate students. We put together an intervention program that included goal setting, mental rehearsal, stress management, and concentration training. Johnson's background enabled him to quickly grasp the underlying principles and training techniques. The next Spring, we went to Spring training in Florida together and did a solid week of staff development workshops and training workshops for the athletes in the various psychological skills. When the season began, Johnson assumed the role of a "roving instructor," rotating among the Astros' seven minor league teams to work with staff and individual players. I supervised his work by telephone and, on a few occasions, in person.

The Astros front office was strongly supportive of the program (though not all of the staff and athletes were initially). One pitching coach complained, "I'm not here to coddle mental weaklings. Baseball is a game of survival of the fittest and always has been." That coach was replaced the next season by one who was "on board" with the concept of mental skills training, and over the years, the Astros assembled a staff that was totally committed to integrating mental and physical skills training and a joy to work with. For his part, Johnson did a wonderful job implementing the program. We published a journal article in *The Sport Psychologist* describing the "organizational empowerment" model of sport psychology consultation that we had implemented (Smith and Johnson, 1990). Indeed, Johnson did so well that when Fred Stanley left the Astros to take a job with another organization, the Astros promoted Johnson to his director's position. At that point, in order to maintain the program, I agreed to assume Johnson's position (with the title of Special Instructor) for the coming season. I went to spring training during our university's spring break to do training workshops, then worked as a roving instructor once classes ended. Typically, I spent four to five days with a team while they were on the road and was easily accessible at the team hotel. I was available to or could access any player who was struggling with performance issues. Despite being a licensed clinical psychologist, I defined my role very specifically as an educational sport psychologist to avoid dual relationships and blurred roles. I referred clinical issues to the organization's Employee Assistance Program, where athletes who needed treatment could be seen on a continuous basis.

As in my work with the Washington football team, I was given permission to do research in order to study psychological variables and to evaluate our program. I therefore undertook a study to assess the role of psychological variables versus physical skills in predicting performance and survival in the organization. The latter was an important practical consideration for two reasons. First, only 5–10 percent of all minor league players make it to the major leagues, and for everyone who does, the organization spends more than $3 million in development costs. To the extent that the success rate can be increased, the organization achieves benefits that far outweigh the costs of a psychological skills training program like ours. Using our Athletic Coping Skills Inventory-28 to obtain self-report data from athletes and a parallel rating form to measure coaches' and managers' evaluations of athletes' psychological skills, we found that even when controlling statistically for physical skills differences, psychological skills predicted both performance and survival as well as or more strongly than did the physical skills ratings that the organization collected from their coaches, managers and scouts (Smith and Christensen, 1995). These findings had a major positive impact on the organization's commitment to the program and on athletes' receptivity to it. Eventually, in an anonymous survey, more than 90 percent of the athletes reported that they were using our training materials to develop at least one of the psychological skills that we taught. Over a five-year period, the Astros organization nearly doubled the percentage of players who reached the major leagues, and it seems likely that the psychological skills and staff development programs contributed to that success.

I planned to work as a roving instructor only one year. To my surprise, I enjoyed it so much that I continued in that role for five more years. Eventually, however, I tired of the traveling, which exceeded 40,000 air miles per year. I wanted to go back to the original organizational empowerment model, but at that point a new general manager appeared on the scene who was not at all supportive of the program. As is typically the case, he brought in new coaches and managers from his former organization and many of my closest coaching colleagues left the organization. I simply did not have the will to start over with a new staff, so I decided to leave as well.

At about the same time, the athletic director at my university who had heard about the Astros program approached me and Frank Smoll about establishing a similar program in her department. She offered to support two of our graduate students on 12-month assistantships. Thus began Husky Sport Psychology Services, which provided consultation to the University's 23 sport teams (see Leffingwell *et al.*, [2001] for a description of the program). For most of its six years of existence, the program was staffed by two clinical psychology doctoral students (Shelley Wiechman and Thad Leffingwell) who had been trained by Jean Williams in the master's program at the University of Arizona. However, when the Arizona sport psychology specialty was eliminated, our pipeline of trained students dried up and we urged the athletic department to hire someone full-time. They eventually did so and sport psychology consultation remains in good hands at our university.

Concluding thoughts

My training as a clinical scientist imbued me with a philosophical commitment to evidence-based practice. I titled my presidential address to the Association for the Advancement of Applied Sport Psychology "Applied Sport Psychology in an Age of Accountability" (Smith, 1989). I argued against "experiential knowledge" as a basis for evaluating our effectiveness, noting that the validity of such knowledge is challenged by the many cognitive distortions that have been proven to exist and by the fact that now-discredited medical practices such as purging, bloodletting, and electroshock therapy for schizophrenics were all supported by the "I've seen it work" personal experience of practitioners. As in medical and psychological clinical science, we must insist that our methods stand the test of scientific scrutiny. As the eminent psychologist Paul Meehl noted, the great strength of experiential knowledge (and the human mind) is for detecting relations or processes that can be the basis for scientific hypotheses; it is a poor basis for testing those hypotheses. If we are to have an ethically-defensible discipline of applied sport psychology, it must be based on empirically-supported principles and methods and conform to "best practice" standards.

The value of doing basic research to inform application has been borne out in both the youth sport work and in the work on psychological skills training. In the coaching research, results from the basic research phase focused our attention onto a small number of key behavior–outcome relations that allowed us to develop a highly effective and economical intervention. We believe the basic simplicity of the intervention is responsible for its efficacy. In the performance-enhancement work in baseball, the compelling results in our research on psychological versus physical skills (which surprised even us) established the credibility of the program beyond any doubt. In a sense, these results supported the famous utterance by Hall of Fame member Yogi Berra: "Baseball is 90 percent mental. The other half is physical." For pitchers, ACSI-28 scores accounted for 13 times as much performance variance as did all of the Astros' ratings of physical skills; for batters, psychological skills accounted for as much variance as did physical skills even when physical skill level was statistically controlled.

On a practical level, effective consultation depends on your credibility and the respect that you command. Neither of these occurs overnight; they must be carefully cultivated until you are viewed as both competent and trustworthy. They have to believe that you are going to help them achieve their goals. Even then, support can be withdrawn in an instant, as was the case with the Astros. The eminent sport psychologist Bruce Ogilvie used to remind his young colleagues that he was fired by nearly 40 different teams over his long and distinguished career. So enjoy it while you can. For me, it's been a great ride that has taken me a long way from who I was when I entered the field as a clinical scientist.

References

Cumming, S. P., Smoll, F. L., Smith, R. E. and Grossbard, J. R. (2007) Is winning everything? The relative contributions of motivational climate and won-lost percentage in youth sports. *Journal of Applied Sport Psychology*, 19: 322–336.

Leffingwell, T. R., Wiechman, S. A., Smith, R. E., Smoll, F. L. and Christensen, D. S. (2001) Sport psychology training within a clinical psychology program and a department of intercollegiate athletics. *Professional Psychology: Research and Practice*, 32: 531–536.

Smith, R. E. (1980) A cognitive-affective approach to stress management training for athletes, in C. H. Nadeau, W. Halliwell, K. M. Newell and G. C. Roberts (eds) *Psychology of Motor Behavior and Sport – 1979*. Champaign, IL: Human Kinetics.

——(1989) Applied sport psychology in an age of accountability. *Journal of Applied Sport Psychology*, 1: 166–180.

Smith, R. E. and Christensen, D. S. (1995) Psychological skills as predictors of performance and survival in professional baseball. *Journal of Sport and Exercise Psychology*, 17: 399–415.

Smith, R. E. and Johnson, J. (1990) An organizational empowerment approach to consultation in professional baseball. *The Sport Psychologist*, 4: 347–357.

Smith, R. E. and Smoll, F. L. (2011) Cognitive-behavioral coach training: A translational approach to theory, research, and intervention, in J. K. Luisell and D. D. Reed (eds) *Behavioral Sport Psychology: Evidence-Based Approaches to Performance Enhancement*. New York: Springer, pp. 227–248.

——(2012) *Sport Psychology for Youth Coaches: Developing Champions in Sports and Life*. New York: Rowman & Littlefield Publishers.

Smoll, F. L. and Smith, R. E. (2012) *Parenting Young Athletes: Developing Champions in Sports and Life*. New York: Rowman & Littlefield Publishers.

15

NO MAN IS AN ISLAND

Building a career in sport and performance psychology through teamwork

Shane Murphy

My first thought when asked to contribute a chapter to this fascinating exercise in self-reflection was, "Am I really that old that I have something to offer to 'aspiring, neophyte and current sport psychologists' from looking back over my career?" (These were my instructions from Paul and Marc.) But I quickly used a self-talk strategy to tell myself that even mid-career sport psychologists who look forward to many more years of active consulting, writing and research may have some insights to offer if they have been as lucky as I have in working with interesting clients. That done, I employed my goal-setting skills to fashion a template for this chapter. I was told that a conversational tone was appropriate, so my chapter is, I hope, just that—a chat with a colleague, reflecting on important "lessons learned" from my years spent working with athletes at the Olympic Training Center, with business professionals from a variety of fields, and with those striving to be the best in creative fields such as music, theater, film and television and digital media.

I can't say that I always wanted to be a psychologist. At various times, my career goals included being an airline pilot, a marine biologist, and a science fiction writer. It was my love of biology that drew me to psychology. As a teen with a voracious reading appetite I stumbled upon *King Solomon's Ring* in my father's library (thanks, Dad!), the warm and funny account of his ethological work by Nobel Prize-winner Konrad Lorenz, and my subsequent interest in studying animal behavior drew me naturally to the field of psychology. In the 1970s in Australia the cutting-edge program in psychology was at the University of New South Wales (UNSW), in Sydney, and so I went there as an undergraduate. The program was very science-based and also cognitive-behavioral in approach, but the main outcome, for me, was that it led me to apply to graduate school in clinical psychology. Since Australia had no applied programs in the field, and because I wanted hands-on training, that meant crossing the Pacific to study clinical psychology in the USA. I chose Rutgers University, because I knew one of the faculty there who had taught at UNSW (thanks, Cyril Franks!), and also because it was close to New York City, and also to my beloved Mets.

Lesson learned 1: take risks

I don't really think of myself as a risk-taker, but I must admit that some of the "leaps of faith" I have made in my life are, in retrospect, breath-taking to me: coming to the USA as a 22-year-old; going to Colorado Springs in 1986 to a new job that was like nothing I had ever done before; leaving the USOC in 1994 and coming to the East Coast with no job and nowhere settled to live to pursue my consulting dreams. Yet they have all worked out. I can't say that taking the riskiest path is always the best advice, but I have observed that to fulfill your career passions it helps to be prepared to make a lot of sacrifices in the initial pursuit of your dreams.

My graduate school experience was pivotal in shaping my approach to psychology, a conclusion I am sure most of us share. The formal training I received in psychological theories, research and interventions was very influential, but perhaps just as much so were the informal experiences offered in graduate school. I had come to a new country, suddenly cut off from my support system of family and friends and I quickly learned that in order to thrive I needed to rely on the support available from my faculty, from my fellow students and from a new circle of friends. I had always been a very competitive individual, often keen to show others that I could succeed on my own merits, with little assistance, but such an approach would have doomed me at Rutgers. The five years of professional development required for a PhD in clinical psychology are a huge commitment and a solo learner approach would have been incredibly stressful. Looking back now, from a sport psychology perspective, I would say that I began to realize how important coaching and teamwork were. Collegiality, social support and teamwork are an integral part of my "professional DNA" today, and I think three specific examples during my years at Rutgers illustrate the important lessons I learned in "how to" succeed in sport psychology.

My first foray into the field was triggered by the collapse of a research project on childhood school refusal which I had been working on for a year. My advisor, Rob Woolfolk, suggested I collaborate with him on an alternative research project he was conducting with another student, Mark Parrish. They were studying the effects of imagery on motor skill performance and as an avid sports enthusiast I had no hesitation about joining the project. My literature review quickly led me to "discover" the large research base on sport psychology, which I had not encountered during any of my previous training. I became fascinated by the issues dealt with in sport psychology and remain so to this day.

Lesson learned 2: stay open to new ideas

Although all my early training was in clinical child psychology, my willingness to learn about other areas of psychology that interested me created the opportunity for a lifetime career in a different area: sport psychology.

A second defining experience occurred when I decided to seek formal instruction in this area. No courses in sport psychology were offered within the graduate school of psychology, but I found an instructor, David Feigley, offering an undergraduate course in the school of physical education. He kindly agreed to allow me to audit the course and his wonderful scholarship opened my eyes to many new areas in the field. Especially influential was the text he used, Terry Orlick's *In Pursuit of Excellence* (1980), which had a great influence on me (and which still sits on my desk today). I quickly saw the many commonalities between the performance enhancement approach Terry described and the cognitive-behavioral approaches to counseling I was being trained in, with their joint emphasis on changing behaviors, tracking behavior change, and helping individuals challenge their beliefs and develop new ways of thinking about their performance. David was a wise mentor throughout my Rutgers years and served on my doctoral dissertation committee (I can never thank you enough, Dave).

Lesson learned 3: don't be afraid to cross disciplinary boundaries

To be honest, there were some in the psychology program who viewed my forays into sport psychology with misgivings and I received advice not to "waste my time" with such research. But I found that other disciplines offer other ways of looking at the world which can enrich the traditional approaches of psychology and I have continued to cross disciplinary boundaries throughout my career, with beneficial results. It proved to be a vitally important attitude when I went to work for the United States Olympic Committee (USOC).

As I learned more about sport psychology, I became motivated to gain some applied experience in the field. Once again the stumbling block was a lack of any such training in the graduate psychology program. This time my savior was a clinical faculty member, Jack Atthowe, who agreed to the polite (but perhaps persistent?) requests of several like-minded graduate students to offer a special course on applied issues in performance enhancement and who also helped us find practicum placements and supervised our efforts. Mine was with Rutgers track and field coach Frank Gagliano, which was another excellent learning experience for me.

Lesson learned 4: if someone else has what you need, ask for their help

Looking back, it was somewhat bold of us to ask for Jack's assistance in such a manner, but it turned into a wonderful experience and convinced me of the wisdom in the adage, "There's no harm in asking."

After finishing my doctoral studies at Rutgers I completed my internship training at the Children's Psychiatric Center in New Jersey and a post-doctoral fellowship with child sex abuse victims at the Crime Victim's Center at the Medical University of South Carolina (MUSC), still on track for my career in child clinical psychology. I wanted to present the results of my sport psychology research at

Rutgers at a professional conference and noticed that a brand new professional organization, the Association for the Advancement of Applied Sport Psychology (AAASP), was holding its inaugural conference at nearby Jekyll Island, Georgia. I submitted two papers, which were both accepted, and not only did I make my presentations, I also met many individuals who were, or would become, leaders in the emerging field of applied sport psychology.

Later that year I applied for the newly created position of Head of Sport Psychology at the USOC in Colorado Springs. In hindsight, those two research presentations were surely the reason I got a "foot in the door" and was among those interviewed for the position. Sometimes luck and fate play a big role in career development, and my good fortune was to be asked to take on the job of creating a role for sport psychology within the Sports Medicine and Science program at the USOC. But it didn't hurt that I had attended and presented at that AAASP conference.

Lesson learned 5: get your work out there

If you're doing interesting or creative work, it helps if others know about it. That doesn't happen by accident. Throughout my career I have found that attending scientific and professional conferences was the best method of presenting my work to a broad audience while also learning about the work of others and hearing about new and emerging trends in the field. Few things are as energizing to my work as several days spent in the company of motivated, energetic colleagues sharing ideas and experiences. Another great way to share your work with others is by writing— for academic journals, books, magazines, sports publications, websites, or wherever your interests take you.

To say that my seven-plus years at the USOC changed my life would be such an obvious understatement as to make it not worth saying. Having the opportunity to work in such a pressure-filled and challenging environment, with some of the greatest coaches and athletes in the world, at such a pivotal time in the history of sport psychology, was a blessing for which I will always be grateful. Such opportunities must be grasped and embraced, and once again, the themes of coaching and teamwork were pivotal in the success of my work at the USOC. Just as I had found at Rutgers, success could only be achieved with the cooperation of many others, and three groups of people contributed to the life-altering learning experiences I had at the USOC.

I had the good fortune when I arrived at the Colorado Springs Olympic Training Center to join a high-performing Sport Science group spear-headed by Chuck Dillman. Within the disciplines of sport physiology and biomechanics there was a well-established "RA" program, in which aspiring graduate students in these fields could apply to become research assistants for a year at the Training Center. I created a similar process in sport psychology and soon there were two graduate students at a time working under my supervision, providing much-needed sport psychology services to the athletes, coaches and programs of the USOC. I believe and hope these RAs would say that their time in Colorado Springs was a great learning experience, but what stands out to me is how greatly I was changed by my experience mentoring these talented, passionate and committed individuals. They gave me energy and enthusiasm every day, they taught me new ways of looking at issues I might have taken for granted, and I learned more about myself than I can describe in being their mentor. And what amazing individuals they were. Just naming some of those RAs is like creating a "who's who" of influential sport psychologists, researchers and counselors, including Kirsten Peterson, Chris Carr, Tom Raedeke, Megan Neyer, Shirley Durtschi, Mike Greenspan, Frank Perna, Doug Jowdy, Vance Tammen, Bob Swoap, Alan Budney, Michael Lesser, and Suzie Tuffey. Of course, I purposely left one name off the list; for he was one of the first of those RAs but is still a dynamic leader in sport psychology at the USOC today, Sean McCann, whose tireless energy and devotion to the needs of athletes and coaches still inspire me today. (Side note: After Sean finished his stint at the USOC, I moved heaven and earth in order to get him back to Colorado Springs as a full-time staff member. Another lesson learned is that people are the most valuable resource we have at work and if you find a special person with talent, do whatever it takes to get them on your team!)

Lesson learned 6: one of the greatest learning experiences is to teach others

After over thirty years in this field I have realized that I will always be most proud of my USOC experience mentoring those wonderful future leaders of our field. That was not at all obvious at the time. None of us knew what might be the outcome of the process to which we were committed. There were many days when we were flying by the seats of our pants! But we did our best every day and loved it, and that was what mattered. To this day, especially in my current position as university professor, I find that I learn more by teaching than from anything else I do. And my students always have a great influence on me, though my job description is to influence them.

It quickly became obvious that there were great needs at the Olympic Training Center which my training had not prepared me to fulfill. Two of the most pressing were the career and life planning needs of the athletes and the issue of dealing with substance abuse and doping, which was already a major problem at the Olympic level, long before it gained notoriety as an issue in professional baseball, cycling and football. I had no training in the former and while I had some excellent training and experience in the latter, the issues the USOC was facing were bigger and more diverse than any I had ever encountered. My learning experiences at UNSW and Rutgers, where I was taught to solve big problems by building a team to tackle them, influenced my instinctive approach to get help in dealing with these issues. Discussions with my RAs at the time helped suggest experts who might be able to assist, some research provided further names, and my contacts from AAASP and my work with Division 47 of the American Psychological Association (APA) gave me other leads. Some begging and borrowing gave me the funds I needed, and soon career development experts such as Steve Danish, Robert McKelvain, Al Petitpas and Dan Gould were working together to create what would eventually become the Career Assistance Program for Athletes (CAPA), a program that not only helped hundreds of Olympic athletes with career issues but became a model for other programs, such as the NCAA's, across the USA and indeed the world (Petitpas *et al.*, 1997). Similarly, we developed a comprehensive substance abuse counseling and prevention program for the Olympic Training Center by bringing together experts in the field from around the country. Dealing with appearance and performance enhancing drugs (APEDs) was a more difficult issue but again we developed sound approaches to education, prevention and treatment by working with our colleagues in sports medicine, particularly the Chief Medical Officer of the USOC, Dr. Robert Voy.

It wasn't just dealing with the big issues that benefitted from working closely with my colleagues in sport psychology. My day-to-day work at the Training Center was heavily influenced by my interactions with the sport psychologists who came to Colorado Springs to work with the many sports organizations that comprise the Olympic movement. To be frank, I stole from the best. I sat in on workshops and training sessions with athletes and coaches offered by some of the best people in our field and whenever I saw a good idea, I took it and copied it. Some of them sat in on my work, as well, and their feedback was extremely helpful to my development as an effective sport psychologist. In these ways I developed my skills in individual work with athletes, I transformed the way I worked with teams and groups, I learned many new ways of effective public communication, and I even gained valuable insights into the working of the complex bureaucracy of the USOC.

My work with individual athletes continued to be guided by the core principles of the cognitive-behavioral approach—careful assessment, identifying specific behaviors to change, identifying the athlete's cognitions that controlled behavior, tracking change over time—but it also became informed by a systems approach. I learned to work closely with coaches, to assess interactions with teammates, and to pay attention to the influence of the reinforcement system inherent in a sport's organizational structure. My team and group work became more and more hands-on and less didactic as I observed the behaviors of those sport psychologists who were most successful with their own sports. Feedback from my colleagues after public presentations helped me develop a more relaxed, informal public presentation style, and I learned from Mo Weiss how to use PowerPoint presentations on a tour of Belgian sports academies.

I also gained a great deal from attending the annual AAASP and APA conferences and from reading the principal journals and books in our field, but the biggest influences on me came from sharing hands-on experiences. Of course there were times when I disagreed or even butted heads with my colleagues, but critical feedback and analysis are often even more helpful in the long term than praise for what we do well.

Lesson learned 7: a collaborative approach works far better than a territorial approach

There is no doubt that the USOC sport psychology program owes much of its great success over the years to its inclusive nature. I realized from the beginning that I didn't have many of the answers, but there were others who could help me find them, and that approach, I believe, carries on to this day. My collaborations with colleagues from a variety of backgrounds, using diverse approaches to sport psychology, have enriched my own approach immeasurably. I feel very lucky to have had the chance to work with some of the best people in sport psychology from around the world and I can't even begin to thank them all enough for the lessons they have taught me. I would try to make a list detailing my debt of gratitude, but I fear I would be guilty of name-dropping. Anyway, my colleagues know who they are—thank you to all.

Over the course of my career, the group which has influenced me the most is my clients. Of course, this is true in any area of psychology, for example, I learned how to better help those who had been sexually abused as children by observing and asking about the coping strategies of those I worked with at MUSC. Yet it seems to be especially true in sport psychology, where the athletes and coaches are so committed and passionate about achieving excellence. These individuals have often learned so much in their careers that, if you are a good listener, observer, and can build good rapport with the athletes and teams you work with, you can truly discover the "secrets of success." Some of the best research ever done in our field has been of this type, carefully interviewing top performers and seeking commonalities in their approaches to success. I am thinking of the early work of Terry Orlick and John Partington (Orlick and Partington, 1988), the terrific research with figure skaters by Tara Scanlan and her colleagues (Scanlan *et al.*, 1989), the extended research by Dan Gould and his colleagues on the mental aspects of success in Olympians (Gould *et al.*, 1999), and the recent work on performance intelligence by Graham Jones (Jones, 2012).

Certainly my clients have been instrumental in changing my viewpoint about the essence of sport psychology. Trained as a clinical psychologist, it was natural for me to see sport psychology through this lens. As a result, I have always emphasized the holistic nature of the consulting relationship, understanding that what happens on the playing field strongly influences what occurs off it, and vice versa. But my specialization in sport psychology made it difficult, at first, for me to see that our large knowledge base could be applied to other areas of human performance. It was my clients who convinced me. First, by asking me to try; try to understand their performance situations, for example, in business, or the performing arts, and try to help them achieve greater success using the knowledge and strategies gained from sport psychology. Second, by showing me; in our work together it soon became apparent that many of the same psychological processes I had studied with athletes were also critical in creating a successful work team at a nuclear energy plant, or also vitally important when going on stage to sing at the Met. In this way I gradually came to see myself as a sport *and* performance psychologist and I have argued elsewhere that where "once an interest in sport and physical activity chiefly defined the field, a movement has been underway to instead define sport and performance psychology as reflecting interest in issues of performance, in sport and other domains" (Murphy and Murphy, 2012, p. xix). I have my clients to thank for this growth in my perspective and approach.

Lesson learned 8: remain open to new ideas

There are many forces in our training and development that encourage a fixed way of looking at performance concerns – our formal education, past successes which suggest that a certain approach is "correct", and the tendency to become more dogmatic as we gain years of experience. But our field is young. It has already evolved greatly and I believe it will continue to grow and change if we ask good questions, stay open to the lessons of research and scholarship and listen closely to our clients.

For all of us, performing at our best, especially in a sustainable and consistent manner, day-to-day and dealing with all the stress that life throws at us, is one of our greatest challenges. Being a student of this field has been a hugely fulfilling and very satisfying career choice. I want to thank Paul and Marc for the opportunity to engage in some rare navel-gazing. Writing this chapter has crystallized some important ideas for me. It's not often I get the chance to reflect on these types of career lessons. I hope you have enjoyed our chat.

References

Gould, D., Guinan, D., Greenleaf, C., Medbery, R. and Peterson, K. (1999) Factors affecting Olympic performance: perceptions of athletes and coaches from more and less successful teams. *The Sport Psychologist*, 13: 371–395.

Jones, G. (2012) The role of superior performance intelligence in sustained success, in S. Murphy (ed.) *The Oxford Handbook of Sport and Performance Psychology*. New York: Oxford University Press, pp. 62–80.

Lorenz, K. (1961) *King Solomon's Ring*. Trans. M. Kerr Wilson. London: Methuen.

Murphy, S. M. and Murphy, B. P. (2012) Preface, in S. Murphy (ed.) *The Oxford Handbook of Sport and Performance Psychology*. New York: Oxford University Press, pp. xix–xxiv.

Orlick, T. (1980) *In Pursuit of Excellence*. Champaign, IL: Human Kinetics.

Orlick, T. and Partington, J. (1988) Mental links to excellence. *The Sport Psychologist*, 2: 105–130.

Petitpas, A., Champagne, D., Chartrand, J., Danish, S. and Murphy, S. (1997) *Athlete's Guide to Career Planning: Keys to Success from the Playing Field to Professional Life*. Champaign, IL: Human Kinetics.

Scanlan, T. K., Stein, G. L. and Ravizza, K. (1989) An in-depth study of former elite figure skaters: II. Sources of enjoyment. *Journal of Sport and Exercise Psychology*, 11: 65–83.

PART VI
Sport Science

16

PRACTITIONER-SCIENTIST OR SCIENTIST-PRACTITIONER?

Chris Harwood

I chose this title because I'm still contemplating the answer to my own identity, and it may be a few more years before I reflect towards a final conclusion. The secondary aim of course is to offer an example to young sport psychologists of two (well, multiple actually!) career roles that feature research and practice. I take a fairly chronological approach, noting all of the key influences, departure points and forks in the road. I hope you enjoy the story so far.

A family affair

I grew up as the eldest of three children within what I suspect was a great example of the 1980s sporty family. My dad was a 'professional cricketer-turned-accountant' and he greatly encouraged me as a multi-sport youngster. He understood the demands of sport as well as the mastery-oriented, intrinsic nature of motivation that was critical if we were to develop our skills and enjoyment of our various sports. His (perhaps) genetic gift to me of natural hand–eye coordination led me towards anything that I could hit. It happened to be tennis to which I ultimately competed at a national level and a sport that still plays a key part in my life as a 'young' veteran!

My mum did not actually take up competitive sport until she was 50, at which point she started a process of completing 20 marathons in various countries over a 12-year stint. Much like Forrest Gump, she diversified from simply running endless miles and ended up representing Great Britain at the Triathlon World Championships in Edmonton as a 57-year-old. She is a feisty, competitive and very resilient woman!

My younger brother and sister found their groove in competitive swimming, and the levels they reached nationally and internationally were only matched by the persistent sacrifice of the archetypal 'swimming parents' that mum and dad became. Both Paul and Kim would follow me to Loughborough University to study degrees in sport science, and both had the rather nerve-wracking privilege of being taught by me while at Loughborough.

It was this blend of strong Lancashire family values – work ethic, respect, dedication, cooperation, alongside a highly competitive streak – that drove me through my mid-to-later adolescent years. These values and experiences have formed my approach to life, to sport, and to my work and career in sport psychology.

I am forever thankful to my parents for a good education, but given that I was a chubby lad at 12 years old with a 'cereal bowl' bobbed blond haircut, I was subject to more than a touch of bullying at school. One of the more affectionate nicknames – 'Sunbeam Helmet!' – has always stayed with me, and many people still wonder how truthful I'm being when I disclose that I was on the rather portly side as an adolescent. Believe me, I definitely carried a few extra pounds!

The bullying didn't make me work hard on my fitness, my intrinsic love of sport took care of that in due course. However, it did mould a very strong 'helping' schema within me. If it's a sad or triumphant moment in film or sport, or when a character suffers from some injustice, then I can feel my limbic system putting the afterburners on. I've never explored myself with a psychodynamic practitioner, but my experiences of adolescent social adversity have certainly left their mark. I count the mark to be positive because, as a sport psychologist, you've got to freely and openly give more than you'll ever, ever take.

This reflective piece at the start of my story is important because my family and upbringing are major reasons why (1) I ended up in sport psychology; (2) I struggle to say 'No' to requests for help; and (3) my research and applied work have tended to focus on the social-psychological issues in elite youth sport. The role of motivation, family, and psychosocial attributes simply resonate with me, alongside the importance of helping others and being a team player.

Education and training

The academic journey

After A-Levels in Latin, French and Ancient History, I bypassed the opportunities to study for an Ancient History degree at Nottingham or Warwick, by grounding my education and training in Sport Sciences and Physical Education at Loughborough University. Following my BSc, life might have been very different if Professor Bob Weinberg had not moved to Miami University as Chair in 1992. I had just gained an MSc and TA post with him at the University of Texas. He was the main man in tennis psychology and I wanted to follow the man as opposed to retain my place at UofT. Finances unfortunately hampered such a move to Miami, and so I continued with my MSc studies in the UK at Loughborough with Dr Graham Jones and Dr Austin Swain. I often wonder how life would have turned out if I'd worked with Bob – my hunch is that I'd be a better tennis psychologist and he'd be a better player!

Multidimensional anxiety research in sport was booming at that time. Graham, Austin, and later a great friend of mine, Sheldon Hanton, were advancing the notion of 'directional interpretations' of anxiety symptomatology. Ironically, my first publication would be in this very area (Jones *et al.*, 1996) and it was the focus of my MSc thesis alongside another area that was rapidly gaining momentum. This area was Achievement Goal Theory (AGT).

My passion for tennis and interest in swimming were exceptional contextual drivers, only outmatched by my drive to study situational factors that impacted achievement motivation. I was gripped by achievement goal theory and greatly respected those leading the advance of that theory at the time: Joan Duda and Glyn Roberts. The first edition of *Motivation in Sport and Exercise* edited by Glyn Roberts in 1992 was a seminal text for me, and I have to say that it was an exceptionally exciting time. AGT was a theory hungry for research support in sport, and I embraced it at the right time during my postgraduate studies from 1993.

AGT grabbed my attention for many reasons. As a tennis player, I felt I was onto something in terms of how changeable perceptions of oneself and one's view of success were in the context of different matches and opponents. This also extended to how changeable cognitions were within matches. I wanted to study these phenomena and investigate what influenced our achievement goals in the context of competition. I saw both of my parents through the lens of AGT. My mum always made elevated comparisons with other players in a manner that innocently set up both of our expectations. There was no player whom I couldn't beat in her mind. My dad offered another perspective with only his presence sufficient for me to appreciate that it was only ever about competing for every ball. The result: I was your classic 'Hi-task/Hi-ego' goal profile – a conscientious and facilitative disposition in many ways, but with uncomfortable side effects to manage on occasions (see Harwood *et al.*, 2008).

The practitioner journey

Unlike my domestic skills, I was a bit of a multi-tasker during my PhD. First, I worked part-time as Head Coach of Loughborough University Tennis, a position that I would continue after my PhD for one more year. At the same time, I also undertook Supervised Experience to become an Accredited Sport Scientist (psychology) with the British Association of Sport and Exercise Sciences (BASES). This served as the sole practitioner qualification for sport psychologists in the UK, until the British Psychological Society title of 'Chartered Sport and Exercise Psychologist' emerged in 2004. With my PhD education, practical experience and progressive knowledge development in cognitive, social and developmental psychology, I attained Chartered Status and subsequently registration as a Practitioner Psychologist with the Health Professions Council in the UK. My dual accreditation also extended to BASES High Performance Sport Accreditation in 2005 which is bestowed on consultants who have demonstrated a range of competencies through extensive work in high performance sport environments.

Early career as a scientist-practitioner (?)

The research methods within my PhD distinctly shaped my applied work as a practitioner. I gained very rich insights into young performers through qualitative interviews, and completed my PhD with an in-depth, multiple baseline intervention incorporating work with players, coaches and parents (Harwood and Swain, 2001, 2002). The meanings, material, resources, methods and insights from this applied research, dating back 17 years, still nourish some of my work today. I think in our twenties, as dedicated and ambitious young researchers, I suspect that many of us are at our most productive and innovative. I encourage all young researchers who believe in their ideas to stay the course and push for themselves to be heard. I don't think we should ever underestimate the capacity and resourcefulness of young researchers and practitioners coming through our field. They can see the world from a different vantage point and with different stressors than more seasoned academics who are often burdened with other priorities.

A developing humanist

My core philosophy as a practitioner is humanistic but I would not have known that back in 1997. Our accreditation and training then were nowhere near as comprehensive as they are now. I definitely consulted with passion, but I was also consulting with a lot of trial and error. I had a strong grasp of mental skills training and performance enhancement strategies, but I was certainly missing core psychology knowledge that I feel is absolutely critical to working with a range of human beings in a range of different contexts. My competencies in terms of counselling performance dysfunction issues and the inevitable transitional, interpersonal and organisational challenges faced by athletes and coaches were limited (Gardner and Moore, 2006). Working with these non-clinical or sub-clinical themes requires confident counselling skills, specific background knowledge and training – and I cannot honestly say that there was a strong focus on any of this in the 1990s. These areas had to be developed on the job by listening to clients, making errors, observing and listening to experts and through additional courses. I think it is these experiences that helped me to understand the person before the performer. It taught me to spend more time in the 'person world' as opposed to simply whether they knew how to 'set goals', 'do imagery', or have a 'routine'.

Loughborough, 1998–2002

Gaining a job as a lecturer at Loughborough University in 1998, my identity card read 'Academic researcher with some consulting on the side'. My dominant model of practice at that time reflected a 'social-cognitive-behavioural' orientation. I believed that thinking processes governed behaviour in athletes; but my achievement goal research reminded me that thinking processes and behaviour can be subject to substantial social influence. Parents, grandparents, coaches, and peers can shape the way we think and act, and my work with an individual would always proactively take account of the behaviour, involvement and interactions of parents, coaches and peers/teammates.

From 1998 to 2000, while publishing on-going work in AGT, I broadened my consulting experience beyond tennis into squash, swimming, golf, equestrian, athletics and even 'baton twirling'! As a qualified coach, I also engaged in coach education work with national federations and clubs, and I still get a buzz from working with motivated and 'new school' coaches. However, I wanted to work within a team sport environment, and the opportunity came when Dr Mary Nevill, head coach of Loughborough University Women's Hockey team asked me to work with her squad. This opportunity would influence my career choices significantly.

I remember Dr Steve Bull, a fellow sport psychologist for English cricket, talking about his 'immersion approach' whereby the consultant essentially embeds themselves into the operations of a team and has to carefully manage the multiple roles that it may bring. Within women's hockey, gaining entry was greatly facilitated by the fact that I had taught many of the players in their degree (and had thankfully done a good job it seemed!). However, it presented a role conflict that I had to carefully manage from an ethical perspective. There was a keenness to build a strong group dynamic and open communication channels, and so I worked mainly with small units and the team as opposed to individual players.

I found myself drawn towards a system of performance management and unit reflection whereby units would set and review the execution of their goals, principles of play and agreed behaviours match after match over the course of the season. To shape this system I managed the production of *Hockey's the Winner*, the team's weekly mental toughness magazine that contained all of the open performance reviews, educational material, coach's report, and humorous columns edited by the players. It was an extensive undertaking, when positioned against attendance at a weekly training session, weekend match observations and post-match reviewing. This experience formed my apprenticeship as a team psychologist over a full season. The title of a later book chapter 'From researcher to water boy' (Harwood, 2008b) reflected the diverse roles within which I engaged to support the players and coaching staff at the university.

New sport, new start, new risks, new life

I have three identities as a sport psychologist. They all matter greatly to me, they all compete for attention, and they can make life stimulating, unpredictable and stressful in equal measure. As an *applied researcher*, I have a responsibility for advancing knowledge; as a *practitioner psychologist*, I relish the opportunity to support teams, athletes, coaches, and families by listening to stories, guiding development and imparting knowledge; and, as a *teacher/supervisor*, I feel responsible for supporting the next generation of scientist-practitioners, and quality assuring them to stakeholders. While I've definitely attempted to keep these three wives happy, there have been several times when I've contemplated divorce proceedings!

Be prepared for disappointment

Academia can be a tough and disheartening industry, and it had taken a piece out of me by 2002. You will learn how to deal with rejection in academia, and you need to interpret this as a 'constructive pin prick' as opposed to a 'dum-dum bullet' through your self-esteem. I was getting used to this. What can be more testing, however, is how you choose to deal with the disappointing behaviour and tone of academics you originally respected. Sometimes it can even get personal! Only recently, one eminent academic in a book chapter presented me as a misguided crusader *against* achievement goal theory's relevance to sport, indeed, a *young and arrogant* one! My advice to the neophyte researcher: Be the person your parents would be proud of, maintain your humility and character and, in true REBT form, be disappointed as opposed to angry with others. It's a far healthier negative emotion to process when these things happen. Either that or read a John Wooden book!

I include this personal story here because it brings me to a basic premise that we have our one life, and this one life progresses through a process of decisions. For me 2000–2002 was a period that challenged my motivation for academia, and philosophically, it made me think a lot more smartly about where to direct my life energies, where I wanted to contribute, and with whom I wanted to spend time in my life.

Nottingham Forest FC and the Football Association

In 2002, new and interesting avenues emerged for me. The manager of Nottingham Forest FC was looking to employ a sport psychologist and I was approached via the club nutritionist who, ironically, I had taught as an MSc student. I was not a football expert, but I saw how much work needed to be done in English football. It needed the appliance of science to blow away old school cobwebs that still enveloped the sport. My services and methods with women's hockey gave me a confidence, and it was time for a change. It was time to shake my life up.

I had been 12 years at Loughborough, and even though I had worked with Professor Stuart Biddle to establish our new MSc programme in Sport and Exercise Psychology, I knew I needed a fresh focus. Timing is everything, and at a similar time, the Football Association were preparing its 'Psychology for Football' strategy. Dr Andy Cale, the FA's Head of Player Development, spearheaded this strategy, and he approached Loughborough to help deliver research elements of it.

To cut a long story short, I reduced my academic contract with Loughborough to 30 per cent, signed a two-year contract with Nottingham Forest as a self-employed practitioner for 60 per cent, and the other 10 per cent represented a blend of Nottinghamshire youth cricket and regional tennis academy work. While now living and working in Nottingham as a single 31-year-old football club psychologist, I still taught my MSc programme at Loughborough and supervised the research students and projects that would kick start the FA strategy (see Pain and Harwood, 2004, 2007).

A tale of two seasons

My years in professional soccer were fascinating, and it was a steep learning curve. I applied some of the same basic principles of team productivity and communication with the senior players as I had with the hockey team. Most importantly, on a three-day-a-week contract, I had the opportunity and time to get my values across as a sport psychologist with each player. To the majority of the players, my non-expert football background was less important compared with being passionate about sport, and my relationships with them were certainly aided by my tennis and fitness levels. The different demands and skill requirements between tennis and soccer became the focus of many healthy debates with players. In addition, due to my mother, I had completed a third London Marathon in 2002 and could hold my own with the players on their training runs.

Down to business

These factors helped me to gain entry into this subculture, and demystifying and simplifying sport psychology jargon led to a number of senior players being more eager to develop their self-regulation skills. I constructed a weekly match review system which, alongside a pre-match primer that I wrote for every home and away game, became the team's vehicle for mental preparation and match reflections to each other. *Hockey's the Winner* was replaced by *With a Goal in Mind* and by the mid-season point, we were third in the Championship division. These pieces of work with senior professionals provided me with valuable material for my educational sessions with younger, more impressionable academy players. I could pick out examples of role model or less appropriate behaviours from the Saturday game and use them during my player development session with the youngsters.

Video highlight compilation tapes were another regular feature to team and individual work. Supported by our video technician, and 'storyboards' that I had crafted, we were able to create some powerful 'identity-developing' and mastery-focused DVDs. In keeping momentum towards the play-offs, the use of music also became an important preparatory feature with both individualised music/imagery scripts and the team's dressing room playlists. When we changed the pre-match 'tunnel' music to the Battle theme from the *Gladiator* movie, you could feel the City Ground shake from the vibrations. Christmas 2003 was a special time and I didn't mind one bit being slagged off by a couple of fans for replacing 'Mull of Kintyre'. Sorry, Paul McCartney!

Footballers are human beings first

We made the Premier League play-offs in 2003 and lost 5–4 in extra time away to Sheffield United. Although rationally we had overachieved for the season for a young team and small squad, it was a very emotional dressing room that night. These players did not represent society's overpaid footballer stereotype. They were respectful human beings and they hurt just like the rest of us. It seems strange to disclose that I faced a major challenge because of this, and it would be my biggest failure as the club psychologist during the second season. In brief, I simply failed at convincing coaches to work on their own human psychology and to individualise their communication, feedback and leadership style to some of the players. My work with a number of players focused on supporting a fragile self-confidence that was getting knocked by emotional criticism. I failed at organisationally influencing the development of a more accurate performance-based (as opposed to purely result-based) culture. During the dark times in 2004, I felt I was fighting through more 'old school' cobwebs than Indiana Jones! I had to own these failures and be accountable to the cardinal error of assuming that I was employed to work with players *and coaches*. I was very wrong. This experience altered the way I negotiated any projects that required coaches to be part of my work.

The senior team avoided relegation with a new manager who had little interest in psychology. Therefore, with my formal contract expiring and an interest from the Forest youth academy to continue, I returned to Loughborough University full time in late 2004 and began a research and support programme with the youth academy.

Back to the future!

During my two years at Forest, the real world of working across the whole 'youth-to-senior' development spectrum inspired me with many unanswered research questions. However, I had to get something off my chest. I had to download my ideas and practices for optimising the psychology of football players, coaches and teams. I figured that at least if these ideas were out there, then readers could make their own judgement. Hence, with the support of Alistair Higham and Andy Cale, *Momentum in Soccer: Controlling the Game* was published in 2005 (Higham *et al.*, 2005). The phenomenon of momentum had featured greatly in my observations of so many football matches, and so had the mental skills required to gain and regain it!

The 5C's and parental roles

Back at Loughborough, important research questions for me from 2005 related to the roles that coaches and parents were really playing in athlete psychological development. Motivational, attentional, emotional and interpersonal skills and attributes appeared relevant and vital in virtually all sport performance contexts within which I had worked. For this reason, I developed a programme called the 5C's (Commitment, Communication, Concentration, Control and Confidence) to help youth football coaches gain greater confidence in integrating behaviours and strategies with added psychological value into their coaching sessions. The educational programme aimed to simplify psychology in a way that was accessible to coaches, parents and young athletes from any sport (see Harwood, 2008a).

In recent years, I have also taken great interest in the investment, experience and plight of parents in sport. It occurred to me that the literature in sport psychology tended to give parents a 'bad rap'. Yet, my experience of working with parents suggested that we needed to understand them before we judged them. Hence, I committed to a programme of research with one of my MSc students, Camilla Knight, that explored parental stressors in tennis and football (Harwood and Knight, 2009a, 2009b; Harwood *et al.*, 2010). We interviewed a lot of parents about their experiences and I encourage all students to conduct qualitative research such as this. The rich insights you gain simply nourish your understanding and offer excellent material for both educational group discussion and longer-term strategy.

Teaching and supervision

My years back at Loughborough between 2005 and 2010 were enriched by some great students and trainees to work with, and the Master's programme that I directed was something that I was particularly proud of. My practical experiences have shaped my teaching and I'm very careful to ensure that philosophy, ethics, counselling skills, and the various dimensions of professional practice represent core areas to challenge students during their course. This continues for the many trainee psychologists that I have supervised over the years. There is no doubt that working with my students has made me a better teacher, researcher and practitioner over the past fifteen years.

Closing out the match

In 2010, the Lawn Tennis Association approached me with a role that was too important and challenging for me to pass up. They wanted me to provide psychological services to their National Tennis Centre in London, and act as lead sport psychologist. The brief included working directly with coaches first and foremost, and I was quick to ensure that this is what the coaches wanted! Loughborough were yet again generous and flexible in allowing me to reduce my contract while ensuring that there were win–wins for the students and for research. So I headed on the 5.50 a.m. train to London for my two days per week and, as you can imagine, bringing my very varied experiences both back into my classroom and to fire up my research ideas.

This is a relationship that has now lasted over two years, but it is not the most important relationship in my life. This I share with Rebecca, my gorgeous wife who has managed my split weeks away as long as she gets to come to some of the better conference locations! Psychologists need a rock to lean against and to help them recharge, and I value the unconditional ways in which she supports my coping strategies.

As I close this chapter, I owe a lot of people a debt of gratitude for making my sport psychology life so colourful and varied, and for your support of the role of sport psychology. You all know who you are and you all know what you have added. Here's to the next 25 years or so…

References

Gardner, F. and Moore, Z. (2006) *Clinical Sport Psychology*. Champaign, IL: Human Kinetics.

Harwood, C. G. (2008a) Developmental consulting in a professional soccer academy: the 5C's coaching efficacy program. *The Sport Psychologist*, 22: 109–133.

——(2008b) From researcher to water boy: reflections on in-depth consulting with an elite British student-athlete team, in U. Johnson and M. Lindwall (eds) *Svensk Idrottspsykologisk Förenings årsbok 2008* [Swedish Yearbook of Sport Psychology], Stockholm: Trydells Tryckeri AB, pp. 28–48.

Harwood, C. G. and Knight, C. J. (2009a) Stress in youth sport: a developmental examination of tennis parents. *Psychology of Sport and Exercise*, 10: 447–456.

——(2009b) Understanding parental stressors in tennis: an investigation of British tennis parents. *Journal of Sports Sciences*, 27: 339–351.

Harwood, C. G. and Swain, A. B. (2001) The development and activation of achievement goals in tennis: 1. *The Sport Psychologist*, 15: 319–341.

—— (2002) The development and activation of achievement goals in tennis: II. *The Sport Psychologist*, 16: 111–138.

Harwood, C. G., Drew, A. and Knight, C. J. (2010) Parental stressors in professional youth football academies: a qualitative investigation of specialising stage parents. *Qualitative Research in Sport and Exercise*, 2: 39–55.

Harwood, C. G., Spray, C. S. and Keegan, R. (2008) Achievement goal theories in sport, in T. S. Horn (ed.) *Advances in Sport Psychology*, 3rd edn. Champaign, IL: Human Kinetics, pp. 157–186.

Higham, A., Harwood, C. G. and Cale, A. (2005) *Momentum in Soccer: Controlling the Game*. Leeds: Coachwise/1st for Sport Publications.

Jones, G., Swain, A. B. and Harwood, C. G. (1996) Positive and negative affect as predictors of competitive anxiety. *Personality and Individual Differences*, 20: 109–114.

Pain, M. A. and Harwood, C. G. (2004) Knowledge and perceptions of sport psychology within English soccer. *Journal of Sports Sciences*, 22: 813–826.

Pain, M. A. and Harwood, C. G. (2007) The performance environment in English youth soccer. *Journal of Sports Sciences*, 25: 1307–1324.

17

BECOMING A SPORT PSYCHOLOGIST

From Don Bradman to Luke Skywalker

Jamie Barker

My beginning in sport

For as long as I can remember, sport has played an integral part in my life – as a player, fan, coach, and now psychologist. I have found and still do find myself consumed by the drug that is competitive sport on a regular basis. Shortly after my sixth birthday I arrived home from school to find a brand new cricket bat, ball and gloves laid out in the garden – my life would never be the same again. At about the same time I watched a TV drama series called *Bodyline*. This series explored the infamous cricket 'Ashes' series between England and Australia in 1932–1933. More importantly, it was my first exposure to the famous Australian batsman: Don Bradman or 'The Don'. Given the new equipment and a hero to emulate, most of my spare time would now involve going to the local cricket club with my dad and trying to hit the ball as far as I could in the nets (just like The Don) and of course trying to bowl as fast as I could.

My dad, a very keen cricket player and follower, encouraged me shortly before my seventh birthday to join the local cricket club with some friends. The local club had a good reputation of coaching and developing some of the best young players in the county – my summers would never be the same again! At my cricket club I started to receive coaching from an ex-county professional cricketer and what he said was undeniably the truth. I hung on his every word and anecdote in my quest for further information to develop my skills. Through his coaching and the hours and hours my mum and dad played cricket with me in the park, I started to realize that I had quite a natural talent for the game of cricket. Moreover, my coach indicated that technically I was very good. At the age of 17, under the instruction of my county coaches (I was now part of the Leicestershire county academy), I moved to one of the best senior sides in the area so that I could further develop my skills and build my experience playing in the local Premier League. It was around this time that I also started to become aware and I guess somewhat interested in the role of the mind in relation to my cricket performance. During practice I would feel great and play really well – lots of confidence, freedom, and expression. When it came to games, on occasions, I started to feel different. What was going on? On occasions, I would walk out to bat and would feel heavy-legged, tense, and concerned about what I was going to do. Some days my batting would go great and I would play naturally and score the runs I so badly wanted. Other days (after a poor performance) I would sit in the pavilion asking questions of myself about technique and preparation, and even blaming my equipment. The game I loved so much and wanted to do so well at had become complicated – and the most frustrating part was that neither I nor my coaches had any answers. Sport psychology was largely on the periphery of professional cricket at this time and so I continued to practise hard and maintain my efforts, but slowly and surely my confidence and enjoyment for the game were dwindling. At the time I had no idea that my experiences would influence my interest in sport psychology and in years to come I would provide psychological support to sports people and in particular cricketers with similar performance-related issues, along with co-authoring a text on the psychology of cricket (Coterill and Barker, 2013).

My beginning in psychology

My involvement with psychology first came during my A-Level Sport Science course. Here I was introduced only briefly to the application of goal-setting in sport and exercise contexts. At this stage I had a genuine interest in all of the sport science disciplines which influenced my decision to study the subject at university.

During my first year at university I came across a sport psychology lecturer who would ultimately have a substantial influence on my career choice and aspirations: Professor Bruce Hale. In my first two years as an undergraduate I was exposed to a wealth of psychological topics spread across the areas of sport psychology, exercise psychology, and motor learning. For example, I learnt about humanistic, behaviourist, and cognitive psychological approaches, the importance of research methods, individual differences, group dynamics, expertise, personality, motivation, confidence, imagery, and so on. At the end of my second year I was very much interested and enthused by sport and exercise psychology – thanks to Professor Hale's enthusiasm. My motivation for the subject would gather further momentum when I approached Professor Hale about supervising my final year dissertation exploring the effects of pre-competitive anxiety on cricket batting performance using the time-to-event paradigm (Jones, 1995). Now under Bruce's guidance I set about collecting data using the Competitive State Anxiety-2 (Martens *et al.*, 1990). In return for Bruce's expert guidance I pledged to educate him on the laws of cricket – a task I still find myself doing to this day on a regular basis. The data from my thesis made interesting reading, so much so that Bruce suggested that we should submit an abstract to a forthcoming Association for Applied Sport Psychology (AASP) conference, which in time was duly accepted and presented.

Bruce's passion and enthusiasm for sport psychology had made a big impression, but more importantly he had helped to enhance my confidence in my ability and encouraged me to consider post-graduate study. During my MSc I would come into contact with Dr Marc Jones, who has arguably had the biggest influence on my career as a sport psychologist. In my initial work with Marc, I was given the opportunity to engage in applied sport psychology research, the result of which was my MSc thesis investigating the effects of a cognitive-behavioural intervention on cricketers' anxiety and performance based on Hanton and Jones (1999). From my MSc I was set on a PhD and thus after attending the International Society of Sport Psychology (ISSP) conference in Skiathos and reading Donald Liggett's (2000) book entitled *Sport Hypnosis* I approached Marc about supervising a PhD in the area of hypnosis. After much amusement about 'clucking like a chicken' and pocket watches, I managed to convince him that it would make an interesting and innovative contribution to the extant literature and so my PhD exploring the effects of hypnosis on sport performers' self-efficacy began. As part of the process I would gather a qualification in clinical hypnosis, along with obtaining British Association of Sport and Exercise Sciences (BASES) accreditation through the supervised experience scheme. As part of the BASES process, I learnt a number of key lessons about being a sport psychologist, but most importantly I undertook a counselling skills course which taught me a lot about myself – both good and bad. This course would have profound effect on how I worked with athletes in the future.

Following the completion of my PhD, I attained British Psychological Society (BPS) chartered status and later would become a registered sport and exercise psychologist with the Health and Care Professions Council (HCPC). I also completed a course in Rational-Emotive Behaviour Therapy (REBT) to further expand my sport psychology tool box and as a precursor to a programme of research. In 2007, Dr Chris Harwood presented me with two fantastic opportunities in professional soccer and cricket (see Barker *et al.*, 2011). Therefore, I have spent time working with academy players at Nottingham Forest Football Club, while working with players (from junior to professional), coaches and parents in my current role as club sport psychologist at Nottinghamshire County Cricket Club. In addition, I have worked as consultant to the England and Wales Cricket Board (ECB), the Football Association (FA), Staffordshire County Cricket Club, and the British Equestrian Federation (BEF). Typically, my roles as a consultant range from providing one-to-one support, parent education, conducting applied research interventions, developing psycho-education programmes, and team-building activities. More recently I have started to apply sport psychology principles to the business world and this has included presentations and workshops on performance psychology to the National Health Service (NHS) and SONY.

Currently, my role as a senior lecturer requires me to teach courses on sport psychology to undergraduate and postgraduate students, PhD supervision, research outputs through my applied research projects, and income generation through consultancy-related activities. At the time of writing I find myself having completed my role as guest editor for a special issue on single-case research methods and preparing a keynote presentation for an international conference regarding the use of hypnosis in sport. In truth, my work is stimulating and different each day and the best bits are I get to talk about sport and particularly cricket each day.

My approach as a sport psychologist

The focus of my applied work has been in the area of performance enhancement with athletes. Typical client groups include athletes and squads (elite/non-elite) who wish to use mental skills to enhance their performance levels. My initial approach to mental skills training was largely influenced by Marc Jones and stems from a cognitive-behavioural perspective (e.g., Mahoney, 1974). Based on a cognitive-behavioural approach I have used many techniques including imagery, self-talk, goal-setting, and hypnosis in my practice.

Recently I have become interested in the use of REBT (Dryden and Branch, 2008) and its application to sport psychology. We have challenged the irrational thoughts athletes have about themselves and sport performance using REBT principles (e.g., Turner and Barker, 2013). In addition, a lot of my practice also relies heavily on person-centred therapy (PCT) principles learnt from the counselling skills course I took during BASES accreditation (see Walker, 2010). To this end, I try to demonstrate genuineness, authenticity, empathy, and unconditional positive regard toward clients, drawing upon key counselling skills including active listening, paraphrasing, and summarizing (Murphy and Murphy, 2010). By adopting these skills, I hope to create a supportive, non-judgmental environment in which I encourage clients to reach their full potential. In PCT the client is the agent for self-change and hence is the one who directs and develops the process and progress of therapy (Walker, 2010). While I have found this approach to be hugely effective with most athletes, it can be a slow and lengthy process and one which is often uneconomical because there is no set number of sessions. Trying to use PCT in an academy set-up is often compromised by time and access constraints. In my current practice where I am frequently dealing with in excess of eight players during a visit, I have started to use solution-focused brief therapy (SFBT).

SFBT focuses on what clients want to achieve through therapy rather than on the problem(s) that made them seek help. The approach does not focus on the past, but instead, focuses on the present and future. The practitioner uses respectful curiosity to invite the client to envision their preferred future and then practitioner and client start attending to any moves towards it, whether these are small increments or large changes. To support this, questions are asked about the client's story, strengths and resources, and about exceptions to the problem (Berg, 1994).

While working with athletes I encourage them to play an active role in identifying and developing the mental skills that they believe are important to successful performance. Consequently, I make particular use of techniques such as performance profiling (Butler, 1989) and the Test of Performance Strategies (TOPS; Thomas *et al.*, 1999) which allows athletes to highlight their own perceived strengths and weaknesses, along with the prevalence of their mental skills usage in training and competition situations. I also look to use innovative methods to get athlete and coach to buy in and facilitate sport psychology education and adherence. For example, colleagues and I have set up a Facebook group at a cricket academy to further increase players' awareness and understanding of sport psychology principles, along with using psycho-physiological markers collected prior to pressure-training situations to demonstrate the link between thoughts and physiological responses.

In my work with teams I have, where possible, adopted an immersion approach, involving me helping to organize training drills, attending meals, squad practice sessions, matches, training camps, tours, coaching staff meetings, and wearing club kit (Bull, 1997). My playing and coaching background has allowed me to fully adopt this approach into my work in cricket and has helped me to develop rapport with players and coaches and, more importantly, allowed me to integrate psychology into their normal routines. Regarding team interventions, I have become interested in the use of personal-disclosure mutual-sharing (PDMS) as a technique with which to enhance group functioning (e.g., Windsor *et al.*, 2011). Therefore, during recent overseas cricket academy tours I have used PDMS sessions as core aspect of our team-building activities.

As I reflected back over my applied work to date, I recognized that I am somewhat eclectic in my consulting, given my use of cognitive-behavioural, REBT, PCT and SFBT approaches. Further, I noticed that I also have a keen eye for adopting techniques less familiar to sport psychology (e.g., hypnosis, REBT, and PDMS). Finally, I recognized that I have, where possible, moved from the more traditional psycho-education to more experiential practical activities and more solution-focused one-to-one sessions.

Evaluating my services

Evaluating the effectiveness of interventions in applied practice and research has been an area with which I have had an interest since I adopted a single-case research design (SCD) in my MSc thesis. Further, SCDs have had a big influence on how I try to structure my applied research and consultancy. The unique feature of SCDs is the capacity to conduct experimental investigations in applied settings with one or a few cases. Central to the method is the ability to rigorously evaluate the effects of interventions. SCDs have therefore been applied to many research contexts, including psychology, medicine, education, rehabilitation, social work, counselling, and sport psychology (Kazdin, 2011). Sport psychologists have been encouraged to use SCDs to provide evidence-based interventions for applied work with sport performers. Not surprisingly, therefore, many sport psychologists also use SCDs to justify the strength of their applied work with sport performers (see Barker *et al.*, 2011, 2013). Where appropriate, I have tried to adopt SCDs in my work with athletes and teams to give me confidence in my consultancy and to demonstrate performance gains (e.g., Barker and Jones, 2006; Turner and Barker, 2013); however, professional practice situations (e.g., crisis interventions) do not always permit the rigours of SCDs.

Most prevalent issues in my practice

The most prevalent performance issue which I work with is that of low sport confidence. I have come across sports people with such low self-confidence that they have considered quitting their sport due to slumps in performance or have developed learned helplessness, where they have a perceived absence of control over the outcome of their sporting situations. I also come across teams with low group confidence typically during crisis situations (e.g., trying to avoid relegation or overcoming a poor run of form). With individual sport performers (e.g., golfers, archers, and figure skaters), I have found a greater prevalence of debilitative cognitive anxiety. To this end, many of my clients often describe having thoughts of failure, worry, and concern about meeting their goals, and what others (including spectators, parents, and coaches) think of them. Linked to cognitive anxiety and worry, I am aware of the irrational thoughts athletes have about themselves and their performances and the associated negative emotions. For example, I used REBT with a cricketer who held beliefs which were firmly embedded in demands (i.e., *musts* and *needs*) to score runs and to be successful. While he firmly believed that his beliefs were appropriate, through REBT he realized that creating demands such as *needs* and *musts* also increased the negative emotions he was feeling prior to going out to bat. In essence, he was experiencing high levels of anxiety because of the demands he was creating. Overtime, he re-evaluated these beliefs to preferences which he described as 'a weight being lifted from his shoulders'.

In my work with academies I also see a lot of players with high expectations and perfectionist tendencies. For example, some players want a perfect performance all of the time and when they fall short of this, they demonstrate feelings of disappointment and dissatisfaction. Therefore, we have worked hard on educating players on perfectionism and the obvious implications in terms of negative mood, low confidence, and burnout (Hill et al., 2008).

Particularly in my work with cricketers, I encounter players (from junior to professional) who become easily distracted while performing because they do not have pre-performance routines (Cotterill, 2010). Therefore, I encourage all players to develop specific and precise routines for the disciplines of batting, bowling, and fielding where appropriate. To illustrate, a player with a lot of potential came to me about his inability to convert 50 runs to 100 runs when batting. After much discussion and observation it was clear that the player did not have a consistent pre-delivery routine. Moreover, the closer he got to 100, the more his focus turned to the scoreboard rather than on task-relevant cues. In time, we developed a pre-delivery routine which focused on his stance, balance, and the cue words of 'watch the ball' when the bowler was running in. The player is now a professional and has recently received international honours. In conversations with him he repeatedly points to his routine as having the greatest impact on the consistency of his batting performances in recent times.

Establishing my values

During the early stages of my consultancy career I naïvely believed that sport psychology should be welcomed by all players and coaches. In carrying this value forward I would often get somewhat downhearted when my enthusiastic and evangelical approach to sport psychology was not shared. Presently, and I guess to a large extent because I have more experience of being around elite and professional performers, I realize that sport psychology is not for all and should be a choice. Moreover, I have a greater understanding that some players will naturally adopt the mental and coping strategies that we often prescribe. I now take a more relaxed approach in presenting my values rather than going for the hard sell. I recognize that my enthusiasm for sport psychology is not shared by everyone and, for whatever reasons, some athletes do not respond with open arms. I now respect athletes' views more and try not to impose my beliefs on to them unduly. It is much more beneficial for me to work with those who see value in my services than to spread myself thinly across an entire squad.

Luke Skywalker syndrome and saving the universe

When I have undertaken one-to-one sessions in the past, I believed that I had special knowledge or powers to save the athletes from their issues and thus had a real 'saviour complex' or Luke Skywalker syndrome, as I like to call it! In essence, I wanted to help everyone I came into contact with and make a difference to them both as people and sport performers. Because I wanted to work effectively with them all of the time in every session, this often led to poor time management along with me presenting too much information and too many solutions. On reflection and going back to the principles of my approach, I now realize that typically sport psychologists do not 'fix' athletes, but provide support and guidance. To this end, when consulting with athletes, I am now keen to establish that my main aims in one-to-one work are to develop self-awareness and self-reflection. By reinforcing this philosophy, I feel more relaxed when working with clients who in turn have helped me to develop rapport with players and coaches.

Conclusion

In my early career I experienced much excitement and anxiety about having the right knowledge, doing the right thing, and working effectively. For example, I often wonder how my approach and services are perceived and valued. I often ask myself the question – am I doing a good job? While I use SCDs, and collect consultant evaluation data to inform me of my effectiveness, I have insecurities about doing a good job, and wonder how the coach and players perceive me. I have concerns about standing still and not being contemporary – what happens if I don't make a difference? From talking with fellow academics and practitioners, it would appear that I am somewhat 'normal' in my thoughts. The challenge is for me to keep them rational. Time to use some REBT!

Throughout my career I have been fortunate in the many opportunities I have had to develop my skills while working at the coal-face. I now feel comfortable in my approach and methods and this gives me confidence when going into new applied endeavours. I continue to be extremely motivated about working in applied settings and trying to maximize my effectiveness as a practitioner through contemporary and innovative methods.

Reflecting on my career has been therapeutic and enlightening. For the reader, I hope it offers some insight and honesty regarding how a sport psychologist may operate in the field, with the operative word being 'may'. As always, after reflecting on my work, I am left with more questions than answers. In closing, I am extremely indebted to the wonderful colleagues and friends I have for their support, guidance and encouragement – you all know who you are!

References

Barker, J. B. and Jones, M. V. (2006) Using hypnosis, technique refinement, and self-modelling to enhance self-efficacy: a case study in cricket. *The Sport Psychologist*, 20: 94–110.

Barker, J. B., McCarthy, P. J. and Harwood, C. G. (2011) Reflections on consulting in elite youth male English cricket and soccer academies. *Sport & Exercise Psychology Review*, 7: 58–72.

Barker, J. B., McCarthy, P. J., Jones, M. V. and Moran, A. (2011) *Single-Case Research Methods in Sport and Exercise Psychology*. London: Routledge.

Barker, J. B., Mellalieu, S. D., McCarthy, P. J., Jones, M. V. and Moran A. (2013) A review of single-case research in sport psychology 1997–2012: research trends and future directions. *Journal of Applied Sport Psychology*, 25: 4–32.

Berg, I. K. (1994) *Family-Based Services: A Solution-Focused Approach*. New York: W. W. Norton.

Bull, S. J. (1997) The immersion approach, in R. J. Butler (ed.) *Sport Psychology in Performance*. London: Arnold, pp. 177–203.

Butler, R. J. (1989) Psychological preparation of Olympic boxers, in J. Kremer and W. Crawford (eds) *The Psychology of Sport: Theory and Practice*. Leicester: BPS, pp. 74–84.

Cotterill, S. (2010) Pre-performance routines in sport: current understanding and future directions. *International Review of Sport & Exercise Psychology*, 3: 132–153.

Cotterill, S. and Barker, J. B. (2013) *The Psychology of Cricket: Developing Mental Toughness*. Birmingham: Bennion Kearny.

Dryden, W. and Branch, R. (2008) *The Fundamentals of Rational-Emotive Behavior Therapy*. Chichester: John Wiley & Sons, Ltd.

Hanton, S. and Jones, G. (1999) The effects of a multimodal intervention program on performers: II. Training the butterflies to fly in formation. *The Sport Psychologist*, 13: 22–41.

Hill, A. P., Hall, H. K., Appleton, P. R. and Kozub, S. A. (2008) Perfectionism and burnout in junior elite players: the mediating influence of unconditional self-acceptance. *Psychology of Sport and Exercise*, 9: 630–644.

Jones, G. (1995) More than just a game: research developments and issues in competitive anxiety in sport. *British Journal of Psychology*, 86: 449–478.

Kazdin, A. E. (2011) *Single-Case Research Designs: Methods for Clinical and Applied Settings*, 2nd edn. New York: Oxford University Press.

Liggett, D. R. (2000) *Sport Hypnosis*. Champaign, IL: Human Kinetics.

Mahoney, M. J. (1974) *Cognition and Behavior Modification*. Cambridge, MA: Ballinger.

Martens, R., Burton, D., Vealey, R. S., Bump, L. A. and Smith, D. E. (1990) Development and validation of the Competitive Anxiety State Inventory-2 (CSAI-2), in R. Martens, R. S. Vealey and D. Burton (eds) *Competitive Anxiety in Sport*. Champaign, IL: Human Kinetics, pp. 117–190.

Murphy, S. M. and Murphy, A. I. (2010) Attending and listening, in S. J. Hanrahan and M. B. Andersen (eds) *Routledge Handbook of Applied Sport Psychology*. London: Routledge, pp. 12–20.

Thomas, P. R., Murphy, S. M. and Hardy, L. (1999) Test of performance strategies: development and preliminary validation of a comprehensive measure of athletes' psychological skills. *Journal of Sports Sciences*, 17: 697–711.

Turner, M. and Barker, J. B. (2013) Examining the efficacy of Rational-Emotive Behavior Therapy (REBT) on irrational beliefs and anxiety in elite youth cricketers. *Journal of Applied Sport Psychology*, 25: 131–147.

Walker, B. (2010) The humanistic/person-centered theoretical model, in S. J. Hanrahan and M. B. Andersen (eds) *Routledge Handbook of Applied Sport Psychology*. London: Routledge, pp. 123–130.

Windsor, P., Barker, J. B. and McCarthy, P. J. (2011) Doing sport psychology: personal-disclosure mutual-sharing in professional soccer. *The Sport Psychologist*, 25: 94–114.

18

'IT TOOK ME 10 YEARS TO BECOME AN OVERNIGHT SUCCESS'

Brian Hemmings

The quote attributed to leading football/soccer manager Jose Mourinho (currently at Real Madrid) resonates with my experience as a sport psychologist. In this chapter on my 20-year career in the field of sport psychology I aim to convey how knowledge, professional training, perseverance, skill, luck, relationships and hard work have enabled me to make the transition from academic and part-time practitioner into my position (over the last six years) as a full-time consultant in private practice.

Early experiences

I was a keen sportsman as a youngster, with a particular liking and aptitude for football and cricket, though I was not quite good enough to seriously contemplate a career playing sport. I became disaffected with school and left aged 16 to do a variety of jobs, such as a window installer, postman/driver, and when travelling round Australia in my early twenties (while still playing football), a variety of manual labour roles. My first knowledge of sport psychology came from the back-page of newspapers; I recall an article on the England cricket team sometime in the late 1980s which had fascinated me.

Academic and professional training/'early' consultancy experiences, 1990–1997

I decided to enter university education as a 'mature' student aged 23, and a degree in the emerging sport-related courses seemed an ideal choice. I chose to do a Sport Studies undergraduate programme in Chichester, West Sussex, and was concerned that after seven years absence from education I might struggle to succeed. As it transpired, I worked tremendously hard and excelled, gaining a first class degree and a university-wide award for academic achievement. The design of the degree programme had enabled me to specialise to an extent in sport psychology. I had found a subject that I really enjoyed, and the tutors thought I produced excellent work. I continued to play football in the 'non-league' (semi-professional) pyramid of English football/soccer, the highlight being an appearance in the FA (Football Association) Cup, the prestigious cup competition. However, I do always joke that it was only the first-qualifying round! A knee injury eventually curtailed my playing during my undergraduate days.

In 1993, after completing my degree and getting married to Kim, and a short spell as a swimming pool manager, I was offered an opportunity to return to the University of Chichester (then the West Sussex Institute of Higher Education) to undertake a PhD. The Project Assistant position was funded by the English Sports Council on the Sport Science Support Programme (SSSP), attached to the sport of Amateur Boxing. The role was 50 per cent support to athletes and 50 per cent research. At that point I had no experience of working with athletes, and no knowledge of the world of amateur boxing. Working immediately in elite sport was a challenge, and on many occasions I felt out of my depth and I wondered if I had made the right career move, as I also considered my research progress was slow. However, although these were difficult times, the good fortune I experienced was to spend some time observing Richard Butler (the originator of performance profiling) who was the main psychology consultant to amateur boxing at that time. Of course, I was too inexperienced to comprehend the esteem with which he was held in the wider sport psychology community. Working with an Olympic sport allowed me access to the British Olympic Association (BOA) Psychology Advisory Group meetings. I really enjoyed attending these as I was able to listen to the views and experiences of some of the best sport psychologists of the time such as Brian Miller, Lew Hardy, Graham Jones, Austin Swain, Steve Bull, Dave Collins and Hugh Mantle, as well as interacting with the younger members of the profession such as Chris Shambrook and Chris Harwood. I successfully became a BOA Registered Psychologist in 1998.

During 1994–1997 I embarked on the British Association of Sport and Exercise Sciences (BASES) supervised experience scheme in sport psychology, which was still very much a developing programme in terms of its clarity regarding competencies and the type of experience needed to become accredited. I was gaining considerable experience in boxing in my SSSP role at training and competitions; had begun to work in motor racing (Hemmings, 1998) and a range of other team and individual sports, eagerly following leads to develop myself. For instance, I did a number of sessions with Cambridge University Women's Boat race crews to gain experience within a coactive team environment. One of my early motorsport clients has gone on to excel in Formula 1, and even today, many word-of-mouth referrals have come through that relationship. I was gaining undergraduate teaching experience at this time, although it was principally in physiology! These fledgling steps into teaching were challenging at times, particularly when teaching a subject that I had only studied to second year undergraduate level myself. I gradually gained more sport psychology teaching experience and with the birth of my first child Harriet (1995), and a PhD nearing completion, there was a need to start earning money. In autumn 1996 I started a temporary sport psychology lecturing position at the University of Winchester (then King Alfred's College of Higher Education).

Tim Holder was a big influence in this stage of my career. Tim had been to the Barcelona Olympics in 1992 as psychologist to table-tennis as part of his SSSP role and his presence at Chichester as a postgraduate facilitated a weekly 'quality circle' meeting which brought together senior members of sport psychology staff: Jan Graydon, Ian Maynard, Terry McMorris and Jane Lomax, and postgraduates Mark Bawden, Iain Greenlees and me. In this group we discussed current issues in sport psychology consultancy, academic papers, gave conference/workshop attendance feedback and reported our research progress. Meeting regularly with a group like this provided a great breadth of expertise when my knowledge and experience were in its infancy. Tim has remained a friend and professional colleague for nearly 20 years, sharing the same cognitive-behavioural approach to our work, and we now increasingly collaborate on projects (e.g. Hemmings and Holder, 2009). Nowadays I facilitate a similar professional practice group that meets every month to discuss consultancy reflections, research and teaching issues. This group is made up of ten sport psychologists and trainees of varying expertise and backgrounds using the blueprint that Tim Holder so effectively introduced to us.

Post accreditation/the 'middle' years, 1998–2005

I successfully achieved BASES Accreditation for the first time in mid-1997 and had also secured a permanent lecturing position at the University of Northampton (then Nene College of Higher Education). I completed my PhD in early 1998, and with a second daughter, Katie, just born, I was also getting busier in a new environment with many requests for consultancy. I started working with Northamptonshire County Cricket Club, and found myself in the slightly surreal situation whereby the head coach was someone I had, as a boy, regularly watched playing for England. The relationship with the club is still ongoing 15 years later (Hemmings, 2009), whereby several of the players I worked with in the late 1990s are now senior coaches at the club.

Although I had become accredited, with a degree and a PhD in sport psychology, I felt slightly uncomfortable using the title psychologist as I had little broader psychology knowledge. In 1999, I undertook an Open University Postgraduate Conversion Diploma to secure British Psychological Society (BPS) graduate registration. I could see the field of sport psychology was gaining more professional recognition and that the BPS would become more influential in the training and registration of British sport psychologists. (I became a BPS Chartered Psychologist in 2003.) However, my main motive was to improve my own knowledge base and while it was incredibly hard work to juggle a full-time lecturing job, consultancy work, research, external examining, professional body committee roles, more study

(I also had to complete a postgraduate teaching certificate) and home life (a third daughter, Natalie, was born in 2000), I gained a distinction on modules on social, cognitive and developmental psychology over a three-year period.

In 1997, I was invited to work for the English Golf Union with their boys' regional squads. This role quickly developed, and the governing body and national coach liked my delivery and rapport with players and coaches (client satisfaction is always a major source of my evaluation of consultancy). In 1999, I was asked to lead the delivery of the men's 'elite' squad and have fulfilled that role ever since, while also coordinating the delivery of sport psychology by other consultants to all national and regional squads. My reputation grew in the sport, and I was asked by the English Women's Golf Association to also lead their sport psychology provision. While I had no prior playing knowledge of golf, I quickly became immersed in the sport and found it a great environment for support work. In other sports, I have on occasion experienced the well-reported stigma toward the discipline; however, in golf it was refreshing to find that psychology was well accepted and almost part of the culture of the game. Search the internet for golf psychology books and the reader will quickly see the wealth of texts aimed at the average golfer, which goes some way to explain the popularity of psychology for many players. In this period it was not unusual for me to be working with squads 60–80 days a year at home and abroad, travelling to competitions, delivering coach education and increasingly working with professional players privately. In 2002, I really enjoyed writing and recording a narrative golf audio CD programme in conjunction with a leading golf magazine, and arranged and hosted two national golf psychology conferences (2002 and 2004) which brought together psychologists, coaches and administrators to listen to leading speakers in our field, such as Joan Duda and Aidan Moran. In 2002, I developed my own golf psychology website (www.golfmind.co.uk) to better publicise professionally trained sport psychologists working in the United Kingdom. I have now written considerably on my golf work and collaborated on golf research projects (e.g. Hemmings, 2003, 2008, 2011; Hemmings *et al.*, 2008; Nicholls *et al.*, 2010). While I had never had an overriding plan to establish a niche as a sport psychologist specialising in golf, opportunities kept presenting themselves, and ultimately it seems that this cycle kept on reinforcing itself the more I worked within the sport. Indeed, in 2000, after the Sydney Olympics I decided to end my eight-year relationship with amateur boxing to focus on my increasing golf work. I had completed two Olympic and Commonwealth Games cycles with boxing. While I helped prepare boxers for these events, I did not attend any of those Games due to accreditation scarcity. However, I had attended European and World Championships and gained extensive experience with elite athletes in a combat sport.

Transition to self-employment and private practice, 2006–present day

In 2006, I received an offer from within golf to increase my consultancy workload, and I felt I had to make a decision whether to leave my university position to go into private practice full-time if I were to accept the invitation. With a mortgage to pay and a family to support, it was an anxious time to leave the security of a full-time salary. I negotiated a one-day-a-week 'sabbatical' with the university for one year to act as a safety net should self-employment not work out, but since then since I have successfully built up my private practice, mainly working in amateur/professional golf (70 per cent of time) and cricket/motorsport. In more recent times I have really enjoyed delivering BPS Learning Centre approved masterclasses in sport and golf psychology for sport psychologists. Here I feel I am able to discuss finer aspects of delivery that may not appear in the literature which, in my opinion, is often too much about 'techniques' rather than the 'process' of consultancy. In 2010, I also developed an online education course (www.golfpsychologycoaching.com) for golf coaches in conjunction with the Professional Golf Associations of GB&I and Europe that is currently being undertaken by coaches all around the world. I do believe there is great potential for coach and athlete online education in well-designed and approved programmes, which are accessible without time and travel constraints. I am also actively involved in research through an affiliation with St Mary's University College in London, and in the supervision and development of sport psychologists (e.g., Katz and Hemmings, 2009). In more recent times I have become a Christian and am exploring the aspects of faith in sport psychology practice where appropriate (e.g., Gamble and Hill, in press; Watson and Nesti, 2005; see also www.bacip.org.uk). Now six years into private practice I can say that the uncertainty which may accompany being self-employed has diminished to a large extent; however, like the experience of so many professional athletes with whom we consult, that uncertainty is always there. In 2010, I was very honoured to receive a BASES Fellowship for 'esteemed personal achievement, skills, knowledge and service to BASES and the sport and exercise science community', and today, a commitment to professionalism is still the mainstay of my working life.

In 20 years of practice as a sport psychologist I have been privileged to work with many world champions, professional and elite amateur athletes and to travel to places in the world I might not have otherwise visited. While there are so many lessons I have learned, here are five that come to mind.

Five specific lessons learned

1 Develop your own approach

In the current masterclasses that I offer on consultancy skills, I talk in depth on developing a personal style of delivery and on working with each athlete as an individual. The sport psychology literature constantly tells us to individualise interventions, yet rarely tells us how to achieve this. I work on something I call the 'Elvis' (Presley) approach. Essentially, this means that just as there was only one unique Elvis, there is also only one of each of us and we should seek to utilise our own particular strengths and personality in our work. For instance, my work often includes humour, creativity and story-telling. Over my career I have sought out workshops on comedy and improvisation skills for trainers, story-telling, and in recent years undertook voice coaching. I have stepped outside of the sport psychology domain in my professional development activities and sought to bring new skills to my practice. The 'Elvis' approach also applies to the individual client (team or individual) with whom you are consulting. I believe my role is to find out what makes the athlete unique and help them shape/believe in that uniqueness.

2   Get peer supervision throughout professional practice

I am a firm believer in good supervision for trainees *and* those already qualified. Since my original accreditation with BASES in 1997, I have undertaken regular (now monthly) peer supervision with a trusted and experienced colleague who brings a different skill set and background (also qualified for clinical work) to his sport psychology practice (he is also self-employed). We supervise one another in a reciprocal fashion depending on which consultancy issues we are facing. I have often stated to others that this supervision has had a big impact on my continuing development as a practitioner. Unlike other psychology disciplines and therapeutic approaches, sport psychology does not insist on regular post-qualification supervision, yet I am convinced peer supervision promotes good professional practice. Many times in this supervision through sharing my concerns, doubts and questions, my own reflections have been deepened and shaped toward more positive actions, and this has led to increased confidence in my practice as a result. Handling disappointments, dealing with conflict, coping with insecurity and personal stress all affect sport psychologists as much as they do athletes and need to be managed. Also being self-employed, talking with someone in a similar position has helped to shape my thinking on business matters, pricing, and general negotiation skills which do not typically form part of sport psychology training.

3   Try and maintain a healthy work–life balance

Like any other working professional, the work–life balance is of importance to sport psychologists (Waumsley *et al.*, 2010). I have had the misfortune to experience depression and some of this mental health issue was due to a poor work–life balance. Wheeler (2007) has noted how therapists and psychologists can be strengthened in their capacity to empathise with clients through their own painful life experiences, and I do believe that my own experience of depression has made me a better practitioner in many ways. With the boundaries between work and life (home/social) becoming seemingly increasingly blurred in many professions, and potentially even more difficult to manage due to the unusual/unsocial hours of sport psychology practice, I would encourage sport psychology training programmes and supervision to consider education to manage the work–life balance in neophyte sport psychologists.

4 Build effective relationships

In my early days as an accredited professional it took time before I realised that the relationship between psychologist and athlete/coach is critical for success (Hemmings, 1999). While the importance of the professional relationship in sport psychology practice is now firmly embedded in the literature, I still feel sport psychology needs to do more to centralise the importance of listening skills and the development of relationships in effective consulting. In our BPS handbook (Katz and Hemmings, 2009) and our BASES counselling skills and working alliance workshops over many years, Jon Katz and I have proposed that for too long sport psychology has been overly focused on 'content' or 'intervention' questions. I believe the successful long-term associations I have had with multiple athletes, coaches and organisations have come about through maintaining human relationships, showing you care, and sustained professionalism rather than through any particular personal excellence in delivering 'techniques'. Many athletes comment that I am a great listener, and this skill should not be underestimated when trying to build effective relationships with athletes.

5 Learn from others

I echo the interview comments made by Dan Gould in a recent edition of the BPS magazine, *The Psychologist* (July, 2012). Dan points out that all aspiring psychologists should recognise that those with whom you work, consult or teach are as much a source of knowledge about psychology as sport psychologists are, and we should continue to learn from all of them. For instance, I sat with a 13-year-old golfer last year who, when discussing his poor performance with me, said, 'I guess a setback is only a setback if you let it set you back.' I loved the simplicity of this statement and have since shared that comment with professional players, who have reappraised their thinking after disappointments through these words. I have also been very honoured to have worked with and listened to so many brilliant sport psychologists over the years. I have sought collaborations with like-minded people, and working closely with others in the same field has brought many rich learning experiences. For instance, last year Ken Ravizza was over in the UK and I took the day away from work and travelled some way to hear him speak, as I had never had the opportunity to do so before. Recently, I enjoyed meeting Richard Cox (also an author in this book) for lunch and it was fascinating to hear of his life experiences and opinions on sport psychology. I maintain contact with my golf book co-author Hugh Mantle, a hugely experienced and successful Olympic coach and psychologist, who has taught me a great deal. Often, being self-employed, I work in isolation, and informally meeting other sport psychologists, peer supervision, the professional practice group activity, and professional development activities present the chances to continue to learn from others.

Conclusion

To conclude, my career in sport psychology has been successful in so many ways. I am fortunate to do a job I really enjoy; more like a hobby I get paid for. The work is both challenging and rewarding and I have met so many great people. My work and ideas are still developing. I am still learning.

References

Gamble, R. and Hill, D. (in press) Revs and psychs: role, impact and interaction of sport chaplains and sport psychologists within English premiership soccer. *Journal of Applied Sport Psychology*.

Hemmings, B. (1998) Applied sport psychology and motor racing: two case studies, in H. Steinberg, I. Cockerill and A. Dewey (eds) *What Sport Psychologists Do*. Leicester: British Psychological Society, pp. 62–67.

——(1999) Making contact in consultancy work: laying the foundations for successful intervention, in H. Steinberg and I. Cockerill (eds) *Sport Psychology in Practice: The Early Stages*. Leicester: British Psychological Society, pp. 16–23.

——(2003) Dealing with distractions, in I. Greenlees and A. Moran (eds) *Concentration Skills in Sport*. Leicester: British Psychological Society, pp. 43–54.

——(2008) Golf: an applied perspective. *Sport and Exercise Psychology Review*, 4(2): 28–32.

——(2009) Managing distractions in test cricket, in B. Hemmings and T. Holder (eds) *Applied Sport Psychology: A Case-Based Approach*. Chichester: John Wiley & Sons, Ltd, pp. 33–50.

——(2011) Sport psychology and the English Golf Union: a case study of a winter elite squad support programme. *Sport and Exercise Psychology Review*, 7: 34–47.

Hemmings, B. and Holder, T. (2009) *Applied Sport Psychology: A Case-Based Approach*. Chichester: Wiley-Blackwell.

Hemmings, B., Mantle, H. and Ellwood, J. (2008) *Mental Toughness for Golf: The Minds of Winners*. London: Green Umbrella.

Katz, J. and Hemmings, B. (2009) *Counselling Skills Handbook for the Sport Psychologist*. Leicester: BPS.

Nicholls, A., Hemmings, B. and Clough, P. (2010) Stress appraisals, emotions, and coping among international adolescent golfers. *Scandinavian Journal of Medicine and Science in Sports*, 20: 346–355.

Watson, N. and Nesti, M. (2005) The role of spirituality in sport psychology consulting: an analysis and integrative review of literature. *Journal of Applied Sport Psychology*, 17: 228–239.

Waumsley, J., Hemmings, B. and Payne, S. (2010) Work–life balance, role-conflict and the UK sport psychology consultant. *The Sport Psychologist*, 24: 245–262.

Wheeler, S. (2007) What shall we do with the wounded healer? *Psychodynamic Practice*, 13: 245–256.

19

A GLANCE AT THE 'TO DO' LIST OF DR ZOE KNOWLES...FROM OLYMPIC PARK TO LOCAL CHILDREN'S CENTRE IN A DAY

Zoe Knowles

As I write this chapter I am travelling by train to the London 2012 test event to work with a Paralympic athlete as his sport psychologist. I have the usual essentials of laptop, mobile and the ever present 'to do' list and hope the timings and requirements of this particular role over two days allow me to tackle some of my other duties that form my 'typical' working week. In looking for a starting point for this chapter (and having attempted to initiate writing several times), I begin with my 'to do' list which in its entirety is in fact a startling representation of all the facets of my role. The list reads: undergraduate exam marking; complete article for *Early Years Educator*; complete amendments for *BMC Public Health* journal article and *JSEP* articles; review article for *The Sport Psychologist*; submit *Reflective Practice* book proposal; arrange meeting with Children's Centre managers; review PhD student's chapter; travel, accommodation and abstract for symposium chair role, ICSEMIS 2012 conference. On the opposite page are: pay dance school fees, school trip money, and book family dentist appointments. It is from here that I start this chapter with a view to explaining chronologically the journey that has created that list.

I studied BSc (Hons) coaching science at Liverpool JMU, then an MSc in sport psychology, and was subsequently employed there as a graduate teaching assistant. I was accredited by BASES in 2000 and was teaching, studying for a PhD and engaged in consultancy full-time. Alongside this, I had success coaching national age group champions and attending the national squad training programs. My work since has been that of juggling these roles of teaching, research and consultancy in varying proportions each new academic year and I still remain at JMU as a staff member. My planning and role are defined by the academic calendar of teaching, the Olympic calendar for consultancy and for research for the Research Excellence Framework. These demands do not always synchronize well; however, I enjoy the variation and skills that each week brings; the regular pay each month, and that no two consecutive weeks are the same. Early experiences in these roles were shaped by opportunities that arose by way of each of these demands and several key people with whom I remain in touch today. My research mentor Professor David Gilbourne arrived at JMU while I was still an undergraduate and our first encounter was when I was reprimanded in class for talking (I still state to this day it wasn't me). My PhD took 10 years in total (for a variety of reasons explained later) and we have continued to write beyond my PhD and are now supervising a PhD student together. We have shared much over the last 16 years, including a drink at my wedding, and I will always be grateful for his influence on my work. Dr Hugh Mantle OBE and Dr Alison Rhodius (JFK University California) were key in shaping me as a consultant. I am a believer in surrounding yourself with positive people and many other mentors/peers have been influential in many ways. My employment brings me into contact with such people daily and I often wonder whether I would have 'made it' in the world of private consultancy which can be inherently isolating. My parents tell me I'm bossy, stubborn and determined by nature, and colleagues would define me as organized and ambitious. I am also a wife to a Grenadier Guard sergeant with extensive operational tour experience, the mother of two girls, and hold several roles within the community.

Sport psychology was never my first thought as a career. I had made university applications primarily for physiotherapy with sports science as a fallback option to then enter teaching. Exam grades hadn't gone according to plan and, in fact, the week before I joined JMU, I was simultaneously considering turf science and golf course management and diagnostic radiotherapy! My own sporting background both as a gymnast and then a coach helped me onto the JMU programme two days before the course started. Coaching continued to be influential in my development as a researcher (see Knowles *et al.*, 2001) and a practitioner when working with other sports. Interestingly, I have never been a consultant in my own sport of gymnastics and didn't mention my professional role while I was still in the national squad system with my performers. Since leaving coaching I have been asked why I didn't 'let on', and fellow coaches have reacted well and been educated by my research work on reflective practice and psychological skills-based studies with gymnasts.

In 1999, I started working with GB archery, where I had no knowledge of the demands, techniques, tactics or structure of the sport. What was accepted straight away was my credibility, having both studied and practised elite coaching and thus gained knowledge and expertise of the realms of elite performance demands and the coaching role. This has been influential in my philosophy ever since, which has been to work with, through, in co-operation or alongside the coach as a psychologist. I have had the privilege of working alongside and learning from excellent coaches and I would suggest all neophyte sport psychology practitioners both gain some coaching experience themselves and/or actively seek out shadowing opportunities in their professional training. I will always remember questioning Dr Mantle about his role as a highly acclaimed canoe slalom coach and his qualifications as a sport psychologist; did they complement or hinder his role? 'Some of the best performance coaches are sport psychologists; we can learn a lot about our work from the way they do theirs,' he said. I agree entirely. The coach can assist with reinforcement of strategies/interventions and being your 'eyes and ears' at the event, and also more recently recognize the need for psychologist intervention and facilitate consultancy at a distance through Skype or phone.

2003/2004 brought a change in the 'typical' work I had known for several years associated with teaching, consultancy and research. The PhD was suspended and I became increasingly involved in supporting GB archery in the approach to the Olympics. Over the summer periods of both years I travelled extensively with the squads in Europe, including periods in the holding camps in Cyprus. This was demanding work on each 16-hour day with attendance at the field in stifling temperatures, managing the team in the absence of others who were struck down with illness, remaining at cross-border checkpoints for hours with athletes who did not have the correct visa, carrying luggage for disabled athletes, shopping for food preferences/forgotten items, and then having individual meetings with archers late into the night. I was not trained for team management, especially that of juniors, and the responsibility of travelling and acting *in loco parentis*. I learned quickly, asked for advice, expected the unexpected and dealt with all that was thrown at me. It is perhaps easy to take the line of 'that's not my role' and contractually that position could have been argued. However, such tasks gained respect, credibility and all helped with the efficient functioning of the team supporting the athlete. Likewise, when appropriate, being able to handle your own at pool, jet skis, card games and 7 a.m. fitness sessions overlooking the Mediterranean all helped too!

Archery had recently made the transfer to being Lottery-funded and was now affluent, with money, support services and high-profile coaches on the back of a system which historically had been funded by individuals, run by volunteers and was steeped in tradition. Supporting this transitional phase was a challenge and, for me, widened the focus of the 'client' being that of the athlete to that of the organization of which the archers were one part. There were organizational changes to new methods, accountabilities, targets, roles and regimes that were influencing the archers and manifesting themselves via underperformance and intra-team issues. In essence, this occurred at a time when (in terms of financial support, coaching and sports science) the archers had never had it so good. It was here I learned that the sport psychologist's role is that which encompasses problem solving and supporting all facets of the system and its personnel, including coaches, committees, the governing body hierarchy, as well as the athletes themselves. I distinctly remember a team meeting over a meal in a backstreet café in Germany where straight talking, conflict and resolution were set out and discussed in line with the servings of starter, main course and dessert. Conflict is productive if managed appropriately, and I still use this technique now as it helps to focus timings and the process.

Some sport psychologists see themselves on the front line wearing a tracksuit and sitting alongside other support personnel ready for instant recognition at points of achievement, but this, for me, has not been the case. That is not to say recognition hasn't occurred, it has, but has been somewhat covert and less brash than a direct mention in a media interview or an acceptance speech. I felt considerable disappointment at not being able to support the team in the 2004 Games itself, due to a lack of accreditation, having invested time and compromised on many other personal life goals to commit to the pre-Olympic period. This lay heavy on me for some time and influenced a change of course in my work. London 2012 has brought less financial and access barriers as regards the UK-based sport psychologist being at the event with the athletes; however, I believe the role will in the future become less about in event services and more about working at a distance with technology (Skype, etc.).

I had returned to JMU in late 2004 with a sense of wanting to complete the PhD exploring reflective practice. I had finished coaching gymnastics, and consultancy was minimal, thus allowing more time for other tasks. My first article in *The Sport Psychologist* journal (Anderson *et al.*, 2004) had created quite a stir in the research community, stimulating comment and inducing others to join the debate, and I was now at a point whereby promotion/progression in the realms of Higher Education Institution required a PhD. The year 2005 brought changes to the family with the arrival of my first daughter and then my second in 2006. I returned part-time which brought its own challenges as regards managing my time, yet the PhD was still vehemently pursued. Since its proposal, my PhD work had moved from its original context of sports coaching to sport psychology, as a consequence of me finishing coaching and developing further as a sport psychology practitioner. I almost felt fraudulent continuing to research this field and concluded this work in print via papers and chapters. I had supervised my first student through to sport psychology accreditation and published a second paper in 2007 reporting on this experience (Knowles *et al.*, 2007). The PhD was completed in 2009 after a turbulent period in my personal life and surviving on approx. 5 hours sleep per night.

I returned to full-time work progressively in 2010 and took stock of my situation and capacities. I was acutely aware of the need to manage my work–life balance, and there was now even less scope to work as a sport psychology consultant which typically demanded evening and weekend contact, flexibility and being always available on the phone as standard. Practically, this now wasn't possible for me to work at these times or in this way. At a personal level I had really enjoyed being in the pre-school 'system' in the UK with sessions at Children's Centres, swimming, activity classes, in essence, being involved in my children's development. I had never really considered the 'exercise' component of the title 'sport and exercise psychologist' and so began discussions with a group of researchers in JMU who researched active play. I began a relationship with this group and have, to date, co-authored seven research papers, several evaluation-based reports associated with pre-school physically active play in childcare environments, playground/recess-based play, natural play environments, and am now embarking on a collaborative project with Liverpool City Council improving fathers' engagement with their pre-school children using active play.

As a sport psychologist, you acquire knowledge and skills that have a transferable quality across domains and populations. Sometimes this isn't obvious and you have to make the conceptual leaps yourself and be creative in your delivery/research methods and interventions. Observing behaviour using systems in coaching bears resemblance to those used to observe playground activity and interactions; working with early years professionals drew on skills I had learned in working with coaches, and parents of inactive, overweight children have the same fears and concerns at working with a psychologist as those of elite athletes. I recognize too the fact that with such projects I was not only a consultant/academic but also a consumer as a parent myself. Working with PhD students who themselves had no children, in such fields, and also that of weight management, I found myself at times advising simply as a parent and as a childcare user. I make no apologies for using some of the ideas from my child-minder, pre-school teacher and drop-in classes at libraries, community centres that I have come across! Perhaps here it is pertinent to note that while sport psychologists (and I include myself here) advocate that within every athlete is a person, and we should attend to that in our work, and that life events, daily hassles, etc., can influence the athlete's performance-based mental state, I would argue that this is also true of the consultant. My role has been shaped by my life experiences and influences on my own identity, yet, it has provided me with opportunities to be innovative, maintain a work–life balance and brought success across domains.

January 2011 brought the Research Excellence Framework to the forefront of the School of Sport and Exercise Sciences' agenda along with other HEIs in the UK. The London 2012 Olympic Games were also less than 18 months away. My employment role, at this point, focused on the former with a need to establish four high quality papers for inclusion in the REF submission. Ironically, these are now focused on physical activity, exercise and health (e.g., Mackintosh *et al.*, 2011) and not sport psychology, and I felt a sense of stability in the timely, significant and positive move to this domain across research, consultancy and teaching. However, I was still, perhaps through history and loyalty, involved in reflective practice research and advising other HEIs and associations (BASES) on the topic area, supervision of pre-accreditation students in sport psychology and undertaking a research project on mindfulness and flow in elite swimmers. In 2010, I was also accepted for Chartered Sport and Exercise Psychologist (C.Psychol.) status with the British Psychological Society.

Within one month in Spring, several opportunities arose which were about to change my role once again. I was approached to supervise a PhD in reflective practice, to edit a book on the topic and to write a further paper in the series of publications in *The Sport Psychologist* with an esteemed sport/clinical psychologist (Knowles *et al.*, 2012). I was also approached through the British Paralympic Association to support via regular consultancy a locally based Paralympian in his approach to 2012. I considered the role I had and the changes that could be made to encompass sport once again. Was it workable in view of time and personal circumstances? My children were older, my husband was now home-based and non-deployable due to embarking on retirement, REF papers were in, and I felt a sense that I had missed this work. Was it appropriate to have such a wide focus across physical activity to sport, pre-school to elite populations? Yes, all were within my skills, expertise and qualifications. Here, unashamedly, I sought advice from line managers and my husband and took the lot on.

Working with the Paralympian came on the back of unsuccessful working relationships he had had with previous sport psychologists, being geographically isolated from centralized support at the National Tennis Centre, and following a referral based on the need to control his behaviour, aggression and being prone to outbursts and non-compliance. He was local to Liverpool, was a former Marine (though was not disabled through this role), and was a devoted family man according to both his Twitter feed biography and the first point he made at our initial meeting. We have worked together since and are achieving great things. I am privileged to work as part of a team including his personal coach, national coach, physiotherapist, wheelchair supplier, strength and conditioning coach and (most recently) his fiancée. We communicate each week, led by the athlete, on progress, issues and updates and are all contributing to a change in the discipline, attitude and compliance to training and authority. This has reaped rewards on the court, coupled with a program of developing awareness of his behaviour, using match analysis to develop on-court decision-making and intervention skills on breathing and timing within a pre-shot routine. The BPA have also been active in advising on a pre-Games 'health check' in view of the home advantage and additional pressures this can bring. This has also informed my work with the Paralympian and for the first time I have felt a part of a 'system' as regards support and the sharing of ideas outside of those I come across daily in my work. I have, however, been unable to attend the face-to-face events hosted by the BPA and this is perhaps as a consequence of the academic cycle I work in being at variance with the pre-event period for London 2012. I have also joined an independent sport psychology peer support group who meet periodically throughout the year and I believe this is an important investment for my accountability, practice scrutiny and professional development.

I want to finish with a few points on consultant effectiveness. How do I know I am good at what I do?, how is it measured?, how is it used? With research output this is easy, peer review followed by acceptance, plus journal impact factors and volume. With evaluation-based project work, further commissions or grant funding indicate effectiveness. With consultancy, this is more opaque and I have always used client recommendation, formal references from funding agencies, together with peer review and reflective practice. I believe a variety of mechanisms can provide a multi-dimensional assessment of effectiveness in consultancy and it is from this we learn about ourselves, our services and hopefully can inform our profession. I will leave the final word to my Paralympian who was interviewed recently about his psychology support work:

> Zoe understands what I need to help me achieve more and pushes me to the next level. She's a great listener and also says the right things at the right

times which is important. Zoe has been giving me habits and routines to help me out during play and turned negative parts of my games into positives. She has helped me with pre- and post-match visualization techniques that help get my mind straight. Since she's been part of my team, my performance has gone up another level and the results speak for themselves.

Now, where's that 'to do' list...?

References

Anderson, A., Knowles, Z. and Gilbourne, D. (2004) Reflective practice for sport psychologists: concepts, models, practical implications and thoughts on dissemination. *The Sport Psychologist*, 18: 188–203.

Knowles, Z., Gilbourne, D., Borrie, A. and Nevill, A. (2001) Developing the reflective sports coach: a study exploring the processes of reflective practice within a higher education coaching programme. *Reflective Practice*, 2: 186–201.

Knowles, Z., Gilbourne, D., Tomlinson, V. and Anderson, A. (2007) Reflections of the application of reflective practice for supervision in applied sport psychology. *The Sport Psychologist*, 21: 109–122.

Knowles, Z., Katz, J. and Gilbourne, D. (2012) Reflective practice within elite consultancy: Diary extracts and further discussion on a personal and elusive process. *The Sport Psychologist*, 26: 454–469.

Mackintosh, K., Knowles, Z., Ridgers, N. D. and Fairclough, S. (2011) Using formative research to develop physical activity. CHANGE!: a curriculum-based health-education intervention. *BMC Public Health*, 11: 8–31.

AFTERWORD

Paul McCarthy and Marc Jones

We are indebted to the contributors for their honest, insightful and edifying reflections on becoming sport psychologists. Not only has this been a fascinating book to edit but we have also learned greatly from their experiences inside and outside sport. What follows is our reflection on these contributions but it is by no means an exhaustive summary of the countless issues that have emerged from the rich diversity of insight.

A debt of gratitude

Sport psychology is a young discipline. Doubtless, part of the reason we belong to such a vibrant and growing discipline emerges from the determination of the pioneers of sport psychology, many of whom have contributed to this book. More than one contributor commented on 'flying by the seat of their pants' as they sought to establish in a habitually sceptical sporting world, their own credibility and often that of the discipline. Their diligent groundwork means that sport psychology is increasingly accepted among the sporting milieu with exciting opportunities available for those wishing to practise sport psychology. Becoming a sport psychologist is much more carefully defined today. Professional bodies outline distinct education and training routes for students who want to become a sport psychologist. For example, the professional organisations listed in the appendix present the education and training routes to become a sport psychologist in the USA, Australia, New Zealand, Canada, Ireland and the UK.

What's in a name?

In Shakespeare's *Romeo and Juliet*, Juliet argues: 'that which we call a rose by any other name would smell as sweet'. In other words, the names of things do not matter, only what they are. Yet, societies and associations in many countries have invested to protect the title 'sport psychologist' for those who have undertaken recognised training and education routes. Ironically, it is sometimes advantageous in sport settings to avoid using the title 'sport psychologist' and use something less imposing such as 'mental skills coach'. We feel, however, that with the prominence of sport psychology programmes at university, accredited training routes and constructive reflections about the work of sport psychologists in the media, people are more aware of *what we are* and how we can support them.

Psychology in, and of, sport

The association between sport psychology and its parent discipline also emerged. Some of our contributors who had studied or trained in psychology wrote about 'stumbling' upon sport psychology. It does seem that the application of psychology to sport is less visible to those who studied psychology compared to those who studied sport science. The relationship between psychology and sport psychology has been debated elsewhere, in which the interdependence between psychology and sport psychology and other disciplines such as organisational psychology were highlighted (see Arnold, 2006; Conroy, 2006; Hardy, 2006; Walker *et al.*, 2006). A consensus in this debate was that sport psychology was an independent discipline, but that it has much to give back to its parent discipline. This interdependence was particularly highlighted by Hardy (2006), when he outlined the contribution of research in sport to stress and performance, meta-cognitive skills, rehabilitation from injury and motor control. From the perspective of practice, Ken Hodge argued that the field of sport psychology has the potential to make a broader contribution to society through the application of techniques developed in sport to a wider client base. Of course, this wider application must be based on a solid foundation and reputation within sport.

Are we 'worth our salt'?

Sport psychologists are constantly challenged by their image and reputation in sport settings. Perhaps the allegory of the medical doctor selling elixirs from a wagon in the nineteenth century shows the time required to establish a respected profession is protracted (Illich, 1976; Meyers, 1997). Similar to medicine, we are improving our product through empirically validated interventions and gaining acceptance by managing the expectations of those we serve, celebrating our achievements and aggregating best practice through scholarly publications. Meyers (1997) argued for higher standards in published research, training new professionals and ethical behaviour. We are moving toward these higher standards. Perhaps there is no better example of how this should be done than what Ron Smith illustrated in Chapter 14 in this volume. The book he co-wrote with Frank Smoll on youth sport coaching was not written when he had the idea, but rather after thirty years of research, so the principles and behavioural guidelines are based on empirical evidence (Smith and Smoll, 2012).

For those working in sports settings, our greatest challenge is showing others that we are *worth our salt*. We have to show people that what we do is worth their time and money. After all, people have played sport successfully for thousands of years. They have trained diligently, coped with adversity and excelled under extreme pressure, so what could a sport psychologist possibly offer them? It seems a reasonable question to ask, especially when one considers that most athletes have a coach or a manager to prepare them psychologically for competition. Former Glasgow Celtic manager, Gordon Strachan, said: 'You can have all the sports psychologists you like but, in terms of motivating people; he [Sir Alex Ferguson] is the best' (Wilson, 2011). As sport psychologists, we know that our role is more varied than motivating athletes for competition. For example, we help athletes to cope with the psychological and emotional consequences of injury; we prepare referees psychologically for competition, and advise coaches about suitable strategies to build cohesive squads. But in an age of science, just listing what we do as sport psychologists is not enough. We need evidence to support the claims we make about our discipline. Those sceptical about our profession should guide our sceptical thinking – to construct and understand a reasoned argument while recognising a fallacious or fraudulent one. The issue is not whether we like the conclusion drawn from our reasoning but whether the conclusion follows from the premise (Sagan, 1996).

Maintaining the instrument

In Chapter 5, David Tod remarked that he was a 'service delivery instrument' and because of this realisation, it was important to maintain himself as you would any other complicated instrument. David, among others, suggested one way to achieve this goal is through peer supervision. From our experiences in applied practice and supervising trainees, we wholeheartedly recommend peer supervision and peer support. These are common features of similar disciplines (e.g., counselling), whose aim it is to create and maintain the highest standards of care for the client and the counsellor. Brian Hemmings advised that peer supervision promotes good professional practice, and because we are accountable for our profession, anything we can do to move ourselves toward best professional practice, then we should do it.

Searching for a madeleine

In *Swann's Way* (Proust, 1928), the author, Marcel Proust, described how the smell of a madeleine biscuit dipped in linden tea aroused deep joy and memories of his childhood in Combray. A time he had long forgotten reappeared without warning. Ironically, when he was a child in Combray, his greatest desire was to escape the small town. His autobiographical memory, then, seemed fraudulent and unreliable but also enlightening because he remembered the past not as it was, but as he is now. The memories shared in this book tell us about the journey to become a sport psychologist; each story as vibrant and educative as the person who wrote it. We hope you enjoyed their stories and learned from their experiences. We finish with these words taken from Mark Andersen: 'We are historical beings. I have the voices of my mentors in my head, and I consult with them all the time.'

References

Arnold, J. (2006) Commentary on Walker, Kremer & Moran. *Sport and Exercise Psychology Review*, 2: 37–39.

Conroy, D. E. (2006) Commentary on Walker, Kremer & Moran. *Sport and Exercise Psychology Review*, 2: 39–40.

Hardy, L. (2006) Commentary on Walker, Kremer & Moran. *Sport and Exercise Psychology Review*, 2: 40–43.

Illich, I. (1976) *Medical Nemesis: The Exploration of Health*. New York: Pantheon Books.

Meyers, A. W. (1997) Sport psychology service to the United States Olympic Festival: an experiential account. *The Sport Psychologist*, 11: 454–468.

Proust, M. (1928) *Swann's Way*. New York: Modern Library.

Sagan, C. (1996) *The Demon-Haunted World: Science as a Candle in the Dark*. New York: Ballantine Books.

Smith, R. E. and Smoll, F. L. (2012) *Sport Psychology for Youth Coaches: Developing Champions in Sports and Life*. New York: Rowman & Littlefield Publishers.

Walker, G., Kremer, J. and Moran, A. P. (2006) Coming of age in sport psychology. *Sport and Exercise Psychology Review*, 2: 30–36.

Wilson, J. (2011) Why Manchester United's Sir Alex Ferguson deserves to be recognised as football's greatest-ever manager. *The Telegraph*, Nov. 3.

Appendix

For those interested in a career in sport psychology or further information about the discipline the following organisations may be of interest:

American Psychological Association	www.apa.org/
Association for Applied Sport Psychology	www.appliedsportpsych.org/
Australian Psychological Society	www.psychology.org.au/
British Association of Sport and Exercise Sciences	www.bases.org.uk/
British Psychological Society	www.bps.org.uk/
Canadian Psychological Association	www.cpa.ca/
European Federation of Sport Psychology	www.fepsac.com/
International Society of Sport Psychology	www.issponline.org/
Sport and Exercise Science New Zealand	www.senz.org.nz/
The Psychological Society of Ireland	www.psychologicalsociety.ie/

INDEX

References in **bold** indicate tables.